Visual Basic® 6
Weekend Crash Course

Visual Basic® 6
Weekend Crash Course

Richard Mansfield

M&T Books
An imprint of IDG Books Worldwide, Inc.
Foster City, CA • Chicago, IL • Indianapolis, IN • New York, NY

Visual Basic® 6 Weekend Crash Course
Published by
M&T Books
An imprint of IDG Books Worldwide, Inc.
919 E. Hillsdale Blvd., Suite 400
Foster City, CA 94404
www.idgbooks.com (IDG Books Worldwide Web site)

ISBN: 0-7645-4679-1
Printed in the United States of America
10 9 8 7 6 5 4 3 2 1
1B/QX/QS/QQ/FC
Distributed in the United States by IDG Books Worldwide, Inc.
Distributed by CDG Books Canada Inc. for Canada; by Transworld Publishers Limited in the United Kingdom; by IDG Norge Books for Norway; by IDG Sweden Books for Sweden; by IDG Books Australia Publishing Corporation Pty. Ltd. for Australia and New Zealand; by TransQuest Publishers Pte Ltd. for Singapore, Malaysia, Thailand, Indonesia, and Hong Kong; by Gotop Information Inc. for Taiwan; by ICG Muse, Inc. for Japan; by Intersoft for South Africa; by Eyrolles for France; by International Thomson Publishing for Germany, Austria, and Switzerland; by Distribuidora Cuspide for Argentina; by LR International for Brazil; by Galileo Libros for Chile; by Ediciones ZETA S.C.R. Ltda. for Peru; by WS Computer Publishing Corporation, Inc. for the Philippines; by Contemporanea de Ediciones for Venezuela; by Express Computer Distributors for the Caribbean and West Indies; by Micronesia Media Distributor, Inc. for Micronesia; by Chips Computadoras S.A. de C.V. for Mexico; by Editorial Norma de Panama S.A. for Panama; by American Bookshops for Finland.

For general information on IDG Books Worldwide's books in the U.S., please call our Consumer Customer Service department at 800-762-2974. For reseller information, including discounts and premium sales, please call our Reseller Customer Service department at 800-434-3422.
For information on where to purchase IDG Books Worldwide's books outside the U.S., please contact our International Sales department at 317-596-5530 or fax 317-596-5692.
For consumer information on foreign language translations, please contact our Customer Service department at 800-434-3422, fax 317-596-5692, or e-mail rights@idgbooks.com.
For information on licensing foreign or domestic rights, please phone +1-650-655-3109.
For sales inquiries and special prices for bulk quantities, please contact our Sales department at 650-655-3200 or write to the address above.
For information on using IDG Books Worldwide's books in the classroom or for ordering examination copies, please contact our Educational Sales department at 800-434-2086 or fax 317-596-5499.
For press review copies, author interviews, or other publicity information, please contact our Public Relations department at 650-655-3000 or fax 650-655-3299.
For authorization to photocopy items for corporate, personal, or educational use, please contact Copyright Clearance Center, 222 Rosewood Drive, Danvers, MA 01923, or fax 978-750-4470.

Library of Congress Cataloging-in-Publication Data
Mansfield, Richard, 1945–
    Visual Basic 6 weekend crash course / by Richard Mansfield.
        p.   cm.
    ISBN 0-7645-4679-1 (alk. paper)
    1. Microsoft Visual BASIC. 2. BASIC (Computer program language) I. Title.
QA76.73.B3 M36492   2000
005.26'8--dc21   99-059505

 is a registered trademark or trademark under exclusive license to IDG Books Worldwide, Inc. from International Data Group, Inc. in the United States and/or other countries.

 is a trademark of IDG Books Worldwide, Inc.

ABOUT IDG BOOKS WORLDWIDE

Welcome to the world of IDG Books Worldwide.

IDG Books Worldwide, Inc., is a subsidiary of International Data Group, the world's largest publisher of computer-related information and the leading global provider of information services on information technology. IDG was founded more than 30 years ago by Patrick J. McGovern and now employs more than 9,000 people worldwide. IDG publishes more than 290 computer publications in over 75 countries. More than 90 million people read one or more IDG publications each month.

Launched in 1990, IDG Books Worldwide is today the #1 publisher of best-selling computer books in the United States. We are proud to have received eight awards from the Computer Press Association in recognition of editorial excellence and three from Computer Currents' First Annual Readers' Choice Awards. Our best-selling ...For Dummies® series has more than 50 million copies in print with translations in 31 languages. IDG Books Worldwide, through a joint venture with IDG's Hi-Tech Beijing, became the first U.S. publisher to publish a computer book in the People's Republic of China. In record time, IDG Books Worldwide has become the first choice for millions of readers around the world who want to learn how to better manage their businesses.

Our mission is simple: Every one of our books is designed to bring extra value and skill-building instructions to the reader. Our books are written by experts who understand and care about our readers. The knowledge base of our editorial staff comes from years of experience in publishing, education, and journalism — experience we use to produce books to carry us into the new millennium. In short, we care about books, so we attract the best people. We devote special attention to details such as audience, interior design, use of icons, and illustrations. And because we use an efficient process of authoring, editing, and desktop publishing our books electronically, we can spend more time ensuring superior content and less time on the technicalities of making books.

You can count on our commitment to deliver high-quality books at competitive prices on topics you want to read about. At IDG Books Worldwide, we continue in the IDG tradition of delivering quality for more than 30 years. You'll find no better book on a subject than one from IDG Books Worldwide.

John Kilcullen
John Kilcullen
Chairman and CEO
IDG Books Worldwide, Inc.

Steven Berkowitz
Steven Berkowitz
President and Publisher
IDG Books Worldwide, Inc.

Eighth Annual
Computer Press
Awards ≥1992

WINNER

Ninth Annual
Computer Press
Awards ≥1993

WINNER

Tenth Annual
Computer Press
Awards ≥1994

Eleventh Annual
Computer Press
Awards ≥1995

Credits

Acquisitions Editor
Greg Croy

Development Editor
Matthew Lusher

Technical Editor
Greg Guntle

Copy Editor
Amy Eoff

Project Coordinators
Linda Marousek
Louigene A. Santos

Quality Control Specialists
Laura Taflinger
Chris Weisbart

Graphics and Production Specialists
Jude Levinson
Michael Lewis
Dina F Quan
Ramses Ramirez
Victor Perez-Varela

Book Designer
Evan Deerfield

Illustrators
Shelley Norris
Mary Jo Richards

Proofreading and Indexing
York Production Services

Cover Design
Clark Creative Group

About the Author

Richard Mansfield (High Point, NC) is an author and programmer whose recent titles include *Visual InterDev 6 Bible*, *Visual Studio 6 For Dummies*, and *Visual Basic 6 Database Programming For Dummies*. While he was the editor of *COMPUTE! Magazine* from 1981 through 1987, he wrote hundreds of magazine articles and two columns. From 1987 to 1991, Richard was editorial director and partner in Signal Research. He began writing books full-time in 1991, and has written 21 computer books.

*This book is dedicated to
my best friend, Jim Coward.*

Preface

If this is your first time working with Visual Basic, you're in for a treat. In my opinion, it's by far the most fun you'll ever have programming. Or, if you're here for a quick refresher course, you'll be reminded of why you chose to come back to VB: It's not only great fun to work with, it's also the fastest route on our planet from programming concept to finished application.

Who Should Read This Book

This Crash Course is designed to provide you with a set of short lessons that you can grasp quickly — in one weekend. The book is for two categories of readers. First, it's for people who want to learn the Visual Basic language fast. You may need to learn it to get a job, to be eligible for a promotion, to pass a course, and so on. You don't have the luxury of taking your time to gain this knowledge. You need to learn it quickly. You may be entirely new to programming, or you may have experience programming in another language and just need to apply your knowledge to a new language.

A second audience for this book consists of people who have some knowledge of Visual Basic, but who haven't used it in a while. You need a quick refresher course.

Whatever your circumstances, you'll find that this book gives you the guidance you need to start working with Visual Basic to produce excellent Windows and Internet applications.

What Results Can You Expect?

Is it *possible* to learn Visual Basic in one weekend? Yes, it is. For one thing, VB is a straightforward, easy-to-understand language. Its vocabulary is quite like English, so you'll often see easily understood lines of programming code like this:

```
If Temperature = 98.6 Then Patient = "Healthy"
```

rather than the crypto-reverse notations of some other languages, where the code can look like this (as you can see, it truly deserves the name *code*):

```
main(int, char **argv)
{
    int  i = 4408;
    int  n = atoi(argv[2]);
```

What's more, this book has been designed so that you'll learn everything you need to know to create fully professional, tested, effective Visual Basic programs. *But you'll learn only what you need to know.* This is not a reference book, so the VB vocabulary has been carefully surveyed to determine which commands you need to know for nearly all programming. VB's vocabulary consists of several hundred commands, but fewer than 50 are essential. The rest are highly specialized or rarely, if ever, used. So, in this book, you'll learn all of the useful concepts and commands — but we will not fog things up with the obscure or the merely technical commands.

Finally, Visual Basic includes dozens of Wizards, add-ins, templates, and other built-in assistants that can greatly simplify common programming tasks. Throughout this book, you'll be relying on these helpful features to get your programs up and running fast. If VB has a tool that makes connecting your program to a database a snap (and it does), why do things the hard way with pages of hand programming? Visual Basic was the first, and is still the best, RAD language. RAD means *rapid application development*. And that's not an empty promise, as you'll see in many of the sessions in this book.

Layout and Features

No one should try to simply propel themselves through this material without a break. We've arranged things so the sessions in this book last about a half-hour each, and they're grouped into parts of two or three hours. After each session, and at the end of each part, you'll find some questions to check your knowledge and give you a little practice exercising your newfound skills. Take a break, grab a snack, refill that beverage glass or cup, and plunge into the next one!

Along the way, you'll find some features of the book that help you keep track of how far along you are, and that point out interesting bits of info you shouldn't miss. First, as you're going through each session, check for this in the margin:

**20 Min.
To Go**

This icon and others like it let you know how much progress you've made through each session. There are also several icons that highlight special kinds of info for you:

This is a flag to clue you in to an important piece of information you should file away in your head for later.

This gives you helpful advice on the best ways to do things, or a neat little technique that can make your programming easier.

SYNTAX ▶

Syntax flags a passage where essential VB syntax is modeled for you. The bar to the left shows you the extent of the passage. Usually, it'll be something like this:

To instruct Visual Basic to check something and make a decision based on it, use the If...Then statement. The If...Then statement works like this:

```
If this is true Then do this
```

Here's an example:

```
If Check1.Value = 1 Then Form1.Text1.FontBold = True
```

VB uses the part after the If as a condition; if the condition is true, VB will do whatever comes after Then.

Conventions Used in this Book

Aside from the icons you've just seen, there are only three conventions in this book:

- To indicate a menu choice, we use the ⇨ symbol, as in:

  Choose File ⇨ Save Project to save your work.

- To indicate programming code within the body text, we use a special font, like this:

  Notice the line at the end: `Form2.Hide`. When the user clicks the OK button, you want Form2 to disappear. The `Hide` command does just that.

- To indicate a programming example that's not in the body text, we use this typeface:

```
Private Sub Command2_Click()
Form2.Hide
End Sub
```

Where to Go from Here

Now you're ready to begin. Stake out a weekend, stockpile some snacks, heat or cool your beverage of choice, and get ready to enjoy accomplishing startling results with what I think is the greatest computer language ever invented. Visual Basic is also, by far, the world's most popular programming language, so a lot of people must agree with me.

Session 1 gets you started by exploring in detail just what it is about Visual Basic that makes it so powerful, effective, and — let's be honest — just plain fun to work with (don't tell your boss).

Acknowledgments

First, I'd like to thank Acquisitions Editor Greg Croy for his thoughtful advice. Development Editor Matt Lusher deserves credit for his discernment, and the high quality of his editing. Technical Editor Greg Guntle carefully reviewed the entire manuscript and made important suggestions. Greg has a remarkable memory, finding inconsistencies across chapters once or twice. Production Coor-di-nator Linda Marousek ensured that this book sailed smoothly through production, and Amy Eoff, copy editor, combed through every line of my prose and made a number of improvements. To all these, and the other good people at IDG who con-tributed to this book, my thanks for the enhancements they made to this book.

Contents at a Glance

Contents

Visual Basic® 6
Weekend Crash Course

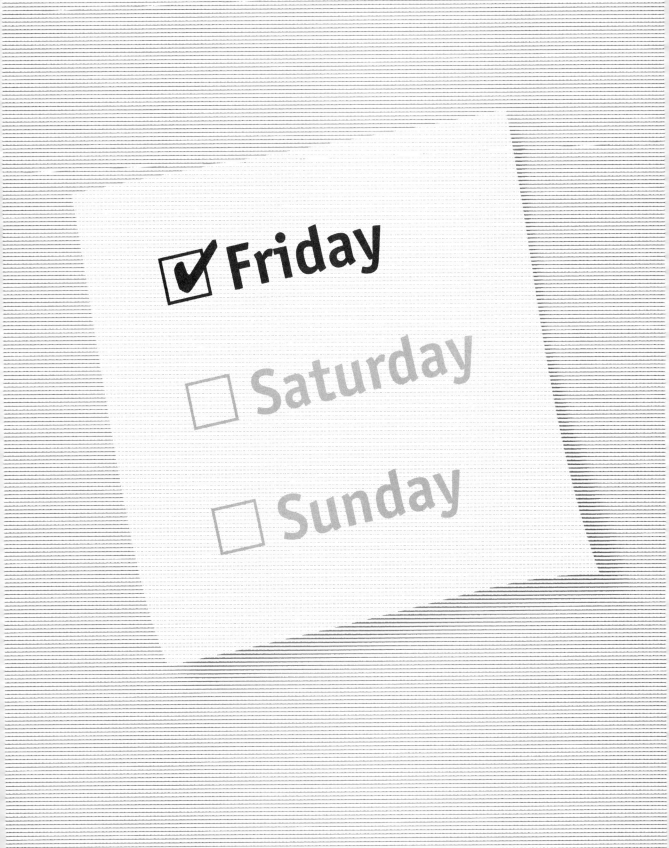

Part I–Friday Evening

Session 1
Computer Programming Fundamentals: Introducing Visual Basic

Session 2
A Tour of the VB Editor

Session 3
Talk to Your User: Creating an Interface

Session 4
Writing Your First Code

PART

I

Friday Evening

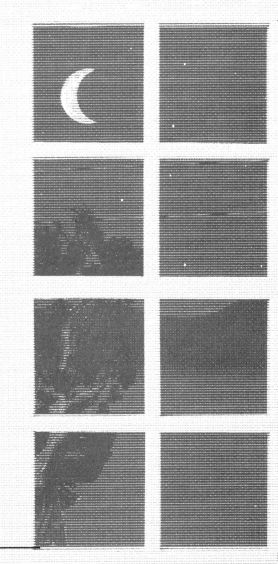

Computer Programming Fundamentals: Introducing Visual Basic

Session Checklist

✔ Designing an application using Visual Basic's built-in components

✔ Drawing the user interface

✔ Understanding Visual Basic's English-like programming language

30 Min. To Go

There are dozens of computer languages — each one has its fans.

My favorite language is Visual Basic (VB), and I'm not alone — it's the most popular programming language in the world. It has more power than most of the other languages, for several reasons. It has continued to be polished for ten years now, improved for a decade by some of the most talented computer programmers currently employed. It's usually the fastest (and most enjoyable) way to get from idea to running application.

One reason Visual Basic is so popular and so effective is that it doesn't ask you to reinvent the wheel. Some elements of any significant programming job are unique, so it's necessary to work those out yourself. But many elements of a job are likely *not* unique. VB is filled with prewritten components: Wizards that step you through many programming jobs (and write the programming for you), templates that you merely customize, and Add-Ins of all kinds that make your programming life easier.

Visual Basic provides such a full set of built-in intelligent tools that creating programs for the Windows or Internet environments can be astonishingly easy. You can just double-click the icons for TextBoxes or PictureBoxes — or dozens of other components — and they're instantly added to your program. These components are fully functional, and you can modify their behavior and appearance in many ways by simply adjusting their properties with a click of the mouse.

With VB, you can write efficient, polished programs that are every bit as professional as commercial applications. Yet, creating a program with Visual Basic is usually much easier than with C or other computer languages.

"Designing" instead of Writing

If you are new to programming, the first phase of writing a program in Visual Basic will seem more like designing a picture than writing out cryptic, half-mathematical instructions for a machine to follow. If you have struggled with more primitive languages, it will seem paradoxical that programming for a sophisticated environment like Windows should prove to be so simple.

Visual Basic contains so many built-in features that creating the user interface for a program is more like picking out lawn furniture from a catalog than building the chairs and tables yourself.

But Visual Basic's tools and custom controls are more than simply nice-looking; they also know how to *do* things. Perhaps the quickest way to grasp what makes Visual Basic so special is to think of it as a collection of prebuilt robot parts. You just choose the parts you want and add them to the surface (the windows) of your program with a double-click of your mouse.

Visual Basic provides all the visual components necessary for computer interaction: listboxes that automatically alphabetize and arrange items in columns, scroll bars, resizable windows, pushbuttons, and more.

These tools come with built-in capabilities

A TextBox automatically wraps words around to the next line and responds to arrow, backspace, delete, enter, caps lock, and shift keys. It would take days or even weeks to hand-program a TextBox from scratch.

In addition, you can customize each tool by selecting qualities from the Properties Window. For example, some of the choices for a TextBox's Properties are

BackColor, BorderStyle, DragIcon, Enabled, FontBold, FontSize, ForeColor, Height and Width, Index, LinkMode, MousePointer, Name, ScrollBars, TabStop, Text, and Visible.

Want to change the background color of a TextBox? Just click BackColor and select from a palette of colors, as shown in Figure 1-1.

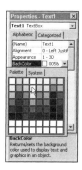

Figure 1-1
Changing an object's colors is as easy as clicking your mouse button.

**20 Min.
To Go**

You can edit objects globally

Want to change the color of five labels? Drag the mouse around them to select them as a group. This is the same way you would group visual objects in a graphics program. You can also group them by holding down the shift key and clicking on each label you want to change. VB is so intelligent that its Properties Window (where the qualities of objects, such as their size or color, are adjusted) will now display the properties that the selected objects have in common. After selecting all of the labels whose color you want to change, just double-click the Properties Window BackColor item. The Color Palette will appear. Click the color you want and, voilà, all the selected labels change from white to magenta. This grouping is also a good technique to use when you want to align controls (give them all the same Left property). When you do that, they'll line up onscreen. As is usual in VB, you can accomplish a goal in more than one way: You can also align components by choosing Format ⇨ Align.

Want to copy a group of selected objects within a given form or from one form to another, or cut and paste them? It's just as easy as copying and pasting text in a word processor. Delete, cut, copy, or paste them using the same Windows conventions that you would with words: Click on a component (or if you want to manipulate a group of objects, drag the mouse around them to select them). Once the component or components are selected, you're then free to copy, delete, or cut them. Remember, if you don't want to drag the mouse around them — perhaps they're not contiguous — hold down the shift key and click the mouse. This adds an object to a selected group.

Then, you can manipulate the selected components just as you manipulate selected text in a word processor:

- The Del key **deletes** the object or group.
- Shift+DEL **cuts** (deletes, but copies to the clipboard for any later pasting you might want to do) the object or group. This is the way you move objects from one window to another.
- Ctrl+Ins **copies** the selected object(s) to the clipboard, from which they can be pasted as often as you want. The properties of the object(s) — qualities such as color, width, text fonts, and so forth — will also be copied. You can also copy with Ctrl+C.
- Shift+Ins **pastes** the object(s). You can also paste with Ctrl+V.

Keep in mind — we're only covering a few of VB's shortcuts and helpful tools in this introductory session. You'll learn about many more before your crash course is over.

Drawing in the Design Phase

One very important Visual Basic breakthrough is a reversal of the normal approach to programming. Instead of spending weeks writing instructions that tell the computer how to make your program respond and how it should look, you simply *draw* the program. You drag the various items you want onto a window (called a *form* in Visual Basic), select their qualities, and then see how your program looks to the user.

This design stage takes very little time. You don't write a single instruction — just click or drag. You can resize, reposition, and delete components very easily. And from each item's individual Properties Window, you can select its qualities to adjust aspects of behavior and appearance. This way of organizing a program and achieving an interface between computer and user is both quick and intuitive. You are, in effect, describing how the program should behave — how it should interact with the user — but you are describing it *visually*. Recall that many of the tools you assemble on a window come from the factory already functional, equipped to react intelligently when the program runs.

This design-first approach encourages you to think your program through before you get down to the details of programming. In Visual Basic, you draw your goals onscreen first so that the final product is there for you to see. You never lose sight of your overall design and the way that components work together to make your application effective.

How about Programming?

**10 Min.
To Go**

Well, you say, that's all good, but what about the actual programming? Isn't programming unforgiving? Yes, in many ways, a computer is the least flexible thing you'll ever try to communicate with. Put a comma — a little comma — in the wrong place and the computer will completely misunderstand what you're asking it to do. Misspell a word, even only slightly, and the computer will not understand it at all. There's no getting around it — at this stage of their development, computers are extremely *literal* critters. Communicating with them means doing it their way, or not at all.

However, in spite of this literal-mindedness, VB helps you out in many ways when you're programming. First, VB's commands — the 300 words in VB's language — are mostly familiar English words like stop, height, line, and timer. Second, it's not hard to learn a language that has only 300 vocabulary words. Third, you combine VB commands into statements that are often quite similar to English sentences, for example: If X = 12 Then Stop.

Sure, punctuation must be exact (a semi-colon means one thing, and a comma means something entirely different to VB). But always remember that Visual Basic hates to let you fail. While you're learning to program, you can turn on various kinds of training wheels that are built into VB. If you make a punctuation error or misspell a command, VB can make suggestions as you type in each line of your program. Features like Auto Syntax Check and Auto Quick Info are always available. Perhaps most experienced programmers might turn them off, but while you're still getting used to the idea of telling a machine what you want it to do (also known as programming), these various kinds of helpers are invaluable.

That's the topic of the next session. In Session 2, you take a tour of the VB editor — or *Integrated Design Environment (IDE)*, as it's sometimes more grandly called. As you'll see, when you program in VB, the editor is there to assist you every step of the way.

Done!

Computers may be highly literal, but they can make up for it by offering you tireless and watchful assistance. If you mistype a VB command, VB itself will immediately show you the error and suggest how to fix it. And if you're not exactly sure what a particular command does — or how to use it — examples and tutorials for each command are only a key press away. Just click a command in your program to select it, and then press F1. With VB, you're never left hanging and twisting in the wind.

REVIEW

You were introduced to the world of Visual Basic in this session. You heard about its integrated design environment and its Toolbox full of prewritten solutions to programming problems, and you learned that this language is packed with templates, add-ins, wizards, and other tools to make a programmer's life easier. Then you saw some ways to efficiently create and modify a user interface using VB's components and the Properties Window. Next you saw how organizing a project graphically during the design phase helps you see the overall structure of your emerging program. Finally, you were warned that computers are very literal, but comforted with the knowledge that VB includes various tools to help you avoid making errors, or at least fix them quickly.

QUIZ YOURSELF

1. What is the purpose of the Properties Window? (See "These Tools Come with Built-in Capabilities".)

2. How would you change the font property of three labels simultaneously? (See "You can Edit Objects Globally".)

3. What does the align feature on the Format menu do? (See "You Can Edit Objects Globally".)

4. When a Visual Basic program runs, what do forms look like to a user? (See "Drawing in the Design Phase".)

5. Commas and semi-colons can be used interchangeably in VB programming. True or False? (See "How about Programming?".)

A Tour of the VB Editor

Session Checklist

✔ How to use the VB Toolbox to add components to your project.

✔ How to add more components to the Toolbox.

✔ What a form is when you're designing a project, and what it becomes for the user.

✔ How to adjust the qualities of components and forms using the Properties Window.

✔ Naming your components.

✔ How the Project Explorer offers an overview of your entire project.

**30 Min.
To Go**

The Visual Basic editor has been modified and improved for over ten years. By now, the majority of programmers consider it to be the world's most comfortable, efficient, and powerful programming editor. You can customize it extensively to suit your personal preferences, and you'll find it loaded with tools that can prevent or solve all kinds of programming problems.

In fact, calling it an *editor* seems insufficient — its proper name is *Integrated Design Environment* (IDE) — and it deserves that more elaborate name.

When you create VB programs, you work in the IDE — so you'll find tips and examples of how to use it throughout this book. In this session, we'll cover the four main visible features in the IDE: the Toolbox, form, Project Explorer, and the Properties Window. These are the primary tools that you'll use in all of your VB projects.

The Toolbox

Click the VB icon to start the editor. You'll likely see the New Project dialog box, shown in Figure 2-1.

Figure 2-1
This set of templates greets you when you first run VB.

The New Project dialog box can also be displayed when you choose File ⇨ New Project. It also appears, by default, each time you run the VB editor. You can prevent the dialog box from appearing by choosing Tools ⇨ Options, and then clicking the Environment tab and then the Create Default Project OptionButton.

Double-click the Standard EXE icon in the New Project dialog box. Standard EXE is the simple, empty template you use to create traditional Windows applications or utilities.

You should now see the VB IDE layout shown in Figure 2-2:

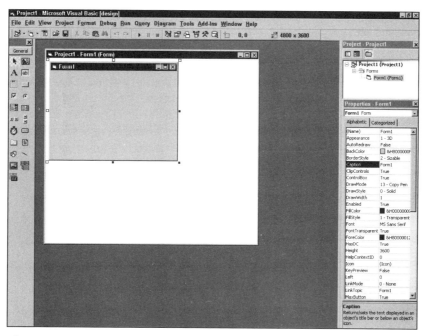

Figure 2-2
*Most programmers use this layout when working in VB, but you can drag
the windows around and position or resize them to suit yourself.*

If you see the Form Layout window, close it. You can do things your way soon
enough, but for now arrange your IDE as shown in Figure 2-2. Put the Toolbox on
the left, the Project Explorer in the upper right, and the Properties Window just
below the Project Explorer. If the Toolbox, Project Explorer, or Properties Window
is not visible, click each of them on the View menu to make them visible.

A collection of components

The Toolbox is where the components (also called controls) sit, waiting for you
to double-click one to place it on the form. Hold your mouse pointer over any
of the icons on the Toolbox to see what each icon represents. The controls you'll
likely use often are clustered near the top: PictureBox, Label, TextBox, Frame,
CommandButton, CheckBox, OptionButton, ComboBox, ListBox, and Timer.

You will probably never use the DriveList, DirList, or FileList Boxes. Their original purpose was to let users browse their hard drive, but these three components have been superceded by a superior approach — the Common Dialog, which you'll learn to use in Session 12.

The ScrollBars aren't of much use — the TextBox, where you're most likely to need scrollbars, includes its own ScrollBars property. The Shape and Line controls have very limited value — they can be used to subdivide a crowded window, as explained in Session 9. The Image control is also explained in Session 9, and it is often used instead of the PictureBox. The Data control is a quick way to connect an application to a database. The OLE control is a quick way to set up communication between your VB application and other applications. The idea was to permit your VB application to borrow, for example, features from other applications. Perhaps you wanted to make a connection to Word's spellchecker so users of your VB application could check the spelling in a TextBox. This feature never really caught on, or perhaps its time hasn't yet come.

Adding more components to the Toolbox

Right-click the toolbox and choose Components from the context menu. You should see the dialog box shown in Figure 2-3.

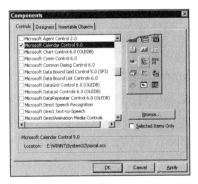

Figure 2-3
Use the Components dialog box to add controls to your Toolbox.

If you want to use any of the many additional components listed in the Components dialog box in your VB project, go ahead and click the CheckBox next to the component's name. When you close the dialog box, that component's icon will be added to the Toolbox.

As you can see in Figure 2-3, I chose the Microsoft Calendar control. Then I double-clicked its icon and, *voila!*, a fully functional calendar is added to my VB project, as shown in Figure 2-4.

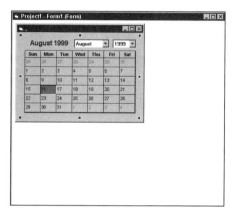

Figure 2-4
Do you want a calendar in the VB application you're building? Just add it to your Toolbox, and it's yours to use.

Precisely *which* additional components are available in the Components dialog box depends on which Microsoft products you've installed on your system (some additional components come with VB; others come with other applications). You can buy commercial components as well. For information on these third-party components, take a look at one of the VB magazines, or try http://www.vb-web-directory.com/software/software.shtml.

**20 Min.
To Go**

The Form and the Properties Window

The second and third of the four main IDE windows are the form and the Properties Window. To illustrate how to use the form, you must also use the Properties Window. So we'll combine these two features into this one section.

A form is Visual Basic's main method of organization. It holds the components that make up the user interface. When your VB application runs, a form is a window that the user sees and can interact with. A VB application can have several forms, just as any other Windows application can have more than one window. Also, as you'll see in Session 4, forms act as containers for your programming.

Your first step when writing a VB program is to add some components from the Toolbox to a form. You arrange the components on the window as you wish — resizing and repositioning them by dragging them with the mouse. If you want to remove a component, just click it to select it and then press the delete key. Only one component at a time on a form is selected — it's the one with eight small squares surrounding it. You can drag those squares to resize the component. Reposition the component by dragging the entire component — click anywhere within the component and hold your left mouse button down while moving the mouse.

You often want several components lined up in a row, and you want them all the same size, same font, and same color. For instance, a group of four CheckBoxes might offer the user four options. Rather than spending the time to adjust each of their Font, ForeColor (text color), and Width properties individually, just make all your changes to the first CheckBox. Then clone it, making as many copies (with the exact same properties) as you wish.

Setting properties and cloning components

This example shows you how to use the Properties Window to adjust the qualities of a component, and also how to clone. (Don't forget that each form also has a list of properties you can adjust. Just click the form itself, and its color and other qualities are listed in the Properties Window.)

1. You want a larger form, so drag the lower-right corner of the form itself to make it bigger. (If you want your form really big, first drag the form's container window to enlarge *it*.)

    Now you've got some room to work with. Remember, the size that you make a form when creating your project is the size that the user will later see when using that form/window in your running application (assuming they use the same screen size that you use).

2. Double-click the CheckBox icon in the Toolbox. A CheckBox control appears in the center of Form1, as shown in Figure 2-5:

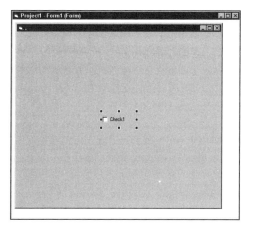

Figure 2-5
When you double-click a component, it appears in the center of the form.

3. I usually change the default font of Labels, CheckBoxes, OptionButtons, and the like from the default MS Sans Serif 8 point (which is tiny) to Arial 11 point (which is more readable). So double-click the word Font in the Properties window, and you'll see the Font dialog box.

   Before changing these properties, first make sure that the title bar of the Properties window says Check1, the name of your CheckBox — not Form1. If it says Form1, you've clicked the form and its properties are now listed in the Properties Window rather than those of the CheckBox. To fix this, so that you see the properties of the CheckBox, click the CheckBox to select *it*. Whatever object is currently selected will be the one whose properties are listed — and can be changed — in the Properties Window.

4. Adjust the font so that Arial is selected and the size is set to 11. Click OK to close the Font dialog box. Now note that the CheckBox's font has grown larger.

5. Double-click the ForeColor property in the Properties Window. Click the Palette tab and click a dark blue for the text color.

 There's a bug in VB6 that sometimes prevents the color palette window from closing. Just ignore it, or save your project with File ⇨ Save, and then restart VB if you want to get rid of that persistent palette window.

6. Adjust any other properties that you want to customize. Now you've got your CheckBox looking just the way you want it. Time to clone three copies of it.

7. You create copies of components much the same way as you copy text or any other object in Windows. First select it, then copy, then paste.

8. Click the CheckBox to select it, and press Ctrl+C to copy it. (You can also choose Edit ⇨ Copy.) Notice that when you copy a component, the component is no longer selected. The *form* becomes the selected object (you can tell because the form now has the eight small boxes — drag handles — surrounding it).

9. Press Ctrl+V (or Edit ⇨ Paste). A message box appears, asking if you want to create a *Control Array* (discussed in Session 13). Click the No button.

   Your new clone CheckBox appears in the upper-left corner of your form. It shares the properties — color, font, size — of its parent CheckBox.

**10 Min.
To Go**

Understanding the Name Property

We'll continue working on this form in a moment, but first note these two important features:

- Visual Basic automatically gives each new component a Name property. The first CheckBox you created by double-clicking its icon in the Toolbox was automatically named Check1, and now its clone is given the name Check2. (TextBoxes are named Text1, Text2 . . . and so on.)

- VB also automatically supplies a default Caption property to each new component that has that property. However, some components, like ScrollBars, don't have a Caption property. The Caption given to new components is, by default, the same as the component's default Name property. You always change the Caption property because it informs the user of the purpose of the components. If a button shuts down your program, you would caption it Exit, so the user knows what it does. Or if you wish, you can delete the Caption property in the Properties Window. Just select it, and then press the delete key.

Sometimes you need to refer to a particular component in your programming. The names of components are the way that you, and VB, tell them apart. You can change the name of a component by merely clicking it in the Properties Window. It's the first property listed, at the very top, unless you click the Properties

Windows's Categorized tab (few people do, because an alphabetized list of properties is almost always easier to work with).

Some programmers like to rename all their components, naming them after the *purpose* of that component. They find that renaming makes it easier to read the source code if it becomes necessary to modify it later. The purpose of this next line of programming is easier to understand:

```
If chkShowThumbnail.Value = vbChecked Then Call ShowIt
```

than this version:

```
If Check2.Value = vbChecked Then Call ShowIt
```

(Really advanced programmers might abbreviate the above programming to this: `If Check2 Then ShowIt`, but we'll get to the ways you can abbreviate in VB in later sessions.)

Other programmers feel that the default names that VB gives components are just fine. In this book, we'll avoid spending the extra time individually renaming components — except in some cases in which I think it's necessary to help avoid confusion.

When you clone components, as we're doing in this example, all properties *except position (Left and Top), TabIndex, and Name* are inherited and therefore identical in the parent and its clone. So, you can see that each new clone CheckBox will have the same `Caption` property — in this case, `Check1`. (Forget about `TabIndex` at this point.)

Now let's return to our form:

1. Drag the clone CheckBox from the upper-left corner of the form, and drop it just below the parent CheckBox. For now, don't worry about making it neat or aligning it.

2. Press Ctrl+V. You should now see that same warning about control arrays, so click No.

    If you don't see the warning message box, one of two things is wrong: A) You need to click the form to select it because components must be pasted into a form, or B) Your original parent CheckBox component is no longer in the Windows clipboard. Click the parent CheckBox to select it, and then press Ctrl+C to copy it to the clipboard. Now press Ctrl+V to paste it.

    Again, a clone appears in the upper-left corner of the form. Drag it down beneath the other two CheckBoxes.

3. Repeat Step 11 to get a fourth CheckBox. Now your form should look something like Figure 2-6.

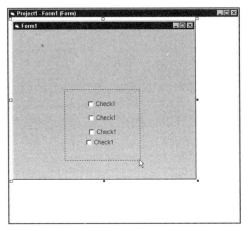

Figure 2-6
Aligning these clones is easy. Just drag your mouse pointer around them until you see the dashed rectangle shown here, and then release your mouse button. Now they're all selected.

4. Align the four CheckBoxes by first selecting them as described in the caption for Figure 2-6, and then choosing Format ⇨ Align ⇨ Lefts. They now line up horizontally.

5. To align them vertically, select individual CheckBoxes, then hold the Ctrl key while repeatedly pressing the up or down arrow keys. Visually align them, as shown in Figure 2-7.

If you're having problems with alignment, choose Tools ⇨ Options@, and then click the General tab and deselect the Align Controls to Grid option.

6. Finally, change the various Caption properties so they describe what each CheckBox does for the user, as shown in Figure 2-7.

Figure 2-7
Now you've got a neat set of choices to display to the user.

If you want to use the special identifier prefixes for the Names of your components, Table 2-1 provides the official list.

Table 2-1
Standardized Naming Conventions

Prefix	Corresponding Object	Example
Acd	ActiveDoc	acdMainPage
Chk	CheckBox	chkBoldface
cbo	ComboBox	cboDropper
cm	ADO command (database)	cmMyCommand
cmd	CommandButton	CmdExit
cmg	CommandGroup	cmgSelectOne
cn	Connection (database)	cnMyConnex
cnt	Container	cntFramed
ctl	Control	ctlSeeThis
edt	EditBox	EdtWrite
fld	Field (database)	FldTitles
frm	Form	frmColors

Continued

Table 2-1   *Continued*

frs	FormSet	frsTypeIn
grd	Grid	grdGoods
grc	Column	grcQuantity
grh	Header	grhYearsResults
hpl	HyperLink	HplURL
img	Image	imgGraphic
lbl	Label	lblContents
lin	Line	linDivider
lst	ListBox	lstNames
olb	OLEBoundControl	OlbInsert
ole	OLE	oleLinker
opt	OptionButton	optGreece
opg	OptionGroup	opgChooseOne
pag	Page	PagTurn
pgf	PageFrame	PgfRule
prj	ProjectHook	prjSuzerine
rs	Recordset (database)	rsTotalSales
sep	Separator	SepZone
shp	Shape	shpRounded
spn	Spinner	spnWatch
txt	TextBox	txtAddress
tmr	Timer	tmrAnimation
tbr	ToolBar	tbrDropThis
tbl	Table (database)	tblTitles

The Project Explorer

The Project Explorer window (see Figure 2-8) is VB's equivalent of the Windows Explorer — it's your viewport into the overall organization of your project. All your forms are listed — and you can quickly switch between them by clicking their names in the Project Explorer.

Also, any other large-scale elements of a VB project are displayed, organized by folders. For example, if you have five forms in a project (your application will have five windows) — you'll see each of these forms contained in the Forms folder in the Project Explorer.

The elements that are displayed in the Project Explorer can include Modules, Class Modules, User Controls, User Documents, Property Pages, and Designers — things you'll learn about in future sessions.

Figure 2-8
The Project Explorer shows you the big picture — all of the major elements of your current VB project.

Done!

In special situations, there might even be two different projects in the VB IDE (and therefore the Project Explorer) at the same time. Interestingly, one category of VB project is designed to work within other VB projects. You can use VB to build your own custom components in the VB IDE. These are called *ActiveX Controls*. An ActiveX Control that you build can be added to the Toolbox just like any other Toolbox component. It can then be added to any form in any standard VB application. To test a custom ActiveX component that you're building, you need to have it in the VB IDE at the same time as a Standard EXE VB application. You need to see how it works when added to the standard application. In this specialized case, the Project Explorer will show these two completely separate projects.

REVIEW

In this session you were introduced to three primary Visual Basic features. The Toolbox is your container for components — useful, pre-built parts that you can assemble into an effective user interface. Then we looked at the primary unit of organization in VB — the form. During the design phase, you use it to create your program's appearance. When the program executes, the form becomes a traditional window. Finally, we looked at the Project Explorer — the tool you use to see the overall organization of your project.

QUIZ YOURSELF

1. What is the Standard EXE? (See "The Toolbox".)
2. How do you put additional components on the Toolbox? (See "Adding More Components to the Toolbox".)
3. What is the value of cloning components? (See "Setting Properties and Cloning Components".)
4. Where do you change the name of a component? (See "Understanding the Name Property".)
5. Name two items that might be found in the Project Explorer window. (See "The Project Explorer".)

Talk to Your User: Creating an Interface

Session Checklist

✔ Understanding Rapid Application Development (RAD)

✔ Manipulating the properties of a TextBox

✔ Listing the features of your application

✔ Adding tooltips to assist the user

✔ Running and testing the application

✔ Saving the application

✔ Adjusting the `TabIndex` properties

**30 Min.
To Go**

Nowadays, the term *Visual* is in the names of dozens of languages and products — Visual C++, Visual Studio, and so on. But back in 1991, Visual Basic was the first language to offer what's now called *RAD* features. RAD stands for Rapid Application Development, and it means a collection of tools that considerably lighten a programmer's burden. What's more, working with RAD is often just plain *fun* (don't tell the boss).

VB has had nearly a decade now to perfect its RAD tools. Those tools — along with VB's English-like vocabulary and syntax — are the primary reason that Visual Basic is by far the world's most popular programming language.

The RAD tools — drag-and-drop, add-ons, wizards, templates, pre-built functionality in components, designers, and other shortcuts — can seriously speed up your programming, and greatly assist with the later maintenance of that programming.

An important component of RAD is its *visual* approach to solving many common programming problems. Need a password-entry box? Don't program it. Don't even copy and paste some programming code. Simply double-click a TextBox to put it onto your form. Drag the TextBox to the size and position you prefer. Then adjust the `PasswordChar` property of the TextBox. You've got your password-entry box up and working in a matter of seconds.

In this session and the next, you're going to build a word processor application. A side benefit of creating your own application is that you can customize it to your heart's content. Do you prefer a particular font or font color? No problem. Would you rather have a larger entry window to type in? A little dragging, and it's done. Your wish is VB's command.

In this session, you'll design the user interface — the components that a user works with. In Session 4, you'll write your first programming code to support the user interface. (You'll be surprised how *little* code is required in VB, even to create a functioning, if simple, word processor!)

Preparing a TextBox

Fire up VB and double-click Standard EXE when the New Project dialog box appears (if it doesn't appear, you automatically have a Standard EXE template by default). A Standard EXE template is merely an empty Form1 and is the starting point for creating an ordinary, traditional Windows application.

You want a fairly large window for this application, so stretch the form's container window, and Form1, so that they are big enough to fill the IDE without covering the Toolbox or Properties Window, as shown in Figure 3-1:

The primary component of any VB text input or word processing is the TextBox control. Double-click the TextBox icon on the Toolbox. Drag the TextBox so it takes up most of the left side of the form, as shown in Figure 3-1.

Almost always, you have to adjust three properties of a TextBox when you first put it on a form: the Text, Font, and MultiLine properties. First, delete the Text property. By default, a TextBox includes a bit of sample text — the default name *Text1*. You never want that to greet the user; instead, you want a blank, empty TextBox ready for *their* text. So click the TextBox to select it, then click the Text property in the Properties Window. Drag your mouse pointer across the default contents *Text1*. Then press the delete key to delete it. Notice that it disappears in the actual TextBox. Usually, changes you make in the Properties Window are immediately reflected in the object itself as well. This is a great feature.

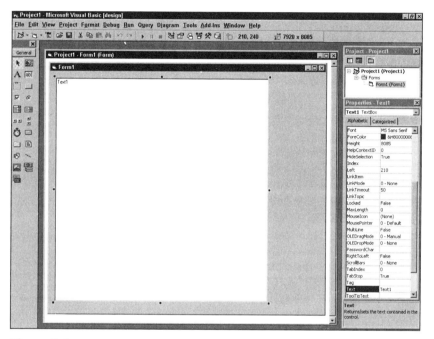

Figure 3-1
Make the form huge, so the user will have a lot of room in which to type.

You can double-click the title bar of the form window, and it will expand to full screen — so you need not drag it. Double-click it again and it returns to normal size.

Next, you'll want to change the font and enlarge the font size from the standard, and tiny, 8 point MS Sans Serif. Double-click Font in the Properties Window and change the font to Times New Roman, Windows' standard serif typeface. Then change the size to 12 and click OK to close the font dialog box.

Finally, the third default TextBox property that nearly always needs changing is the MultiLine property. Double-click MultiLine in the Properties Window so it changes from the default False to True. When this property is set to False, a TextBox only displays a single line of text. If the user keeps typing after the first line is filled, the line scrolls. Put another way, there is no automatic word wrap, and pressing the enter key does not move you down a line. There is only one single line.

Now that the TextBox is in good shape, you can add some CommandButtons to handle the various features you want to offer your user.

In this example, you'll use an alternative approach to application design — using CommandButtons to trigger features, instead of putting those features into menus. CommandButtons are more often used in smaller windows, with smaller ambitions than word processing. You've seen the smaller windows — usually dialog boxes — that often include three standard buttons: OK, Cancel, and Apply. Larger applications like word processors usually avoid buttons and hide their many options within menus.

Even though it's in a large window, we'll consider this "word processor" example as a small-scale utility. So we'll use CommandButtons instead of menus. That's our excuse and we're sticking with it. Seriously, if you're writing an application for your own use, go ahead and do what feels most comfortable to you. I personally enjoy seeing an application's options all lined up in the form of buttons whenever possible. Menus, and especially submenus, are to me a necessary evil. They're just harder to use, but I know that in applications of any complexity, menus are required because there are just too many options and features to put them all on buttons.

Deciding Which Features You Want

20 Min. To Go

Recall the cloning technique you learned in Session 2, in which you defined the properties for a single component, and then used it to create copies that inherited those properties.

Let's say that you decide you want a series of CommandButtons lined up on the right side of the form for this word-processor application. This sounds like a good candidate for the cloning technique.

Double-click the CommandButton icon on the Toolbox to put a new CommandButton on the form. Drag the button over to the right side of the form so it's not covering the TextBox. Then widen the button a bit. Enlarge its font by double-clicking the Font property in the Properties Window. Change the font to Arial and the font's size to 12 point. Click OK to close the font dialog box.

Naturally, you need a Close button to shut the application down. What other buttons would be useful? Surely you'll want New, Save, and Open buttons. A button for Import and Export would be nice (to paste and copy text to the clipboard). Sure, you can just use Ctrl+C or Ctrl+V for these features, but we've got room so let's add those buttons. While we're at it, why not create a Notepad button to bring up Windows Notepad? It's often a useful alternative text-entry utility. And, of course, you want

Print. Finally, how about Options? At the least, you'll want to let them have the option of changing the font and font size.

OK. You've thought it over and you want to have a total of nine buttons: Close, New, Save, Open, Import, Export, Notepad, Print, and Options.

In this example, you can follow the naming conventions to give each CommandButton a meaningful, easily recognizable name. So change the name of the existing CommandButton from the default Command1 to cmdClose. Click the button to select it, then locate its Name property in the Properties Window and make the change. Now click the Caption property and change it from Command1 to Close.

Now follow these steps to clone eight copies:

1. Click the CommandButton to select it.

2. Press Ctrl+C to copy it.

3. Press Ctrl+V to paste it.

4. A message box appears asking if you want to create a control array. Click No.

5. A new clone button appears in the upper-left corner of your form.

6. Drag the new button over to just underneath the existing buttons.

7. Change the new clone button's Name property to cmdNew (or cmd plus whatever the button's function is).

8. Change the new clone's Caption property to its function.

Repeat Steps 1-8 until you've created buttons captioned for each feature in your application: Close, New, Save, Open, Import, Export, Notepad, Print, and Options.

It's nice to arrange buttons in logical order. On most Windows application's menus, New, Open, and Save appear in that order. Close should be at the bottom of the form (at the end of the column of buttons). Also, it's useful to organize some of the buttons into logical groups. New, Open, and Save should be closer together than the other buttons — so they form a group of related features. Similarly, you might want to group the Import and Export buttons. When you're done rearranging the buttons, they should look something like the organization in Figure 3-2.

One final step — horizontal alignment: Drag your mouse pointer around all of the buttons to select them. Choose Format ⇨ Align ⇨ Left to horizontally align the buttons.

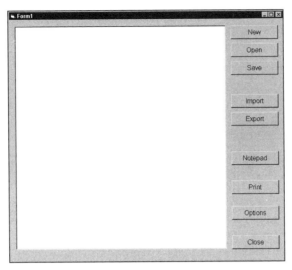

Figure 3-2
Your new word processor application looks like it's ready to work.

When you finally have the components positioned just the way you like them on your form, you might want to lock them down. It's easy to accidentally click and move a button or some other component, messing up your careful, clean layout. To lock all the components in place, choose Format ➪ Lock Controls. You can tell that the controls have been locked because now when you click one of the buttons, it displays white drag handles instead of black ones. And more importantly, you can no longer drag or resize it.

Adding Mini-Help Tooltips

Users appreciate tooltips, those little boxes that pop out when you pause your mouse pointer on a button, toolbar icon, or other component. It's a handy feature that can remind you, with a succinct description, of the purpose of each component.

Adding tooltips to your buttons is a snap. Click each button, and then in the Properties Window type a description into its ToolTipText property.

**10 Min.
To Go**

Testing Your Application

Any time you want to see how your VB application works, you can run it. What you see is precisely what users will see when they run the application; it looks and acts just as it will later after you officially compile and distribute it.

How do you run it? Press F5. Suddenly you see the window you've been working on as a real Windows application. Click the buttons — they move down and up just like real Windows buttons (because they *are* real Windows buttons).

Test the tooltips you just added by pausing the mouse pointer over one of the buttons. You see a tooltip pop out, as shown in Figure 3-3.

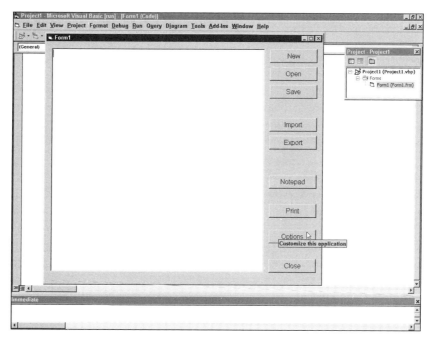

Figure 3-3
Your application is now running, so the tooltips you added to these buttons will pop out when you pause the mouse pointer over them.

Notice that the Toolbox and the Properties Window disappear when you put VB in run mode. You can't use them anyway while the application is being tested. Also note that a window named *Immediate* appears down at the bottom of the IDE. You'll find out how to use this window in Session 20.

When you're finished running the application and playing with the tooltips, shut the application down by clicking the X icon in the upper-right corner of Form1 — or select Run ➪ End in the VB editor window.

Saving Your Work

You've gone to the effort to make a nice, thoughtful user interface. In the process, as a welcome byproduct, you've also defined what your program will do for the user when it's finished.

Now save your project to your hard drive. If lightning strikes and you lose power between now and Session 4, you won't have to repeat Session 3. When you're ready for Session 4, you can just reload the project back into VB. In Session 4, you will fill in the programming that makes all your CommandButtons actually do what their captions say they can do.

To save your project, first run Windows Explorer and create a new folder on your hard drive named *CCourse1*. Now, in VB, choose File ➪ Save, browse your hard drive until you find the CCourse1 folder, and then click the Save button on the Save File As dialog box. This saves Form1. Now you must click the Save button a second time to save the project (Project1). Finally, the dialog box closes, and your work is secure.

Courtesies for the Keyboard-bound: Adjusting the TabIndex Property

You should add two final niceties to your application before considering the user interface finished. Some people like to use the Tab key to move between the components. Each time they press Tab, the focus moves to the next component (as defined by the TabIndex property of each component). Pressing the spacebar triggers the component that currently has the focus. For example, when one of your CommandButtons has the focus, pressing the spacebar will depress that button, just as if the button had been clicked with the mouse. Some people prefer to leave their hands on the keyboard when using a word processor, so you always want to take into account the TabIndex.

By default, each newly added component gets the next higher TabIndex. However, recall that you rearranged the buttons after creating them. So the TabIndexes are scrambled. In this application, you want to have the tab simply move down the buttons in order. So leave the TextBox's TabIndex property alone — it's 0 (the first, lowest index number), and that's fine. That is what you want. It means that when this application first runs, the TextBox will have the focus, and the user can start typing right away without having to click the TextBox or tab to it. You can only type into a TextBox if it has the focus.

However, the buttons' TabIndexes are messed up. So click each button in turn, starting with New at the top of the column of buttons, and adjust their TabIndex properties from 1 to 9. VB is smart enough to prevent any of them from being duplicated — so by the time you get to the last button, Close, it will automatically have been changed to TabIndex 9.

A second courtesy for keyboard-bound users is to add a shortcut keypress feature to each of your Captions. Consider how menu items and button captions usually have one letter underlined — for example, *File*. This permits people to keep their hands on the keyboard, yet still activate a menu or button by pressing Alt+F to trigger *File*, for example, or Alt+E for *Edit*, and so forth.

You add these underlined shortcuts to each button's Caption property by adding an ampersand (&) immediately preceding the letter you want to underline. So change the captions of each button to: &New, &Open, &Save, &Import, &Export, No&tepad, P&rint, O&ptions, and &Close. (Notice that we had to use some interior letters, so that each button has a unique shortcut letter. New uses up the N̲, so with Notepad put your ampersand before the t̲.)

Now, to be on the safe side, save your work again. Choose File ⤳ Save Project.

Press F5 to run the application and try tabbing to make sure that the TabIndex series works correctly, and try pressing Alt+C to see if the Close button gets the focus. Hopefully, all is well.

Done!

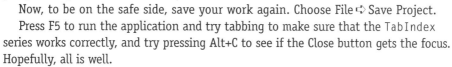

REVIEW

This session was intended to give you an idea of the powerhouse you're tapping into when you use Visual Basic. You can create a text-entry utility of surprising capabilities with very little real effort on your part. You saw how to get some of the benefits of RAD. Then you adjusted the properties of the TextBox and a set of CommandButtons. You also saw how to run and save your new project, as well as how to provide the user with three nice features — tooltips, shortcut keys, and intelligent Tab-key cycling through the components on the form.

QUIZ YOURSELF

1. Name three features in Visual Basic that are considered RAD. (See the introduction to this session.)

2. What three of its properties do you nearly always have to change when adding a TextBox to a project? (See "Preparing a TextBox".)

3. What's the advantage of "cloning" a component? (See "Deciding Which Features You Want".)

4. What does the ToolTipText property do for the user? (See "Adding Mini-Help Tooltips".)

5. What symbol do you add to a component's Caption property to create a shortcut key? (See "Courtesies for the Keyboard-bound: Adjusting the TabIndex Property".)

Writing Your First Code

Session Checklist

✔ Knowing how to use the code window

✔ Understanding the four basic programming steps

✔ Learning how to assign text to a TextBox

✔ Interacting with the user through CommondDialog components

**30 Min.
To Go**

O K. We've been hanging around the shallow end now for three sessions. It's time to move to the deep water. Sure, Visual Basic makes life easy by doing a lot of the grunt work for you, but a programmer *programs* by definition. You have to know a computer language and how to use it to make the computer do precisely what you want it to do.

It's fine to type in a caption like *Close* on a CommandButton, as you did in Session 3, but now you have to write the code that actually shuts down a program when the user clicks that button.

In Visual Basic, you write most of your code in procedures called *events*. Each component has a whole set of events available for your use, if you wish to use them (although normally you only use one or two events in a typical program).

Events are things that can happen to a component — there are Click events, MouseOver events, LostFocus events, KeyPress events, and many others.

What do you want your application to do if the user clicks the Close button? You want the application to end. There is an End command in VB that does precisely that — shuts down the application. To program the behavior of the Close button, you put the End command into that button's Click event.

Using the Code Window

Let's see how this works. If you have shut down VB, restart it (if the New Project dialog box appears, just click Cancel to close it).

Select File ➪ Open Project. Browse your hard drive to find the CCourse1 folder you created in Session 3, then double-click the file Project1.VBP to bring in the word processor application you started in Session 3. By default, all projects you start in VB are named Project1. The .VBP extension stands for Visual Basic Project.

The file dialog box closes when you double-click the .VBP file. At this point, you might see the code window, or no window at all. In any case, you want to see Form1, which contains all of your CommandButtons, so click the Forms folder in the Project Explorer (the Explorer-like window in the upper-right corner just above the Properties Window). If you don't see the Project Explorer window, select View ➪ Project Explorer. You should see Form1 listed, followed by its filename (Form1.frm). Double-click Form1 in the Project Explorer, and your design window opens, showing you the mini word processor application you designed in Session 3.

Now you can open the VB code window in which you will actually write your programming. When you want to do some programming for a component, just double-click that component in the form design window, and the code window opens, as shown in Figure 4-1:

Notice that you see a new window with the following code already typed in for you:

```
Private Sub cmdClose_Click()

End Sub
```

A Sub is a little program within a program (the *sub* is short for *subroutine*). Whatever programming you put between the Sub and End Sub will wait to be activated by some outside event. In this case, you named the Close button cmdClose, and this is its Click event. So if this Close button is clicked while this program is running, VB will carry out any instructions that you've written in this Click event.

Figure 4-1
Double-click any component to open the code window on that component's most commonly used event.

Let's try it. Type the command End inside this event, so it looks like the following:

```
Private Sub cmdClose_Click()
End
End Sub
```

Now press F5 to run and test this application. Click the Close button. What happened? Your application stopped running, and you're back in the ordinary VB design environment. In other words, the End command was executed when you clicked that Close button. The program closed, just as if you'd clicked the X in the upper-right corner of Form1, or selected Run ➪ End, to stop the program.

Congratulations! Your first programming code — written and successfully tested.

The four basic programming steps

Of course, this isn't the most demanding programming that you'll come across in your career. As you'll see in the rest of the sessions in this book, there is still more to learn about Visual Basic code. But you now know the fundamentals of coding in VB:

1. Double-click a component.
2. Decide in which event to write your program code.
3. Write the code.
4. Press F5 to test your code, to see if it does what you expect it to do.

When you double-click a component, VB chooses one of its events to display (often it's the Click event). The chosen event represents VB's guess as to which event you want to use based on statistics. For instance, by far the most common behavior with a CommandButton is that the user clicks it — so when you open a code window by double-clicking a CommandButton, VB shows you that button's Click event.

VB made a good choice. You'll put all of your programming for this application in the Click events of the buttons. Let's do the programming for the button captioned *New*. It's supposed to provide the user with a new, blank document — in other words, it's supposed to clear the TextBox of any text.

You can get to the cmdNew_Click event for this button by double-clicking the New button on the design window. There's also another way. Notice that there are two drop-down listboxes at the top of the code window. Drop the left listbox, as shown in Figure 4-2:

Click cmdNew in the left listbox. Now the code window displays two Subs and two Click events, like this:

```
Private Sub cmdClose_Click()
End
End Sub


Private Sub cmdNew_Click()

End Sub
```

You can now program the Click event for the New button. By the way, if you drop the listbox on the right side, you'll see a list of all the events available to whatever component is currently selected in the *left* listbox.

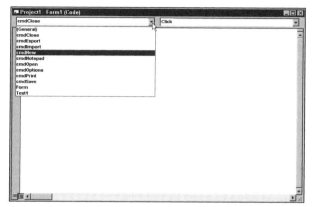

Figure 4-2
The left listbox displays all of the components on this form. Click any component to get to its default event.

**20 Min.
To Go**

Assigning text to a TextBox

We're only interested in reacting to clicks in this application, so what do we do to clear the text from a TextBox?

A TextBox can contain text that the user types into it, but there's another way to add text to a TextBox. You, the programmer, can assign text to the TextBox, like this:

```
Text1.Text = "Helloooo!"
```

What you're saying here, with this equals sign, is something slightly different from what the equals sign means in arithmetic. In arithmetic, when you say $a = b$, you mean that both a and b are the same number. What you mean by Text1.Text = "Helloooo!" is: *When* this line is executed, the contents of this TextBox *will change to* Helloooo!.

You want to remember this distinction: An equals sign used this way in programming indicates *assignment* rather than equality. It means that if this line of programming executes, the text "Helloooo" will be placed (assigned) to this TextBox.

SYNTAX ▶

The equals sign is *sometimes* used in programming to mean what you expect: equality. In a line of programming *that tests something*, the = symbol really does mean equals. Here's an example: If X = 12 Then DoSomething. That means that if X equals 12 then carry out some job. When a test is taking place, you'll always find one of the *conditional* commands: If, While, or Until in that line of programming. Just remember that X = 1 is an *assignment* of the value 1 to the variable X. Check1 = True causes (assigns) that CheckBox to be checked. Check1 = False assigns False (unchecks) to the CheckBox. But *IF* X = 1 or *WHILE* X = 4 are *tests,* not assignments. In these instances, you're actually asking whether or not there is equality, whether or not X currently holds the value 1 or 4. Don't panic. We'll go over all this in detail in later sessions.

So, whew! How do you remove all of the text from a TextBox? Just assign nothing, an empty quotation, "" to the TextBox. Here's the programming that causes the TextBox to empty when the user clicks the New button:

```
Private Sub cmdNew_Click()
Text1.Text = ""
End Sub
```

Using Common Dialogs

**10 Min.
To Go**

Moving right along, what programming shall we put into the Open button so the user can load a file into the TextBox? Luckily, VB provides a component that handles common dialog boxes for you — it does all of the programming required to display the standard Windows Print, File Save, and File Open dialog boxes (and a few others, like Font and Color). So you can use the Common Dialog component to display familiar dialog boxes to the user for the Open, Save, and Print buttons on your application!

The Common Dialog control isn't on the Toolbox by default, but remember that you can add components to the Toolbox by right-clicking it, then choosing Components from the context menu.

Do that now, and in the Components dialog box locate Microsoft Common Dialog Control 6.0 in the list. Click the checkbox next to it to check it. Click OK to close the dialog box. Notice that you now have the Common Dialog icon on your Toolbox.

Double-click Form1 in the Project Explorer so you're looking at the design window (you can see your form and all of its buttons). Now double-click the Common Dialog icon on the Toolbox to add a Common Dialog component to your form. Finally, drag it off to the side somewhere (if your controls are locked in place, choose Format ⇨ Lock Controls to release them).

This Common Dialog icon (like the Timer icon and a few others) is never visible to the user when the program runs. It just offers features. So you can put its little icon anywhere on your form — the icon serves as a reminder that you've added its features to your bag of tricks, that's all.

The programming to display a dialog box and get back the user's response is fairly straightforward. Double-click the Open button on your form and type the following into its `Click` event:

```
Private Sub cmdOpen_Click()
CommonDialog1.ShowOpen
Text1.Text = CommonDialog1.FileName
End Sub
```

That's all there is to it! You use the ShowOpen command to display the standard Windows Open dialog box. Then your program pauses until the user clicks the Open or Cancel button on the File Open dialog box (or double-clicks a filename). At that point, the dialog box closes, and the next line in your code is executed. That next line assigns the contents of whatever file the user selected (`CommonDialog1.FileName`) to your TextBox.

Try it out. Press F5. Click the Open button. You see the typical Open dialog box shown in Figure 4-3.

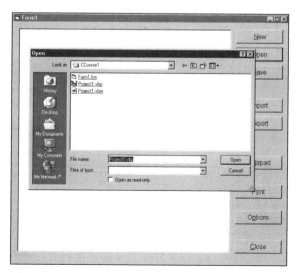

Figure 4-3
You (with Visual Basic's help) can display this dialog box with a single line of programming.

Try double-clicking a .TXT or .VBP filename. The dialog box closes, and the text appears in your TextBox. Now try it again by clicking the Open button a second time, but this time click the Cancel button on the Open dialog box. Notice that there's a little flaw in our programming. Our programming is just too simple. (You knew this was just too easy to be true, didn't you?)

The flaw is that when users click Cancel they expect that whatever text was already in the TextBox will *remain*. But pressing Cancel puts an empty piece of text (remember the ""?) into the Filename property of the CommonDialog. So, when you assign, you're assigning "" to the TextBox, and, as with the New button you programmed earlier, this has the effect of erasing whatever was in the TextBox.

If the user clicks the Cancel button in the dialog box, then this line of code, `Text1.Text = CommonDialog1.FileName`, assigns "" empty text to the TextBox.

To avoid the problem, change that line to the following, which will test the contents of the FileName property:

```
If CommonDialog1.FileName <> "" Then Text1.Text =
CommonDialog1.FileName
```

Put this all on a single line in the code window — don't press Enter to make it two lines. That's very important. VB executes programming one line at a time and considers each line to be a separate, complete statement — just like an English sentence. You must not break lines of code, any more than you would break a

sentence like this by pressing Enter when typing. If you must break a line for readability, or because you don't like it to scroll off the code window, there is an optional symbol you can use — the underscore character. But you must precede the underscore with a space, like this:

```
If CommonDialog1.FileName <> "" Then _
Text1.Text = CommonDialog1.FileName
```

VB will see the space and underscore at the end of the line and understand that you want these two lines to be interpreted as a single "logical" line of code (a single sentence, so to speak).

You'll learn all about the important command IF and the other aspects of this line of code in future sessions. (Hint: <> means *does not equal*.) For now, let me translate what this line of programming means to Visual Basic:

If the FileName property is not equal to nothing (in other words, if the FileName does *contain some text), then go ahead and assign that text to the TextBox.*

What does VB do if the FileName *is* empty? It does nothing. VB goes to look for the next line of programming, but in this case there is no next line, just `Exit Sub`.

So VB does nothing at all — and any text that was in the TextBox remains in the TextBox. Problem solved. Your code window should now look like this (notice the use of the line break character following `Text1.Text =`):

```
Private Sub cmdClose_Click()
End
End Sub

Private Sub cmdNew_Click()
Text1.Text = ""
End Sub

Private Sub cmdOpen_Click()
CommonDialog1.ShowOpen
If CommonDialog1.FileName <> "" Then Text1.Text =
CommonDialog1.FileName
End Sub
```

Done!

Select File ➪ Save to save today's work. Tomorrow morning, in Session 5, you'll finish this word processor application and add some nice extra touches to it that users will thank you for.

REVIEW

In this session, you officially started programming. You learned how to open, and use, the VB code window — the place where you compose and edit programming code. You got your first taste of telling Visual Basic what you want it to do when an event is triggered. Then you saw how to assign text to a TextBox, and discovered the subtle (but significant) distinction between using the equals sign to mean *assignment* as opposed to *equality*. Finally, you tried using the CommonDialog component. I think this component is so important and useful that we'll return to it and spend all of Session 12 getting to understand it better.

QUIZ YOURSELF

---

1. What is an event in VB? (See the introductory paragraphs in this session.)
2. What is a .VBP file? (See "Using the Code Window".)

3. How would you explain the difference between *assignment* and *equality* — the two ways that an equals sign can be used in VB programming? (See "Assigning text to a TextBox".)

4. Why would you add a component to the VB Toolbox? And how do you do that? (See "Using Common Dialogs".)

5. What happens when the following code executes?

```
Text1.Text = CommonDialog1.FileName
```

(See "Using Common Dialogs".)

PART

I

Friday Evening Part Review

1. Create a user interface with two TextBoxes, two Labels, and a Listbox. Align these components so they look neat, and group them by dragging your mouse around them so you can change all of their Font properties at the same time to Arial 11pt.

2. Create a second form and copy all of the components you used in question 1 onto the second form.

3. Explain in a couple of sentences the uses of the Project Explorer window.

4. What kinds of names does VB provide for components by default? For example, if you add two TextBoxes, what are their default names?

5. The cmd in the name cmdExit is the abbreviation some programmers use when renaming a CommandButton that shuts down a program. The cmd identifies the component as a CommandButton. What are the standard abbreviations for the CheckBox, ListBox, Label, and Image components?

6. Is it ever possible to design two different projects at the same time in the Visual Basic Editor? If so, why would you do that?

7. Define IDE and RAD. How are they related?

8. What key do you press to start a VB program running in the editor? How do you stop VB?

9. What is the purpose of the TabIndex property?

10. What's the difference between how the equals sign (=) is used in math and how it is used in programming?

11. How do the VB design window and code window differ?

12. What is the definition of a *sub*?

13. How do you add a component to the VB Toolbox?

14. What does the CommonDialog component do?

15. How would you define the phrase *logical line*?

16. Write the programming that displays a File Open dialog box to the user.

17. Explain what the following programming does:

    ```
    If CommonDialog1.FileName <> "" Then Text1.Text =
        CommonDialog1.FileName
    ```

18. What does a pair of double quotes ("") mean in VB programming?

19. What VB command shuts down a running program?

20. If you had to describe the concept of an *event* in VB to a non-programmer, what would you compare it to?

21. Describe the quickest way to get from the design window to a CommandButton's Click event.

☑ **Friday**

☑ **Saturday**

☐ **Sunday**

PART

II

Saturday Morning

Fleshing Out Your First Application

Session Checklist

✔ Understanding the testing process

✔ Employing the Auto Syntax Check and Auto List Members features

✔ Saving and Printing text

✔ Importing and exporting from the Windows Clipboard

✔ Launching a separate application from within VB

*30 Min.
To Go*

Last night you shut down your programmer's workshop with your mini-word processor application only partly finished. Now it's time to finish writing the code that makes most of the buttons do their jobs. We'll also introduce a couple of VB features that may seem like training wheels to expert programmers, but can be lifesavers to a beginner: Auto Syntax Check and Auto List Members.

When you finish this session, you'll have a good overview of the process of designing, coding, and refining that produces VB applications. You'll also find out whether you feel comfortable using those training wheels.

The Testing Process

What about testing your application? Everybody knows that no program of any complexity is ever *completely* bug-free. After all, teams of the finest programmers available spend years testing major Microsoft applications like Word, yet bugs remain and pop up only after the product is sold to the public. The frequent need for "Service Packs" that fix problems after the sale testify to the never-ending process of software testing.

A decision you need to make when programming is: Should I test each piece of code as I finish it, or should I wait until I've programmed the entire application? Recall that several times in Session 4 you pressed F5 to run your application to see what an individual button did when clicked. You had just finished writing a little programming that made that button do what you wanted, but you tested it to be sure that your intentions were, in fact, being carried out.

These mini-tests of small pieces of code are so easy to run that many programmers like to check each little piece of programming as they complete it. Others prefer to formally test after all of the coding is complete.

Which approach you choose is purely a matter of personal preference. If you're not sure that you used the right command in a particular event (Sub procedure), go ahead and press F5 to see what happens. Some programmers argue that only when you've finished programming can you test for unintended interactions between perhaps widely separated bits of code. That's true, but there's no reason that you can't run mini-tests while programming, and then perform larger-scale tests at the end of the programming process. So I guess it's apparent that I favor the test-as-you-go approach.

This distinction is rather like the two ways people use their spell-checkers when word processing. Some people leave the spell-checker on all the time, so it checks each word as it is typed in, and a misspelling is flagged at once. Other people prefer to leave the check-spelling-as-you-type feature off — claiming that they cannot concentrate on the larger issues of logic and organization if they have to stop and respond to every little typo. This kind of writer prefers to wait until the document is finished before running the spell-checker globally. It's up to you, but if you're a beginner I think you'll probably *learn* the language faster if you run frequent mini-tests. I also suggest that you use VB's equivalent of the check-spelling-as-you-type feature. VB calls this feature *Auto Syntax Check*.

Using Auto Syntax Check and Auto List Members

Choose Tools ⇨ Options. Click the Editor tab. Click the Auto Syntax Check and the Auto List Members checkboxes.

Auto Syntax Check watches as you type in each line of code. As soon as you finish a line, it checks the line to see if you mistyped anything, or made some other kind of error such as leaving out something necessary. (VB knows you're finished with a line because you press the Enter key or click the mouse pointer on some other line.)

If the syntax checker has a problem with the line, it turns the line red and also displays a message box like the one shown in Figure 5-1.

One rule in VB is that when you use the IF command, you must follow it by a THEN or GOTO command. So, if you type this line:

```
IF X = 2
```

then press the Enter key, the syntax checker will display the message shown in Figure 5-1.

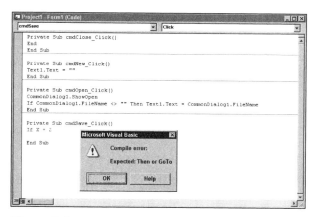

Figure 5-1
The Syntax Checker's error messages can be quite helpful and descriptive.

We'll discuss what the Auto List Members feature does in a moment. First, let's do some more programming

And remember: At this point in the Crash Course, you aren't expected to know which programming commands will accomplish which jobs. For example, when I say it's time to write the programming that displays a Save dialog box, you're not expected to know that you must use the *ShowSave* method. You'll learn VB's programming commands throughout the Crash Course — and by the end of this book, you *will* know that CommonDialog1.ShowSave displays the classic Windows Save dialog box, End shuts down the application, Loop means keep repeating something until I say to stop, and all the rest of them. For now, just relax and go along. Now let's display the Save dialog box.

**20 Min.
To Go**

Programming More Events

Let's move closer to finishing up the mini-word processor you started in Session 3. Start VB. (If the New Project dialog box appears, just click Cancel to close it.) Choose File ⇨ Open Project. Browse your hard drive to find the CCourse1 folder you created in Session 3, then double-click the file Project1.VBP to bring in the application. The file dialog box closes when you double-click the .VBP file. At this point, you might see the code window or no window at all, depending on the state of the IDE when you shut down VB.

You want to see Form1, which contains all of your CommandButtons, so click the Forms folder in the Project Explorer and then double-click Form1. The design window opens, showing you the user interface of the application you're building.

When we left this project, you had just added the CommonDialog that opens a disk file, and you had written the programming that assigns a file's contents to your TextBox. Now it's time to use the CommonDialog to save and to print.

Notice that even though you shut VB down at the end of Session 4 and restarted it just now, VB remembers that you had added the CommonDialog to your Toolbox. The state of VB is saved each time you save a project.

Saving a file

Double-click the Save button on Form1. You see the cmdSave_Click event. Type in the following code:

```
Private Sub cmdSave_Click()
    CommonDialog1.ShowSave
    Open CommonDialog1.FileName For Output As 1
    Print #1, Text1.Text
    Close 1
End Sub
```

Using the Open, then Print #, then Close commands is a common way to save data to a disk file.

...es, but there are other things you can do with the ...easier for the user. Like many components, the ...abbed Properties dialog box you can use to customize ...boxes are similar to the Properties Window — and con-...rties, whereas the Properties Window contains *all* of the ...es dialog box is sometimes a little easier to work with ...properties in logical ways.

...open a Properties dialog box for a component. Right-click ...on Form1 (not in the Toolbox), then choose Properties ...; or, drop the listbox at the top of the Properties Window, ...log. Now the component's properties are displayed in the ...uble-click Custom in the Properties Window. (See Figure 5-2.)

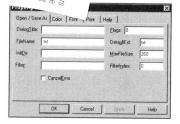

Figure 5-2
Properties dialog boxes can make adjusting the features of a component easier.

For the Save CommonDialog, let's assume you want to display a default file extension of .TXT — a TextBox's contents are plain, unformatted text, just like Notepad's contents. By changing the FileName property, you cause the CommonDialog to display a default filename. The DefaultExt represents the extension that is automatically added to whatever filename the user types in. This property is not shown to the user; it's just added during the filesave. So you want to put TXT in that property and leave off the "." period. By the way, it's easy to see what the rest of the CommonDialog component's properties do: Just click the Help button, or press F1.

Printing text

Printing is easy. Just use the Printer object and tell it to Print. Double-click the Print button on Form1 to get to its code window, then type the following code into the click event:

```
Private Sub cmdPrint_Click()

If Text1.Text <> "" Then
    Printer.Print Text1.Text
    Printer.EndDoc
End If

End Sub
```

Aha! As soon as you type the period (.) following Text1, you should see the Auto List Members feature sprint into action. A *member* is a property or method of a component (or other object). Technically, events are also considered members.

Anyway, what you should notice at this point is that when you type an object followed by a period (.), you're telling VB that you are going to use a property of that object, or perhaps a method. Objects generally have many properties, and only a few methods. Properties are qualities (like size or color), while methods are actions that the object knows how to do. For example, you can use Text1.Move 43 to make the TextBox move 43 units from the left of the form.

The point of Auto List Members is to provide you with a quick reference of *all* of the properties and methods of the object. Notice in Figure 5-3 that methods are indicated by what looks like a flying green eraser icon, while the properties icon is a finger poking the sprocket of a cassette tape (or something).

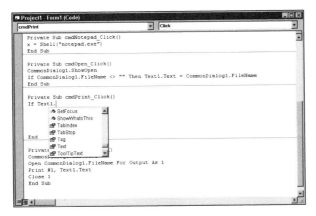

Figure 5-3
With the Auto List Members feature turned on, you never need to wonder which properties and methods are available for your use.

Notice the EndDoc command in the programming above. It tells VB that this document is now complete and can be sent to the Windows print manager. Alternatively, if you don't want to end the document yet, but do want to force a page to eject and start on a new page, use Printer.NewPage.

SYNTAX ▶

The If...Then...End If structure is pretty easy to understand. To avoid accidentally printing a blank page, we added a couple of lines to this procedure. The first line says: If the text in the TextBox is not empty, then go ahead and print. (Remember that <> means *is not equal to*.) Should the If test fail — should there be no text in the TextBox — VB will ignore all the lines between If and End If. In this procedure, VB will not print anything.

Whenever you start an If zone in your programming, you must tell VB where the If...Then zone ends. To show where it ends, use End If. The reason for this is that you can put additional lines between If...Then and End If. Perhaps you always want to end any text you print with your name, the time, and date. You can add this line just above the End If line: Printer.Print "Richard" & Now. (The VB Now command displays the date and time.) You can add as many behaviors as you want between If...Then and End If. There *is* one way to use If...Then without End If: Put the entire zone on one line, like this:

```
If Text1.Text <> "" Then Printer.Print Text1.Text
```

When you put your entire test (if <>) and the response (Then Print) on a single line, you leave off End If. However, whenever you end a line with Then, you must include a line somewhere further down in your code with End If on it.

Notice that, by convention, programmers indent the behaviors between If and End If. This makes it easier to see what will happen should the If test pass and those indented lines therefore get executed. VB doesn't care whether or not you indent. It ignores blank spaces or tabs at the start of programming lines.

Clipboard: importing and exporting

**10 Min.
To Go**

Double-click the Import button on Form1. Type the following code into its click event:

```
Private Sub cmdImport_Click()
```

```
    Text1.Text = Clipboard.GetText
End Sub
```

Double-click the Export button on Form1 and type this in:

```
Private Sub cmdExport_Click()
    Clipboard.SetText Text1.Text
End Sub
```

Like the `Printer` object and its `Print` method you used just a bit earlier in this session, the `Clipboard` object has a couple of methods you can make use of — `GetText` and `SetText`, which are self-explanatory.

Running a separate application

The Notepad button is supposed to bring up the Windows Notepad utility. You can start a program running in VB with the Shell command. Double-click the Notepad button, and then type this in:

```
Private Sub cmdNotepad_Click()
X = Shell("notepad.exe", 1)
End Sub
```

If, when you execute this event, you get a "Compile error: Variable not defined" error message, it means that this line of code is at the very top of this form's code window:

`Option Explicit`

Delete that line. Select Tools ⇨ Options, then click the Editor tab and deselect the *Require Variable Declaration* checkbox. We'll explain all about Option Explicit at the end of Session 14. For now, just leave it out of your programming.

Now, to be honest, I couldn't remember how to use the Shell command when I was writing this session. However, it's simple enough to get answers when you get stuck. Just type in the word **Shell**, then, with the cursor still on the word (or highlighted with the mouse), press F1. When I did this, I instantly saw that I had to use this format — `Shell(pathname[,windowstyle])`. The brackets mean that the *windowstyle* parameter is optional. However, if you leave it out in this case, the default is rather bad: Notepad runs, but it only appears on the taskbar, not as an opened window the user can see. So you want that *1* in (`"notepad.exe", 1`) to force it to be a normal, visible window when it runs. Also, notice that the `Shell` command is a function, which means you must write it in the format `X = Shell` rather than just using `Shell`. You'll find out all about functions in Session 12. Anyway, what I really wanted was a quick example, so I clicked the Example hyperlink at the top of the Shell Help screen. I immediately found precisely what I needed: the full, precise syntax:

```
RetVal = Shell("C:\WINDOWS\CALC.EXE", 1)
```

You can use `X` or `RetVal` or any other name you want for the variable at the start of this line — just don't use a word that's in the VB vocabulary, such as `End`, `Print`, or `If`.

Done!

Select File ➪ Save Project. We'll leave creating the programming for the last button, Options, in our mini-word processor project for Session 6. In that session, you see how to use several kinds of input components — CheckBoxes, OptionButtons, and custom dialog boxes, all of which make life easier for the user.

REVIEW

This session takes your first application well on its way to completion. You saw how to write code to make the Save, Print, and other buttons do their jobs. You also learned how to use the Auto Syntax Check and Auto List Members features to assist you in your programming. Above all, you came away from this session understanding that you cannot know or remember everything about the Visual Basic language — you must be prepared to press F1 from time to time to summon help.

QUIZ YOURSELF

1. Conducting frequent mini-tests on individual events is one approach to testing a program. What is the other main approach? (See "The Testing Process".)

2. What can Auto Syntax Check do for you? (See "Using Auto Syntax Check and Auto List Members".)

3. What can Auto List Members do for you? (See "Using Auto Syntax Check and Auto List Members".)

4. What code would you write to print the contents of a TextBox named Text1 to the printer? (See "Printing Text".)

5. Can you put an entire If...Then structure on a single line of code? (See "Printing Text".)

Easy Choices: OptionButtons, CheckBoxes, and Simple Dialogs

Session Checklist

✔ Using more than one form

✔ Grouping OptionButtons within a Frame component

✔ The effect of a Cancel button on your programming

✔ Using the Show and Hide commands with forms

✔ Understanding CheckBoxes

✔ Why you can't remember everything, and shouldn't try

**30 Min.
To Go**

Computer applications generally involve an exchange, a kind of conversation, between the user and the application. The user clicks buttons, types in data, or otherwise provides information, and the application processes that information.

In previous sessions you've worked primarily with a TextBox, the CommonDialog component, and CommandButtons as user input devices. In this session, you'll see how to use CheckBoxes and OptionButtons to create a custom dialog box that gets information from the user.

You only have one more feature to add to the simple word processor that you've been building since Session 3. What happens when the user clicks Options? A dialog box should appear, allowing the user to specify some preferences about how the application behaves. Let's get started:

1. Start VB running. (If the New Project dialog box appears, just click Cancel to close it.)

2. Select File ⇨ Open Project.

3. Browse your hard drive to find the CCourse1 folder you created in Session 3, then double-click the file Project1.VBP to bring in the application.

   The file dialog box closes when you double-click the .VBP file. At this point, you might see the code window, or no window at all, depending on the state of the IDE when you shut down VB.

4. Double-click Form1 in the Project Explorer to open the design window.

When the user clicks the Options button, you want to display a small window (in VB, a form is a window) that includes several options the user can select from. A VB application can have as many forms as you wish. In this case, you'll add a typical dialog box.

Adding a Second Form

Select Project ⇨ Add Form to add a new form to this project (by default, it will be named Form2). The Add Form dialog box appears, displaying the various kinds of form templates offered by VB. Just double-click the first icon, Form — a plain form.

Form2 appears in its own design window. It's just about the right size for a dialog box, but you might want to stretch it a half inch or so wider.

Use the Toolbox to put two CommandButtons on Form2, and use the Properties Window to Caption them OK and Cancel. All dialog boxes have those two buttons at the bottom, though some dialog boxes also add a button captioned *Apply*, which is used to make the changes the user selects in the dialog box without closing the dialog box.

Now add two Frame components to Form2 by double-clicking them on the Toolbox. The primary use of a frame is to act as a container for a group of OptionButtons. Change the `Caption` property of Frame1 to *Color* and the `Caption` of Frame2 to *Border*. Your Form2 should look something like Figure 6-1.

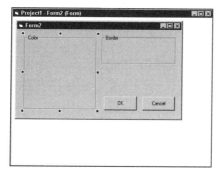

Figure 6-1
Use Frames to group OptionButtons.

Grouping OptionButtons on a Frame

OptionButton controls are *mutually exclusive* when you group them. This means that when the user clicks any one of the OptionButtons, none of the other OptionButtons in its group will be selected. Put another way: Selecting one automatically deselects any previously selected OptionButton in the group. This exclusiveness is useful when you present the user with a set of options, only one of which can be in effect at a given time.

In this example, you will create a group of buttons that lets the user choose between a 3D or Flat frame around the TextBox. You will then create a second group of buttons that lets the user choose blue, red, green, or black as the text color. Note the mutual exclusivity in these groups. The text is going to be entirely green or red — it cannot be mixed. Likewise, the TextBox is either 3D framed or flat, not both.

Now add four OptionButtons to the Color frame. Note that you must not double-click the OptionButtons in the Toolbox — if you do so, they won't be grouped in the frame. Instead, you must use the alternative technique of *drawing* each OptionButton within the frame. To do this, click the OptionButton icon in the Toolbox, then drag your mouse pointer *inside* the Color frame. When you drag your mouse, you will see a solid box that shows what size the component will be, and the mouse cursor changes to a cross, as you can see in Figure 6-2.

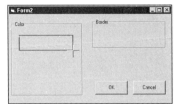

Figure 6-2
Draw each OptionButton onto the frame to group them within the frame.

When you release the left mouse button, the OptionButton appears within the frame. Repeat this three more times: Click the icon and then drag, so you have a total of four OptionButtons inside the Color frame. Change the Caption properties of the four buttons to Blue, Red, Green, and Black.

Change the Value property of the Black OptionButton to True (just double-click the Value property in the Properties Window). This has the effect of selecting this OptionButton (a black dot appears in the button indicating that it's been selected). Black is the default color of the text, so have this button selected when the user first sees this dialog box.

Now repeat this procedure to draw two OptionButtons on the Border frame, and caption them *3D* and *Flat*. Change the 3D button's Value property to True.

Programming with a Cancel Button

Now it's time to make the user's choices happen — by writing the programming that changes the text color (the TextBox's ForeColor property does this) or changes the border around the TextBox (use its Appearance property).

Your first thought is: OK, I can just put each OptionButton's programming in its Click event, like I did with the CommandButtons on Form1. That would work fine if the only thing you had on this dialog box was a Close or OK button. However, things get a little more complicated when you have that Cancel button.

Cancel means that the user decided to make *no changes* — even though the user may have clicked some of the OptionButtons before deciding to cancel. Therefore, if you programmed the text to change to blue when the user clicks the Blue OptionButton, you would be jumping the gun. When there is a Cancel button, you must put all of the programming into the OK button's click event. OK means make the changes; Cancel means do nothing. So you must write the programming in such a way that nothing happens until (and if) that OK button is clicked.

How do you write this kind of programming? Remember the If...Then command? You simply poll the entire status of all the OptionButtons on Form2. Just below is the programming you should type into the OK button's Click event. We'll leave the default name *Command1*, just because we feel like it. Whether you change the Name property of components to make them more descriptive is a matter of personal preference. (Also notice that I use some "constants" like vbBlue and vbGreen in the following code. For now, just go along with me on this — trust me. You'll see how to look up VB's built-in constants in Session 10 in the section titled "Understanding Parameters.")

Private Sub Command1_Click()

```
If Option1.Value = True Then Form1.Text1.ForeColor = vbBlue
If Option2.Value = True Then Form1.Text1.ForeColor = vbRed
If Option3.Value = True Then Form1.Text1.ForeColor = vbGreen
If Option4.Value = True Then Form1.Text1.ForeColor = vbBlack

If Option5.Value = True Then Form1.Text1.Appearance = 1
If Option6.Value = True Then Form1.Text1.Appearance = 0


Form2.Hide


End Sub
```

In programming, you often find that several lines are nearly identical. Programming can be repetitive, as it is in this example. VB's editor is like a word processor in many ways, and one thing you can do to save time with repetitive coding is to type in the first line:

```
If Option1.Value = True Then Form1.Text1.ForeColor = _
   vbBlue
```

then drag your mouse over it to select it. Press Ctrl+C to copy it, then press Ctrl+V five times to generate six lines of programming. Then you only need to change the *1* in Option*1* to the correct name for each OptionButton, and change the ForeColors or BorderStyles.

Notice that if you're referring to components on a different form than the one where you are writing your programming, you must identify the form name, separated by a period, and then the component name — Form1.Text1.ForeColor, for example. If that TextBox were on the same form as the programming referring to it, you could simply write Text1.ForeColor.

Showing and Hiding Forms

Notice the line at the end: Form2.Hide. When the user clicks the OK button, you want Form2 to disappear. The Hide command does just that. In fact, that's all the programming you need to put into the Cancel button's Click event, so type the following code in:

```
Private Sub Command2_Click()
Form2.Hide
End Sub
```

The only thing you need to put into the Options button's Click event on Form1 is the Show command, so double-click Form1 in the Project Explorer, then double-click the button captioned Options on Form1 and type in the following code:

```
Private Sub cmdOptions_Click()
Form2.Show
End Sub
```

At this point, why not test your application? Press F5, type some text into the TextBox, and click Options. You see Form2, as shown in Figure 6-3. Click the Red button (notice that the Black default button is automatically deselected the minute you click the Red button). Now click the Flat button. Click OK. The dialog box disappears and you see that the text has turned red and that the TextBox's frame has gone from a 3D effect to just a simple line.

You can tell when a set of components has been grouped — they all move together. Stop the program from running by selecting Run ⇨ End. Then double-click Form2 in the Project Explorer. Now drag Frame1 (the Color frame) to move it. Notice that all of the OptionButtons inside it move with it. If one of them doesn't move, it wasn't properly drawn and is merely resting on top of the frame rather than contained by it. To fix that, click the offending OptionButton to select it, press the Del key to delete it, and then look earlier in this session for the instructions on proper component drawing technique.

It's not necessary to use a frame if you're only presenting the user with a single group of OptionButtons. All OptionButtons placed on a form are considered grouped by that form — and they will work together just as if you'd contained them within a frame.

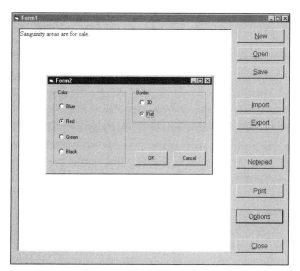

Figure 6-3
Your Options dialog box in action; everything works as planned.

Using CheckBoxes

CheckBoxes are quite similar to OptionButtons, except that CheckBoxes are used for non-exclusive choices — things that can be true for all, some, or none at the same time. For example, text can be bold, or italic, or both bold and italic at once. So the user can select a Boldface CheckBox and at the same time select an Italic CheckBox. Selecting one does not automatically deselect the others.

**10 Min.
To Go**

To see how to use CheckBoxes as a way of presenting the user with non-exclusive choices, put two CheckBoxes on Form2. Caption the first one Boldface and the second one Italic.

Now add the following programming just above the Form2.Hide line in the OK button's Click event:

```
If Check1.Value = 1 Then
Form1.Text1.FontBold = True
Else
Form1.Text1.FontBold = False
End If
```

```
If Check2.Value = 1 Then
Form1.Text1.Font.Italic = True
Else
Form1.Text1.Font.Italic = False
End If
```

You need to notice some peculiarities about this programming. Recall from a previous session that when you have a multi-line If...Then zone, you need to end the zone with End If. Also notice the new command Else. This command enables you to specify what VB should do when the If condition is false. What you're saying is: *If* Check1 is selected, *then* make Text1 boldface, or *else* (if it isn't selected) make it not boldface.

True Confessions: You Can't Remember Everything

One final thing you should notice here. You might have assumed that you can program If Check2.Value = True. But with CheckBoxes, you can't use True or False as the test of their status. CheckBoxes (unlike OptionButtons) can have three Value states: 0, 1, or 2, and they mean: Unchecked, Checked, and Greyed. (Greyed means the option is currently unavailable. You could set the Value to Grey to indicate to the user that they are using a typeface that doesn't have a bold style, for example.) But what I want you to really notice is that I didn't know all this.

I've been actively using Visual Basic for ten years, and the BASIC language itself for nearly 20. But you simply can't — and don't need to — remember all of these little variations and exceptions. Testing in VB is so easy (just press F5), and Help is so full of details (just press F1).

I have to admit I *did* first write If Check2.Value = True when I was working on this chapter, and when I pressed F5 it failed to turn the text bold. After some puzzling, I still couldn't figure it out. I took a look at Help, but it wasn't much help in this case (because when I looked up the Value property, it applied to several components, so it didn't tell me anything).

Next, I put a breakpoint on the line and stepped through the code until I saw that even when the CheckBox was selected, VB still went down to the Else line. I was really puzzled now. (Breakpoints and stepping are explained in Session 20.)

Then I looked at the Properties Window and saw that the Value property for a CheckBox had three possible states: 0, 1, or 2. Eureka! True and False can't work if there are three states.

The point of this confession is that you don't need to feel it's important to learn all of the components, as well as their properties, methods, events, and all the rest. You must remember the main ideas (If...Then...Else is an example of a main idea). However, the tri-state Value property of a CheckBox is, decidedly, not a main idea. It's easy to use Help, the Properties Window, or some other feature of VB to figure out how to fix it if your first guess about how it's programmed is wrong.

Select File ⇨ Save Project to save your work. You'll be asked if you want to save Form2 in the same CCourse1 folder that you've saved the rest of this project in; go ahead and do that.

Done!

REVIEW

You saw how to work with more than one form in a project and then how to group OptionButtons to provide the user with a set of mutually exclusive choices. You worked out the Cancel button problem by putting source code in the OK button rather than in the events of each OptionButton. You learned how to display and hide forms, and also when you should use CheckBoxes as an input device instead of OptionButtons. Finally, a word to the wise — don't think you can possibly memorize everything; rely on VB's Help for details about the various commands and components.

QUIZ YOURSELF

1. What is the difference between OptionButtons and CheckBoxes? (See "Using CheckBoxes".)

2. What containers can you use to group OptionButtons? (See "Grouping OptionButtons on a Frame".)

3. How do you handle it in code when the user clicks a Cancel button on one of your forms? (See "Programming with a Cancel Button".)

4. What's one way to tell if several OptionButtons are grouped together? (See "Showing and Hiding Forms".)

5. What are the three value states of a CheckBox? (See "True Confessions: You Can't Remember Everything".)

Working with TextBoxes and Their Properties

Session Checklist

✔ Understanding the default TextBox

✔ Common changes to a TextBox's properties

✔ Learning the use of every TextBox property

✔ Understanding that most properties are rarely used

✔ Discovering how to use the Properties Window

✔ Changing several properties at once

**30 Min.
To Go**

This session has two purposes: to make you more familiar with the important TextBox component, and also for you to learn all about using the Properties Window.

The TextBox is probably among the most used Visual Basic components — second only to the CommandButton, I would guess. You already worked with a TextBox in the project you built in previous sessions, but the TextBox is so important that learning some new techniques, and some review, are valuable.

Recall that a TextBox behaves like a simple word processor, but it does have its limitations. For instance, at any one time it can only display a single font and a single type style (such as italics). Also, it can display only one size of text at a time. You can change the font, style, and size by changing the TextBox's properties — but the *entire* contents of the TextBox will change. You cannot change a single word, for example, to italics. It's all or nothing.

TextBoxes can be used for both input and output: They can display text or accept the user's typed text. However, if you're merely identifying the purpose of, say, a CheckBox, use a Label instead. A TextBox would be overkill.

Adjusting TextBox Properties

Let's try using a TextBox. It is such an important component that we'll spend this session looking closely at it and its properties. Start Visual Basic and double-click the TextBox icon on the Toolbox.

Stretch and position the TextBox to make your form look the way you want. After that, there are several steps to clean up some default property settings — which, at least with the TextBox component, aren't usually what you want.

Many Visual Basic components have quite a few properties — just as the TextBox does. However, you usually don't have to change most of them. Each property defaults to its most common value. The Visible property defaults to True, rather than False, for instance. This is because you almost always want your components visible to the user.

However, some defaults will be wrong for your project. And a *few* defaults are nearly always wrong for any project. One of these infamous defaults is the TextBox's Text property. It defaults to the name of the TextBox (Text1, for example), and it's doubtful that any programmer ever wanted to display that to a user.

Our first job is to get rid of that default text, which says *Text1*. The default should have been a blank, empty Text property, but unfortunately, we're stuck with always having to remove *Text1* for each TextBox we create.

Note that there are two primary modes in the Visual Basic editor. While you're adding components to a form — or dragging them to change their shapes, or using the Properties Window to change their properties — you are in *design mode*. However, as soon as you press F5, you enter *run mode* and become an "imitation" user who is able to interact with your running application just as a user would. During run mode, you cannot use the Properties Window, any more than a regular user could.

Tip

Sometimes you'll see a phrase like, "You can't change this at run time." Run time means the same as what we called *run mode* in this session (in other words, while the application is running). Similarly, sometimes you'll see a message that says, "Change the property at design time." Design time refers to what we call *design mode* (the application is being worked on in the Visual Basic editor, but is not running). Some properties (such as the Name property) can be changed only at design time. Other properties (such as the Text property) can be changed either during design time or run time. Yet other properties (like the contents of a ListBox) can be changed only during run time — by the programming you write. Every property you see in the Properties Window can be set at design time, at least.

It's important to understand that components like TextBoxes start out with all of their properties in one state or another. The Width property, for example, is set to some width, and the Text property contains (or doesn't) contain some text. In any case, the condition of the properties determines what the user first sees when the application runs, or how the component first behaves.

You don't want users to be greeted with *Text1* (the default) sitting in your TextBox each time they run your application. So click the TextBox to select it (remember that this causes its properties to be displayed in the Properties Window). Then click the Text property in the Properties Window and drag your mouse across the right column where you see *Text1* so that you've selected it. Press Del. It disappears.

The second property that you usually have to change is the MultiLine property. By default, it's set to False, which forces all of your text onto the first line, no matter how high the TextBox actually is. Take a look at Figure 7-1.

Figure 7-1
With the MultiLine Property set to the default, there is no word-wrap, and everything typed appears on a single line.

Double-click the MultiLine property in the Properties Window and toggle it to True.

After you've cleaned up the Text and MultiLine properties, you'll still want to fix the Font property — it defaults to a small size. I generally change it to a more readable 12-point size. Double-click the Font property in the Properties Window, and you'll see the dialog box where you can change several qualities of the font. Change it to 12 in the Size list, and then click OK.

Now you've got a good, usable TextBox. Remember, if you're going to use more than one TextBox in a project, you can avoid having to set all of these properties for each TextBox. Simply click the TextBox you just finished cleaning up and press Ctrl+C to copy it. Then click the Form and press Ctrl+V to paste a new TextBox with all of the same properties inherited from its parent.

Some Important TextBox Properties (and Many that Aren't)

**20 Min.
To Go**

Now we're going to dive into the TextBox's properties. We'll discuss each one in turn. Many of these properties are properties of other components, as well as being properties of a form. For example, the BackColor property is fairly universal — most components have this property so you can change their color. But the main lesson I hope you learn from the following in-depth survey is that the majority of properties are of little use. I'll tell you which ones are valuable, and which ones you can just forget.

A TextBox has many properties, but generally only a few of them are of much value in most projects.

There's an Alignment property, but it merely offers two alternatives to the traditional left-justify (default). You can center or right-justify the text, but such adjustments are rarely of any use.

The Appearance property should remain set to the default — 3D. If you try changing it to the alternative Flat, you'll turn back time to pre-Windows 95-style user interface design.

If you want to, you can change the BackColor property to pink or blue or some other color (but it's best to leave it white in most applications). Similarly, you can change the text color by adjusting the ForeColor property. Again, you should probably leave well enough alone. The default black text on a white background is not only more readable, it's also more dignified.

Leave the BorderStyle property alone. It provides part of the 3D framing effect.

The `CausesValidation` property can remain set to True, with no harm done. When set to True, the `Validate` event will be triggered when the focus shifts from the TextBox to the other component (when the user clicks it or tabs to it). This property only comes in handy with database work. Forget about it for now.

There are four database-related properties; each begins with the word *data*. We'll get to them in the last group of sessions, where you'll build a database application.

The `DragIcon` property enables you to specify an icon that replaces the mouse pointer to show that an object is being dragged. Just leave it set to the default (none). That way, the standard Windows drag icon (the arrow inside a rectangle) will be used if the TextBox is dragged.

The `DragMode` property can be set to Automatic (1) to enable the TextBox to be dragged around the window while your program is running. When the `DragMode` is set to the default, Manual (0), the item will not be draggable unless you write special instructions in your programming. In either case, you must provide additional programming to make a TextBox (or other component) drag and drop. Just changing the `DragMode` property only allows the user to drag, not drop. However, I suggest you avoid dragging and dropping in VB. It's not widely used, nor is it often necessary.

The `Enabled` property, if set to False, prevents users from typing anything into the TextBox (it is said to be *disabled*). Its text will appear light gray rather than black to indicate that the TextBox is disabled. Components are disabled when it makes no sense for the user to try to use them. For example, suppose you have several TextBoxes on a form on which the user is supposed to fill in data about himself or herself, and they fill in the TextBox for their age with 44 years. You could then disable a checkbox in which they are supposed to indicate whether or not they are members of AARP. You have to be over 50 for AARP, so it makes no sense to leave that checkbox enabled. `Enabled` is often used in programming in response to situations as the one described in this AARP example. The code for this is `Text1.Enabled = False`.

The `Font` and `ForeColor` properties are defined earlier in this session.

The `Height` and `Width` properties describe the size of the TextBox. The `Left` and `Top` properties describe the width of the TextBox. The default unit of measurement for these properties is the *pixel*, the smallest dot on a monitor. Using the pixel gives you very precise control over size and position.

The `HelpContextID` enables you to provide a help feature for the TextBox — this property is nearly universally ignored.

The `HideSelection` property is yet another highly esoteric option. Text can be selected within a TextBox — by programming (as is done by a spell-checker to signal a misspelled word) or by the user dragging the mouse over some text. In either case, the text is highlighted. `HideSelection`, when set to False, means that selected text in your TextBox remains highlighted, even if the TextBox loses the focus (the user clicks some other form to give *it* the focus).

I can't really think of a use for this HideSelection **property, and, as you've seen in this session, many properties are just like it: highly specialized. I suggest that you not clutter your memory trying to memorize these rare birds. What you** *do* **need to remember is that VB contains hundreds of programming features, and if there's something highly specialized you want to do, you probably can. The way to find out how to accomplish your specific goal is to press F1, then click the Search Tab in Help and type in some words that describe your highly specialized job.**

The Index property is used with control arrays, and is covered in Session 13.

The four properties that begin with the word link are nearly universally ignored. If you want to use them, read about them in VB's Help.

The Locked property is similar, but less drastic, than setting the Enabled property to False. When set to True, Locked permits the TextBox's text to be scrolled, and even highlighted, by the user. It also permits you, the programmer, to change the text: Text1.Text = "This new text." The text is not changed to a gray color. However, as when Enabled is set to False, the user cannot edit the text.

The MaxLength property enables you to specify that the user can only enter a particular number of characters into the TextBox. This is useful if you want them to enter information like their zip code, the length of which you know in advance.

The MouseIcon property enables you to define a custom icon for the mouse pointer (if you also set the MousePointer property to 99). I suggest you leave well enough alone and just use the traditional mouse icon. The MousePointer property enables you to write programming that changes the mouse pointer to different styles (I-beam, Arrow, HourGlass). This can be helpful to the user as visual feedback. For instance, if you expect an operation to take a while, go ahead and program the pointer to change to an hourglass, using this code: MousePointer = 11. You don't, however, use the Properties Window to change it. You make the changes in your programming, and when the long operation finishes, you restore the default pointer, using the following code: MousePointer = 0. However, in general, you can let Windows and Visual Basic handle any changes to the mouse pointer. Most of the time it's not necessary to manipulate this property. For example, when you press F5 to run your VB program, you'll notice that if you move the mouse pointer onto a TextBox, the mouse pointer changes from an arrow to an I-beam automatically. The I-beam pointer is the classic Windows cue that you can type text into the component over which the mouse pointer is hovering.

The two properties whose names begin with OLE can be safely ignored. They tell VB whether you, the programmer, or the component itself is supposed to deal with dragging and dropping activity. Again, I recommend you avoid the whole drag-and-drop behavior in your VB projects.

The PasswordChar property enables you to specify which character should appear visible to the user when he or she types in a password. In other words, if you want to use a TextBox as a password-entry field for the user, you can type in a * symbol as the PasswordChar. If you type in any character as the PasswordChar, the TextBox will display only that character as the user types: ***********, like that. You know the routine. I've always wondered whether this subterfuge is all that necessary. After all, do you have people hovering over your shoulder all the time, just waiting to see your password? I suppose it's better to hide it though. There *are* lurkers.

Note that the MultiLine property must be set to False for the password feature to work properly.

For an English speaker, the RightToLeft property has no value and should be left at its default. However, some languages such as Arabic and Hebrew run text from right to left. You would set RightToLeft for those languages so vertical scroll bars will appear on the *left* side of a TextBox.

The Scrollbars property enables you to add horizontal or vertical scroll bars to your TextBox so the user can employ them as a way of moving through text that exceeds the size of the TextBox. However, even without them, the user can always press the arrow keys, the PgUp and PgDn keys, the spacebar, and so on to move around through text that's not shown within the visible opening of the TextBox.

We looked at the TabIndex property in a previous session — it defines the order in which components get focus as the user repeatedly presses the Tab key to move among them.

The TabStop property, when set to False, removes the component from the TabIndex list. TabIndex is useful because it offers a quick way for the user to move among the input components (TextBoxes, CheckBoxes, and so forth) on a form — all without having to remove his or her hands from the keyboard and reach for the mouse to click a component into the focus. However, there are some components, like a PictureBox, that are not usually employed as user-input devices. So you can set their TabStop properties to False to eliminate them from the TabIndex group. Components such as Labels that can *never* be used as input devices simply have no TabIndex property in the first place, and are therefore never included in the tabbing.

How can a PictureBox ever be used as an input device, you ask? A simple example is that if the PictureBox is clicked at all, anywhere, something happens (because you put some programming into its Click event). You might display several small PictureBoxes, each containing a different image — perhaps a car, a bus, a train, or a plane. When you click one, a phone number where you can arrange for that kind of transportation is displayed.

Here's a more sophisticated example: Put a map of Italy into a PictureBox in a cookbook application, let the user click on whatever location on the map they choose, and then display a list of recipes typical to the locale that they clicked. (There is an *x* and *y* coordinate for the MouseDown event that tells you exactly where, on a graphic, the user clicked.)

The Tag property is a kind of Post-It' note that you can attach to a component. You can type in some unique text as a way of identifying it when it is passed to a procedure. The Text property is the actual text that appears within the TextBox, visible to the user.

The ToolTipText property is the small help phrase that pops up to inform the user about the purpose of a component when the user pauses the mouse pointer on top of the component.

The Visible property determines whether or not the user can see the TextBox. During design time, components are always visible. But during run time, if you set the Visible property to False, the user cannot see the component. When would you want to make a component invisible? There are at least a couple of uses for this property.

Although it's not traditional, Microsoft and other developers recently started using a new style of user-interaction. For example, a CommandButton is labeled "Additional Features." If the user clicks it, that CommandButton is set to Visible = False and is replaced with two or three OptionButtons from which the user can select additional preferences. Those OptionButtons were always sitting there, but their Visible property was False until (or if) the user clicked the CommandButton, revealing them.

A second use for Visible is when you want to use a feature of a component, but you don't want the user to see that component. The most frequent use of this trick is to employ an invisible ListBox. ListBoxes can alphabetize. You can hand one a list of names, and it will organize them for you. However, the user never needs to see the ListBox.

Note that you often do want to display or conceal forms. Most applications begin with a single form, so as not to confuse the reader. But a project of any complexity likely has additional forms as well. For example, a user may have to fill in three forms worth of data, but only the first form greets them when they start the application. When the user completes the first form, perhaps they click a Next button. The first form is made invisible, and the second form is made visible. You can use the forms' Visibility properties to do this, but it's more common to use the forms' Show and Hide methods, like this: `Form1.Hide: Form2.Show`. The results are the same as if you used this code: `Form1.Visible = False: Form2.Visible = True`.

The `WhatsThisHelpID` property is rarely used. It works with a help feature, the small button with a ? on it that you see on some windows next to the x (that closes a window) in the upper-right corner. Clicking the ? changes the mouse pointer to an arrow with a ? attached. Then when you click a component, a small window appears with a brief description of the component. Note that this description is generally more detailed than the single phrase displayed with the similar *Tooltip* feature described earlier in this session.

Working with the Properties Window

Notice that the Properties Window has two columns. On the left is the property name, and on the right are the values, the actual current status of that property.

10 Min. To Go

Adjusting values

In many cases, double-clicking in either pane changes the value of the property. For instance, double-click the `Visible` property and it switches from its default True to False. Double-click it again, and it goes back to True. Properties with more than two possible values usually cycle through their various possible settings as you double-click them.

When you single-click a property, sometimes a button appears in its right pane. A down-arrow button means that you can click it to drop down a list of values for that property. An ellipsis (...) button means that if you click it a dialog box will be displayed. (See Figure 7-2.)

You might see several kinds of dialog boxes if you click an ellipsis button. When changing the `Picture` property of a PictureBox, you'll see an Open File dialog box you can use to find a graphics file to fill the PictureBox. The `Font` property is somewhat unusual because it actually defines several related properties: `Font`, `FontSize`, and `FontStyle` (italics and bold). If you click its ellipsis button, you see a dialog box in which you can select the various font-related properties all at once.

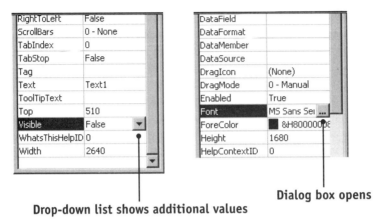

Drop-down list shows additional values

Dialog box opens

Figure 7-2
Drop-down lists and dialog boxes help you quickly change a property's value.

Changing several components at once

Sometimes, you want to change the same property for several components at the same time. We covered this in an earlier session, but here's a reminder of how it works: Imagine that you have two OptionButtons, three Labels, and a TextBox on a form. They all need larger fonts so the user can more easily read them. You want to change all of their Font properties from the default 8 to 11. You can do this in two ways:

1. Click the Font property for the TextBox. Change it to 11. Then click an OptionButton to select it (so its properties fill the Properties Window). You'll see that VB has already selected the Font property for you. Whatever property that was last selected remains selected, even as you move from component to component. Sometimes, two components don't share a property, so in those cases, the default property is selected.

2. The second and fastest way to change a property simultaneously for multiple components is to drag your mouse around the components. This selects all of them (drag handles appear around all selected components). When you do this, the Properties Window displays *only those properties that all of the selected components have in common* (see Figure 7-3). When you change the Font property with several components selected, for example, that property changes for *each* of the selected components.

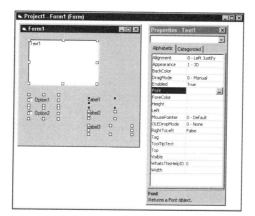

Figure 7-3
When you select multiple components, the Properties Window displays whatever properties they have in common.

Done!

The categorized view

I don't find the feature useful, but some programmers like to click the tab at the top of the Properties Window and switch to *Categories*. This rearranges the properties into groups: Behavior, Appearance, and so on. However, the Miscellaneous category is so large — and so *very* miscellaneous — that I prefer to leave the list displayed alphabetized. But which view you prefer is, as usual, your decision. As I've often said — VB is marvelously flexible.

REVIEW

In this session, you saw how to work with a TextBox. You learned which of its properties almost always need to be changed from their default, and how to use the Properties Window to change them. Then — because the TextBox's set of properties are also the properties used with many other components — you learned about them, their uses, and their relative value. You also learned that some are just plain rarely used at all. Finally, you saw how to change the same property in several components simultaneously.

QUIZ YOURSELF

1. Describe the difference between run time and design time.
    (See "Adjusting TextBox Properties".)

2. What are two (of the three) TextBox properties that you almost
    always have to adjust? (See "Adjusting TextBox Properties".)

3. What is the Enabled property used for? [See "Some Important TextBox
    Properties (and Many that Aren't)".]

4. What does the ToolTipText property do? [See "Some Important TextBox
    Properties (and Many that Aren't)".]

5. If you click an ellipsis button in the Properties Window, what do you see?
    (See "Adjusting Values".)

Labels, ListBoxes, and ComboBoxes

Session Checklist

✔ Adding Labels to inform the user

✔ Formatting Labels to make them look nice

✔ Watch out when adding new text at run time

✔ Working with ListBoxes and ComboBoxes

✔ Ignoring the DriveListBox, DirListBox, and FileListBox components

**30 Min.
To Go**

L abels are generally used simply to identify the purpose of other components or entire forms. Some components such as CommandButtons, OptionButtons, and CheckBoxes are self-identifying because they have a `Caption` property you use to display their purpose to the user. However, a TextBox doesn't have an exterior caption, so you might want to put a label near it to describe what it does.

Use Labels to Describe Something's Purpose

You might want to identify a whole form with a label, as in Figure 8-1.

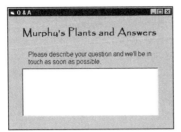

Figure 8-1
Labels can describe what a form does, and what individual components do.

Figure 8-1 shows a form the user is supposed to fill in. Two Labels are on the form. The top one is in a large, special typeface and titles the form, providing the name of the company. The second label describes the purpose of the TextBox and gives the user instructions. If you want to use various fonts or typesizes, you must use more than one label. As with a TextBox, you cannot mix and match character sizes or styles within a single Label.

Notice that the Caption property of the form itself was also changed (click on a form and its properties fill the Properties Window). The title bar displays the caption you give to a form (in this case, *Q & A* rather than the default, Form1).

Formatting Labels

Labels can be formatted in a variety of ways. You can set the Alignment property to Left, Center, or Right. The AutoSize property, when set to True, causes the Label to grow or shrink to fit the text that is inside. This can be useful if you plan to dynamically add text (add it during run time) without knowing in advance how much text there will be.

The BackStyle property, when set to Transparent, permits graphics, text, or colors underneath the Label to show through. The text in a Label is never transparent, but it almost always looks best if you don't let the entire rectangle of the Label cover whatever might be underneath. On the other hand, the default BackColor of a Label is precisely the same gun-metal gray as the Windows standard — which is the default background color of all other components and forms. So unless you've changed the Form to pink, or are using a graphic as wallpaper on the form (this is rarely done), the Label background will match the form it's sitting on.

There's also a BorderStyle property that puts a simple black line around the Label or a 3D-effect sunken frame, depending on the setting of the Appearance property. This property is nearly always left set to False. Labels usually look best unframed, and even the 3D frame can miscue users because sunken objects are supposed to cue the user that the sunken component is an input device, something they can interact with. (True input devices — the box in a CheckBox, the whole TextBox itself, and several other user-input components — appear engraved, a bit sunken into the background, if their Appearance property is set to 3D).

The last major Label property is WordWrap, which, by default, is set to False. This property is easily confused with AutoSize, and the two interact, as we will see in the next section.

A problem: Adding text during run time

If you don't plan to dynamically assign text to a Label (you aren't going to change its Caption property in your programming), go ahead and just stretch the Label so it's big enough to display its permanent caption. But if you plan to assign a new caption at run time, you've got some questions to answer.

Set AutoSize to True, but leave WordWrap set to False, and the Label will expand horizontally, *but not vertically*. It could shoot off the form to the right, but no matter what, it will remain on a single line, as you can see in Figure 8-2.

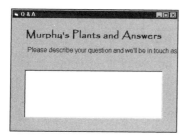

Figure 8-2
If you type too much text with AutoSize set to True, the Label shoots off the right side of the Form.

Another problem with AutoSize = True is that your Label might cover up any components to its right when it expands.

Now, if you leave AutoSize set to False, and if there is too much text to fit inside the Label's existing dimensions, the text will truncate, as you can see in Figure 8-3.

The third possibility is to set both AutoSize and WordWrap to True. In this case, if too much text is stuffed into the Label, it will expand vertically. Taking this approach means that the text usually won't shoot off the side, or be cut off on the bottom. However, this tactic, too, has a weakness — the expanding Label might cover components below it as it expands downward. In most cases, you don't want your Label to suddenly cover other components.

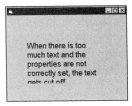

Figure 8-3
With AutoSize set to False, a Label's contents can be cut off.

The solution: Use a TextBox instead

To me, there is only one good solution to this problem: Avoid using a Label at all if you must add text to it during run time. Sometimes you want to display data from a database or other source, and maybe you let a user click buttons to move through the records in that database. Some records may be larger than others (fields such as notes, descriptions, and so forth are not of predictable length the way that a telephone number is). In those cases, I recommend that you use a TextBox. A TextBox doesn't need to expand. It will scroll if the contents overflow its boundaries, and you can also provide an optional scroll bar by setting the ScrollBars property if you wish. But even without a scroll bar, the user can still use the arrow keys and other keys such as PgDn to see the hidden text.

**20 Min.
To Go**

Using ListBoxes and ComboBoxes

The ListBox component is used to display a list of information to the user. It can be a list of names of business contacts, a list of books for sale, or whatever. The user can click on one of the items, and your programming can detect which item was clicked. If the number of items in the list is larger than can be displayed, a scroll bar is automatically added to the ListBox.

Where does the information come from that appears in a ListBox? You can use the VB Array command to hold the list right inside your Visual Basic program. This approach is good for lists that are short and that do not get changed (the data is hardwired in your programming — so changing that data requires that the program itself be modified, then recompiled).

More commonly, though, you'll have a database from which to draw. Data in a database is kept in a file or files separate from your program. Because it's held in an independent file, a database can be modified without requiring that your program itself be modified. You'll see how to use databases starting in Session 21.

For now, you can just use the Array command to see how to contain data inside a VB program, and then fill a ListBox with that data.

If you wish, you can type in a list of data using the Properties Window. You can use this somewhat unusual technique, instead of using the Array **command, to add short lists of built-in data. To do this, double-click the ListBox's** List **property in the Properties Window. A TextBox drops down. Type in your data, pressing Ctrl+Enter each time you finish an item. However, in this session, we'll use the** Array **command instead in our experiments with the ListBox.**

Start a new VB Standard EXE project (File ⇨ New Project), and then put a ListBox on Form1. Double-click Form1 so you get to the code window, and the Form_Load — a form's default event — is displayed. Recall that each component and all forms have a default event, which is its most commonly used event.

If you double-clicked the ListBox instead of the form, you'll see the List1_Click event, so go back to the design window and double-click the form itself.

Type the following code into Form1_Load:

```
Private Sub Form_Load()


MyList = Array("Bob", "Sandy", "Julie", "Fred", "Sam")
For i = 0 To 4
List1.AddItem MyList(i)
Next


End Sub
```

You'll find out about the important For...Next technique in Session 17. For now, let's briefly consider the Array command. It puts data into a variable. The variable in this example is called MyList, but you can give variables any name you want as long as you don't use one of the words in the Visual Basic language (such as Stop or For or Private).

The data in the code above is a list of string (text) data: five names. By typing them within parentheses following the Array command, and using quotation marks and commas to separate them, you put them into the MyList array.

Arrays are special kinds of variables that contain more than one piece of data. Each piece of data in an array is identified by an index number: `MyList(0)` holds Bob, `MyList(1)` holds Sandy, and so on up to Sam in `MyList(4)`. Notice that arrays begin counting with an index number of zero.

We'll talk about arrays in more depth in Session 13. Let's move on to consider the `AddItem` method. In this example, you use the `AddItem` command to add each item from your `MyList` array. This happens because the `For...Next` loop repeats the `AddItem` command five times (from 0 to 4), and each time through the (i) represents a different index number: 0, 1, 2, 3, and 4 — thereby putting each piece of data into your ListBox.

Using a loop is just a shortcut. You can achieve precisely the same result as the above loop by using this code instead:

```
Dim MyList(4)

MyList(0) = "Bob"
MyList(1) = "Sandy"
MyList(2) = "Julie"
MyList(3) = "Fred"
MyList(4) = "Sam"
```

But as you can see, this is repetitive and would be really tiresome if you had a large list to put into an array. (That `Dim` command tells VB that you're going to use the variable `MyList` as an array name. This isn't necessary if you use the `Array` command.)

Don't worry if your understanding of arrays and loops isn't clear yet. We'll cover them thoroughly later. First, let's try this example. Press F5. You should see the list shown in Figure 8-4.

Figure 8-4
Use the AddItem command to fill a ListBox with data.

If you want to add a new item to the very top of the list in a ListBox, use a zero following the command, like this:

```
List1.AddItem "James", 0
```

Automatic alphabetization

Notice that the items in the ListBox are not alphabetized; they are listed in the order that you added them (which in this case is the same order as they appear in your array). Sometimes this is desirable, but usually it's easier for a user if you alphabetize. A ListBox can automatically alphabetize quickly. To alphabetize, change the ListBox's Sorted property to True in the Properties Window. Capitalization is ignored.

Removing items from a list

How do you think you remove an item from a ListBox? How about using the RemoveItem command?

It's not all that common, but sometimes you might want to remove one or more items from a ListBox. You identify the item you want removed by using its index number. Each item in the ListBox has a different index number given to it by the ListBox. The ListBox maintains an array. The name of the array is List(). The index of the List() array (the number of the currently selected item) is called the ListIndex.

Double-click the ListBox to get to its Click event, and then type in the following code:

```
Private Sub List1_Click()

List1.RemoveItem (List1.ListIndex)

End Sub
```

Press F5. Click any item in the ListBox, and that item will be removed.

Sometimes you want to clear out the entire contents of the ListBox all at once, in preparation for refilling the ListBox with a whole new list. To do that, use the Clear command:

```
List1.Clear
```

The Checkbox-style ListBox

There are some different ways you can display your lists. Change the Style property to Checkbox, and small boxes appear next to each item, as you can see in Figure 8-5.

Figure 8-5
The Checkbox style ListBox lets the user select multiple items.

This style of ListBox permits the user to select as many items as the user wishes. To detect which items the user has selected, you use the Selected property. Let's try it. Make sure you've got the Style property set to Checkbox, then delete the previous contents of the ListBox's Click event and replace it with the following code:

```
Private Sub List1_Click()
If List1.Selected(3) = True Then MsgBox "Sam is selected."
End Sub
```

The MsgBox command displays a simple dialog box. It's sometimes quite useful when you're programming and want a quick way to see if you're getting the results you want. Just display something, as we did here, and you can see if things are OK.

Press F5, then click several of the names in the ListBox. As soon as you click Sam, the message box will pop out.

Using multiple columns

You can adjust the ListBox's display in a couple of additional ways. Set the Columns property to 1, and you get a horizontal rather than a vertical scroll bar if the contents are too large to fit. This is pretty counterintuitive, because when the user scrolls horizontally, the list moves vertically. I would avoid this option.

If, however, you set the `Columns` property to any number greater than 1, you get multiple columns, and a horizontal scroll bar, if a scroll bar is needed, as shown in Figure 8-6.

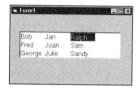

Figure 8-6
If you want data displayed in more than one column, set the Columns property to any number greater than 1.

**10 Min.
To Go**

ComboBoxes, a Variation on the ListBox

The ComboBox is quite similar to the ListBox. It uses the `AddItem`, `RemoveItem`, and `Clear` methods. Both components also have a `Sorted` property that behaves the same way, and so forth.

The primary difference is that a ComboBox has a small TextBox at the very top, as you can see in Figure 8-7.

Figure 8-7
A ComboBox has a TextBox attached to it, where the user can type in an item.

Sometimes you want to let user add their own items to the list you display. Perhaps you show them a list of travel destinations, but you also want to permit them to type in their own destination if it's not in the list. Another feature of a ComboBox is that user can select from the items in the list by typing only the first letter or first few letters, and then pressing enter.

A ComboBox only displays one item — user doesn't see the list unless the down-arrow button is clicked next to the TextBox. The Style property determines a couple of behaviors of a ComboBox. Change the Style to 1, Simple Combo, and the drop-down button disappears, though the user can still scroll through the list with the arrow keys on the keyboard. Change the Style property to 2, which is the drop-down list style, and the user cannot type something new into the TextBox. In any configuration, a ComboBox's great advantage, in addition to letting users type in a new item, is that it takes up less real estate on the screen than a ListBox. The ComboBox shows only the one, default item until the user clicks the drop-down button.

The default item that is the only thing the user first sees is whatever you've typed into the Text property in the Properties Window for that ComboBox.

Directory-, Drive-, and FileListBoxes

In the early days of the 1990s, Visual Basic programmers frequently used DirListBoxes, DriveListBoxes, and FileListBoxes. They were the best way to give the user access to disk drives. VB programmers used these three components to build Save, Save As, and Open dialog boxes so users could load and save files.

However, each programmer's file dialog box looked different from the ones built by other programmers. Understandably, users like to learn how to work with a single utility that looks and works the same way in all of their applications. About the time that Windows 95 came out, dialog boxes that behaved in uniform, logical ways became the norm.

Visual Basic provides a whole collection of these now-standard dialog boxes (Print, Select Colors, Choose Font, Save File, and so on) in a feature called the CommonDialog component, the subject of Session 11.

Done!

So, even though the DirListBox, DriveListBox, and FileListBox are sitting there on your basic VB Toolbox, it's best to ignore them. They're a legacy of a less sensible approach to file access.

REVIEW

All about Labels, ListBoxes, and ComboBoxes, this session explored two of the most useful components Visual Basic offers. I say "two" because the ComboBox component is merely a variation of the ListBox. You saw how to format a Label and how to add a caption to one. You understood when it is best to abandon the Label component in favor of the TextBox. Then you discovered how best to take advantage of the ListBox's alphabetizing capabilities, as well as how to add and remove items from the list. Then some variations on the ListBox were introduced: the CheckBox-style, multiple columns, and ComboBoxes. Finally, you were warned against resorting to the now-passé Directory-, Drive-, and FileListBox components. Sure, they're on the Toolbox, but they are now rarely employed. Use the CommonDialog component instead (see Session 12).

QUIZ YOURSELF

1. You'll sometimes want to adjust the BackStyle property of a Label. Why? (See "Formatting Labels".)

2. Why do you have to worry if you need to change the Caption property of a Label during run time? (See "A Problem: Adding Text during Run Time".)

3. Where do the items displayed in a List- or ComboBox usually come from? The user? An array in the program? A database? (See "Using ListBoxes and ComboBoxes".)

4. How does the user benefit if you employ the CheckBox-style ListBox? (See "The CheckBox-style ListBox".)

5. Why should you avoid using the Directory-, Drive-, and FileListBox components? (See "Directory-, Drive-, and FileListBoxes".)

All About Graphics: Adding Images, Pictures, and Shapes

Session Checklist

✔ How to display graphics

✔ The differences between Image and PictureBox controls

✔ Changing graphics at run time

✔ Simple animation

✔ Adding graphics to other controls, such as CommandButtons

✔ Using the Line and Shape controls to subdivide a form

**30 Min.
To Go**

This isn't really a session; it's more like recess. You'll find out how to use graphics to jazz up your applications, and make them look more professional. It's fast, and it's about the most powerful effect you can achieve in VB in less than ten seconds.

All you do is double-click a PictureBox icon on the Toolbox, double-click the Picture property in the Properties Window, find a graphics file, and double-click its name. You're done. What could be simpler?

Before getting deeper into graphics, you need some actual graphics to work with, right? If you've got picture files on your hard drive, by all means use them. If you chose to install graphics during your setup of VB or Microsoft Office, you'll find them on your hard drive in \Program Files\Microsoft Visual Studio\Common\Graphics, or \Program Files\Microsoft Office\Office\PhotoDraw\Content. And don't forget: The Internet is loaded with great drawings and photos only a download away.

Using a PictureBox

Recall that a PictureBox is an all-purpose graphics container. You can use it to display the contents of .BMP, .GIF, .JPG, .WMF, or .ICO graphics files. Try displaying a graphic by following these steps:

1. Double-click the PictureBox icon in the VB Toolbox. A PictureBox appears on the form.

2. Double-click the Picture property in the Properties Window. VB displays the Load Picture dialog box so you can browse your hard drive for a graphic file.

3. Locate, then double-click, the name of one of the following graphic file-types supported by VB 6: .BMP (ordinary bitmap), .CUR (cursor), .DIB (legacy format not in use), .EMF (older format), .GIF (ordinary bitmap), .ICO (icon), .JPG (popular compressed format — often used on the Internet), or .WMF (a Microsoft format for resizable drawings that never really caught on).

After you double-click a graphics filename in the file browser dialog box, the image will be loaded into your PictureBox control, as shown in Figure 9-1.

In Figure 9-1, I used the ROLODEX.WMF file from \Program Files\Microsoft Visual Studio\Common\Graphics\Metafile\Business — a collection of cartoon drawings that comes with VB.

Notice that a PictureBox can distort a .WMF drawing until you drag the corners of the PictureBox to resize it, as shown in Figure 9-2.

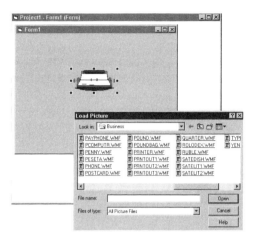

Figure 9-1
Adding drawings or photos to a VB project is a snap.

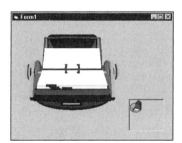

Figure 9-2
A .WMF graphics file will resize itself to fill a PictureBox. However, most graphics files — like the .BMP in the PictureBox on the right — do not resize themselves.

Notice in Figure 9-2 that if you add a second PictureBox, and then put a .BMP in it (or any other graphics filetype besides .WMF), the graphic has a fixed size. No matter how you stretch the PictureBox, the graphic remains the same size. Also notice the 3D-frame effect around the graphic on the right — you get a frame like that by setting a PictureBox's `BorderStyle` Property to Fixed Single.

If you want the PictureBox to size itself to fit precisely around a .BMP, .JPG, or any other graphics format other than the resizable .WMF type — just change the PictureBox's `AutoSize` property to True.

The Image Control

Is there a way to stretch or enlarge a .BMP, .JPG, or other graphic? Yes; use an Image control instead of a PictureBox, and set that Image control's Stretch property to True.

Beware of overstretching a graphic

Most graphics become distorted or grainy if you enlarge them too much or stretch them to the wrong shape, as shown in Figure 9-3.

Figure 9-3
Don't go wild with the Image control's Stretch property or you'll get ugly results like this.

Image and PictureBox compared

An Image control works practically the same way as a PictureBox control, but the Image control has several advantages:

- An Image control draws onscreen faster.
- An Image control uses fewer of the computer's resources (such as memory) because it is less complex and has far fewer properties than a PictureBox. For one thing, an Image control cannot accept graphics drawn (using the Line, Circle, or PSet commands) or text printed (using the Print command). A PictureBox can, but few people use the drawing or printing features in VB because they are relatively primitive. For graphics, you're better off using a graphics application — then saving the results of your creativity into a .BMP or .JPG file that you can then load into your VB application in an Image or PictureBox. For text, it's more efficient to edit the Caption and Font properties of a Label control rather than using the Print command.

- Graphics placed in an Image can be freely resized. You can stretch or shrink the graphics to suit your needs by setting the Image control's Stretch property to True.

- Other controls can be *grouped* or contained within a PictureBox (the Frame control can do this too). The value of this grouping is that the contained controls then act in concert. This containing behavior is generally used to define a group of OptionButtons, only one of which can be selected at a time. When a program runs, if the user clicks one OptionButton, all other OptionButtons in its group are automatically deselected. An Image control cannot contain other controls, but programmers usually employ a Frame control instead of a PictureBox to group OptionButtons. A Frame uses few resources.

Today's typical computer is quite powerful. The idea of avoiding PictureBoxes when possible to conserve resources is no longer as compelling as it was seven years ago when Image controls were first introduced. For ordinary desktop applications, you likely need not concern yourself with the resources problem. However, if you're writing an application that will be used on the Internet or a local network, memory size and other resource issues *can* be significant.

20 Min. To Go

Changing Graphics while a Program Runs

You can copy a graphic, erase it, load a new one, or import a graphic from the Windows clipboard — all while your VB program runs.

Copying

To copy a graphic, try typing this into the Form_Click event:

```
Private Sub Form_Click()
Picture1.Picture = Image1.Picture
End Sub
```

Press F5 to run the program, then click the form's background, and the graphic in the Image control is copied to the PictureBox control.

You can freely copy graphics between Forms, PictureBoxes, and Image controls. For example, Image1.Picture = Form2.Picture **copies a Form's background into an Image control.**

If you do choose to use the Print or Line, Circle, or PSet commands with a PictureBox, you can copy that content by using the Image property in conjunction with the Picture property, like this: Picture1.Picture = Picture5.Image.

Erasing

To erase a graphic, just use the LoadPicture command with empty parentheses, like this:

```
Private Sub Form_Click()
Picture1.Picture = LoadPicture()
End Sub
```

Replacing

The LoadPicture command can also be used to replace a graphic while a program runs:

```
Private Sub Form_Click()
Picture1.Picture = LoadPicture("E:\Program Files\Microsoft Visual
Studio\Common\Graphics\Metafile\Business\CALCULTR.WMF")
End Sub
```

Importing

You can import a graphic from the Windows clipboard by using the GetData command. To try the following example, first press the PrintScrn key to ensure that there is a graphic image in the clipboard, then press F5 to run this little program:

```
Private Sub Form_Click()
If Clipboard.GetFormat(2) Then
    Picture1.Picture = Clipboard.GetData
End If
End Sub
```

If you want your program to make sure that the clipboard contains graphics rather than text, you can use the GetFormat command, as illustrated in the previous example. The GetFormat command can identify the following kinds of contents in the clipboard:

GetFormat(1)	Text
GetFormat(2)	Bitmap Graphic (.BMP)
GetFormat(3)	Windows Metafile (.WMF)
GetFormat(8)	Device-Independent Bitmap (.DIB)
GetFormat(9)	Color palette
GetFormat(48896)	Dynamic Data Exchange link (DDE)

Animation

You can achieve animation in various ways. One way is to turn on and off the Visible properties of two or more superimposed graphics (use a VB Timer control to govern this). Or you can use the Move command (and a Timer) to make a graphic slide across the screen. Another way to move a graphic is to change its Left or Top properties.

Yet another animation effect, illustrated in the following example, merely rearranges superimposed graphics, as you would by putting different cards on top of a deck. If a set of PictureBoxes are all the same size and in the same place on a form, they act like a deck of cards, and which PictureBox is on top (and therefore visible to the user) at any given time is governed by each PictureBox's ZOrder property.

In this example, each time you click the Form, the ZOrder of a PictureBox switches between 0 (on top) and 1 (next to the top). Since there are two PictureBoxes of the same size and in the same position — this has the effect of toggling them.

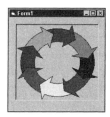

Figure 9-4
Each time this form is clicked, two pictures switch places.

Put two PictureBoxes on a form, and then change their `Picture` properties to fill each of them with a different graphic file. Type the following code into the `Form_Load` event. It causes `Picture2` to be in the same position, and the same size, as `Picture1`:

```
Private Sub Form_Load()
Picture2.Left = Picture1.Left
Picture2.Top = Picture1.Top
Picture2.Height = Picture1.Height
Picture2.Width = Picture1.Width
End Sub
```

Then type this into the `Form_Click` event to produce the animation:

```
Private Sub Form_Click()
Static toggle As Boolean

toggle = Not toggle

If toggle Then
    Picture2.ZOrder 1
Else
    Picture2.ZOrder 0
End If

End Sub
```

Notice that the higher the `ZOrder` number, the lower in the "stack of cards" the object sits. You can manipulate the positions of any objects that have a `ZOrder` property by merely adjusting these numbers, which makes objects overlap each other in various ways.

In the `Form_Click` event, a variable named `toggle` was defined using the `Static` command. Session 13 explains the idea of *scope*, but it's worth briefly noting now that ordinarily when you define a variable in a procedure (between the `Sub` and `End Sub` or `Function` and `End Function`), that variable is extinguished when VB moves out of the procedure.

Ordinarily. But if you use the `Static` command to declare a variable in a procedure, that variable *retains its value* even when execution of the program leaves the procedure. Each time you click the form in this example, execution enters the `Form_Click` procedure, then execution leaves the `Click` procedure after switching the `ZOrder` of `Picture2`. However, because the variable `toggle` is defined as

Graphics Everywhere

In addition to PictureBoxes, Images, and Forms, several other controls also have a `Picture` property. If a control has a `Picture` property, you can add graphics to it if you wish, as visual cues as to the status or purpose of the control. Among the most popular controls with `Picture` properties are the CheckBox, OptionButton, and CommandButton.

Many programmers get confused, though, because with these three controls not only must you make the `Picture` property point to a graphic file, *you must also set the control's* `Style` *property to* `Graphical`. The CommandButton shown here contains an icon of a printer.

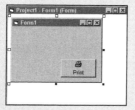

You can assign a different picture to be displayed only when the user clicks the button. To do this, use the DownPicture property.

`Static`, the variable "remembers" whether it holds True or False (the only two values that a `Boolean` variable type can hold).

The `Not` command switches the value in the variable `toggle` between True and False — just like flipping a light switch up or down. If `toggle` holds True, then when the line `toggle = Not toggle` is executed, the contents of `toggle` become False, and vice versa.

**10 Min.
To Go**

Shapes and Lines

You may have noticed the Shape and Line controls on VB's Toolbox. They aren't used much, but they do have one specialized function: subdividing a form. If you have a relatively complicated form, you can organize it visually by using Shape or

Line components to group related items. Typically, an options or preferences dialog box includes various sections that lend themselves to discreet zoning, as you can see in Figure 9-5.

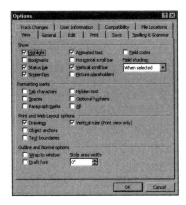

Figure 9-5
Use Line or Shape controls to subdivide a complex window into logical zones.

In Figure 9-5, there are four groups of options, separated by four lines. These visual cues help the reader more quickly understand the contents of a complicated form. However, notice that the lines used (by Microsoft Word) in Figure 9-5 are actually composed of two lines, creating a 3D effect. You can do this quite easily with the Line control in VB.

To create attractive divider lines, like the bottom line in Figure 9-6, put two lines next to each other. Then set the top (or left-side) line's BorderColor property to dark gray and the bottom (or right-side) line's BorderColor to white.

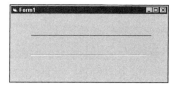

Figure 9-6
By itself, a single VB Line control is crude looking (top). Use two Line controls — one gray, one white — and you get the subtle effect used in most commercial applications (bottom).

To reposition a control on a form with great precision, click the control to select it, and then hold down the Ctrl key while repeatedly pressing the arrow keys. (To resize the control, hold down the shift key while pressing arrow keys.) If you're having problems precisely positioning a control on a form, you probably have the Snap-to-grid feature turned on. Select Tools ⇨ Options, and then click the General tab. Deselect the *Align controls to grid* option.

Use the Shape control (which has six Shape properties) in the same way as you use the Line control. With its Shape property set to Rectangle or Square, or the rounded versions of those two shapes, you can subdivide a complex form much the same way you would with simple lines. Also, try slightly offsetting two Shape controls and coloring them dark gray and white, as described above for the Line control (see Figure 9-7).

Done!

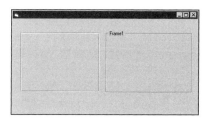

Figure 9-7
You can also zone your dialog boxes with Shape or Frame controls.

You might want to consider the Frame control rather than the Shape control when zoning a window. A Frame automatically creates a 3D effect, as you can see in Figure 9-7. It has the additional advantage of enabling you to identify the zone it encloses with a caption. Or, if you prefer, delete the Frame's Caption property to get a solid frame.

REVIEW

In this session, you learned how to add visual effects — photos, cartoons, divider lines — to your applications. You saw how to resize and reposition graphics, and how to copy, delete, and replace them while a program runs. The tradeoffs between the Image and PictureBox controls were explored — so you can decide which control is best for your purposes. You now know how to use graphics to liven up an application, and to provide the user with visual cues as to the purpose of a button or a group of options.

QUIZ YOURSELF

1. When is an Image control a better choice than a PictureBox? (See "Image and PictureBox Compared".)

2. How can you enlarge a regular .BMP graphic? (See "The Image Control".)

3. Can you import a graphic from the Windows clipboard into a PictureBox? (See "Changing Graphics while a Program Runs".)

4. What does the Static command do to a variable? (See "Animation".)

5. Can you add graphics to any other components besides PictureBoxes, Images, and forms? (See "Graphics Everywhere".)

6. What's the one main use for Line and Shape controls? (See "Shapes and Lines".)

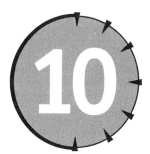
Adding Menus the Easy Way

Session Checklist

✔ Identifying the basic menus

✔ Using the VB Application Wizard

✔ Attaching programming to menu items

✔ Working with the Menu Editor

✔ Adding a context menu

✔ Understanding parameters and constants

**30 Min.
To Go**

Visual Basic makes the job of adding menus to your projects quite straightforward. You're given a choice of two approaches You can start a new project with the VB Application Wizard, which steps you through the process of creating standard menus, toolbars, and certain form templates. After you're done, the Wizard leaves behind a set of Click events for you to fill with your programming — one Click event for each menu item you specified in the Menu Editor. Never was constructing the user interface of a sophisticated application so swift.

The second approach is to use the VB Menu Editor. It's less automatic than the Wizard, but more flexible. Also, you can use the Menu Editor any time to change the menus you offer. But note that, like the Wizard, the Menu Editor merely leaves behind the shell structures (the events); it's up to you to fill in the programming code that actually *does something* when the user clicks your Save As option in your File menu. Fortunately, several of the most common menu options — File Open, Save, Print, Change Fonts — can be handled rather easily with the CommonDialog control, as you'll see in this session and again in Session 12.

Let's go off to see the Wizard to start this session, and then we'll take a look at the Menu Editor.

The Basic Menus

Nearly all Windows programs include at least the basic four standard menus: File, Edit, Window, and Help. File generally contains disk file operations and a print option. Edit includes text manipulation commands (cutting, pasting, selecting all, and search). Window includes options for arranging or sizing the window the user works with, and Help provides answers to user questions. Of course, you can add any additional menus that you choose, to let your users exploit all of the features of your application.

Using the Application Wizard

Let's create File and Edit menus. To understand how to use the Application Wizard to get your new project off to a flying start, follow these steps:

1. Select File ⇨ New Project.

   You see the New Project dialog box.

2. Double-click VB Application Wizard in the New Project dialog box.

   The Wizard's first screen appears.

3. You probably have no profile (a file containing the choices you made when/if you used this Wizard previously). Even if you do have a profile, don't use it. Just click Next.

   You see the page where you can select MDI (which can have several small windows within a single large container window, like VB itself), SDI (each window is separate; no window is contained within another), and browser-style.

4. Choose SDI, leave the name set to the default, *Project1*, and click Next.

   Here you go! This is where you choose which menus you want, and which standard options you want to include within each menu.

5. Check only File and Edit, then select the following options:

For the File menu: Open, Close, Separator (a separator is a line in a menu used to set the options apart in logical groups), Save, Save As, Separator, Print, and Exit. (Note that you can rearrange any of these items by dragging and dropping them within the list.)

For the Edit menu: Undo, Separator, Cut, Copy, and Paste.

6. Click Next.

You see the Toolbar builder, but in this example, you don't want additional complexities. We'll ignore the toolbar the Wizard can create. The Wizard can also add a status bar onto the bottom of the form, but we'll ignore that as well.

7. Click the double-arrow button (<<) in the middle of the Customize Toolbar page.

All the buttons are removed from the list on the right. Now there's no Toolbar to distract us.

8. Click Finish to skip a few additional complexities involving a Resource file and the Internet.

A dialog box appears telling you that your new project has been created.

Take a look at the application, as shown in Figure 10-1.

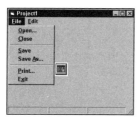

Figure 10-1
You now have a set of menus, thanks to the Application Wizard.

As you can see, the two menu structures that you requested have been created. However, at this point, if a user clicked a menu item, nothing would happen. The shell is there — there's a `Click` event now for each menu item — but there's no code to actually *do* something when the user clicks a menu item.

Understanding Menu Code

Double-click Form1 so you can get to the code window. Ignore the `GetSettings` and `SaveSettings` code. That code is just a way of saving the size and position of the form when the user shuts down your application, and then, when it's restarted, recalling those settings so that the window looks as it did when the application was last used. The Registry holds this information, but ignore this for now. Saving the size and position is not even a requirement when you're creating an actual VB application, though it's a nice feature for the user to remember the last status of the window. (We'll cover the `GetSettings` and `SaveSettings` commands, and how to work with the Registry, in Session 27.)

As you can see by scrolling down the code window, most of the menu events include merely a comment (a line of non-code that begins with a single-quote symbol (')). Any time you want to clarify what your programming does, make a note by preceding it with a single quote mark. The user never sees that; it's just inside your programming code to remind you of things, or to define the purpose of some code.

You also see a `MsgBox` command. When this program runs, if you click one of the menu items, the message pops up, saying: Add such and such code.

However, at the very bottom of the code window, the Wizard did you the favor of filling in the File Open code. Notice that the Wizard also added a CommonDialog component to your project (its icon is on the form, and you can see it in the design window).

You've typed in code that uses the CommonDialog component in previous sessions. Here's a simple example from Session 4 where what you wanted was to put any opened file into a TextBox:

```
CommonDialog1.ShowOpen
Text1.Text = CommonDialog1.FileName
```

But there's no provision for what happens if the user clicks Cancel on the file-open dialog box, so you want to add a line that tests the contents of the `.FileName` as the Wizard did with `If Len(.FileName) = 0`, then exit the `Sub` if the filename is 0 characters long (another way of saying empty). That's just what the Wizard did in its version of this code.

Notice one final thing about the menu `Click` events. Each one is named after the job it does, and each begins with a `mnu`, for menu. This approach to naming makes it very easy to immediately understand that `mnuFileSaveAs`, for example, is a menu item and its purpose is to display the `FileSaveAs` common dialog box.

Using the Menu Editor

Remember that you use the Menu Editor to either modify existing menus, or to create new ones. Let's try creating a new File menu to see how it's done.

Select File ⇨ New Project and double-click the Standard EXE icon to get a blank, standard VB project going.

Press Ctrl+E and the Menu Editor runs, as you can see in Figure 10-2 (the design window must be the active window, or the Menu Editor won't be displayed).

Figure 10-2
Use this utility to create or modify menus.

Type **&File** in the Caption field at the top. The & will cause the letter that follows it (*F* in this case) to be underlined, and to automatically drop this menu if the user presses Alt+F. If a menu is already open, the user can select one of the submenus or listed options by merely pressing the underlined letter, without pressing Alt.

After you type it in, the name *File* will be echoed in the box at the bottom that displays your menu structure. You also want to give this menu a name so that its Click event is well named. (The name you give a menu item later appears as the name of its Click event.) Name it mnuFile in the Name field.

The Caption appears onscreen for the user to see, but the Name is only used by your program, and identifies in the code which menu item the user clicked.

Adding choices or submenus

Now click the Next button and click the right-arrow icon near the Next button. Clicking this right-arrow icon indicates that you want to create a submenu or an option. It inserts some dots in the lower box, moving the submenu over to the right underneath the File menu. This means the next entry will appear as a choice on the parent menu item — it's subordinate.

Type **&Open** as the Caption and **mnuOpen** as the Name. Click Next and type **&Close** as the Caption and **mnuClose** as the Name.

Adding a separator bar

Now you want a separator bar, so type a single hyphen (-) in the Caption box and give it a name like mnuhy or something (a name is required, but never used later because a separator has no Click event), and then click the Next button.

Continue on typing in **&Save**, **mnuSave**, **Save &As** (note the ampersand moved because the Save menu is already using the *S* as a shortcut), **mnuSaveAs**, separator (a hyphen), **mnuhy1, &Print, mnuPrint, &Exit,** and **mnuExit.** Your editor should now look like the one in Figure 10-3.

Figure 10-3
After you've filled in all the menus and submenus, you see the structure graphically in the bottom box of the Menu Editor.

You've got your menu the way you want it, so click the OK button to close the Menu Editor. You can see the results of your work in the design window, as shown in Figure 10-4.

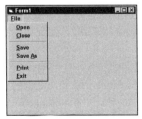

Figure 10-4
You've built a workable File menu.

Double-click the form to see the code. All you'll see is the Form_Load, so click the ListBox in the upper left of the code window to drop down the list of all your events. There they are, as shown in Figure 10-5.

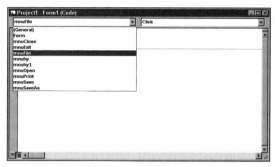

Figure 10-5
The Menu Editor created a Click event for each of your menu items.

Some Tips for Using the Menu Editor

Here are some things to remember when using the Menu Editor:

- Use the Insert and Delete buttons to add new menu items, or delete them, from the list in the box at the bottom of the Menu Editor. Click an item to select it, then click Delete to get rid of it, or click Insert to put a new menu item just above it.

- Move a menu item by clicking it to select it, then using the up- or down-arrow button.

- The Shortcut feature (the drop-down list just above NegotiatePosition in the Menu Editor) allows you to give the user a somewhat faster way to launch frequently used options such as Save. These shortcuts use the Ctrl key plus some other character. Almost everyone who uses Windows knows at least some of them. You might want to use these classic shortcuts for things that people do frequently:

Ctrl+X	Cut
Ctrl+C	Copy
Ctrl+V	Paste
Ctrl+Z	Undo

Take a look at Microsoft Word or some other popular application to see which Ctrl+ keys are traditional for these shortcuts. When you assign a Ctrl shortcut, it will appear on the menu on the far right to alert the user that they can activate that option directly, without having to open the menu at all.

- Sometimes a menu item makes no sense in the current state of the application. If the user hasn't typed any text into a TextBox yet, for example, the Cut and Copy features are useless. Typically, an application makes such inappropriate options unavailable to the user, and indicates this to the user by making the text gray (disabled). Clicking a gray option does nothing. To disable a menu item, you can write some code in the Form_Load event so that the item starts out disabled when the program first runs:

```
mnuCut.Enabled = False
```

But as soon as the user types something into a TextBox in your application, you can enable it, with this code in the TextBox's Change event:

```
Private Sub Text1_Change()

If Text1 <> "" Then
   mnuCut.Enabled = True
Else
   mnuCut.Enabled = False
End If

End Sub
```

Which means: If Text1 is not (<>) empty ("") then enable that menu item; otherwise (Else), disable (gray) it and make it unresponsive to clicking.

- Some menu items, such as a group of three font sizes (Small, Medium, Large), should display to the user which of them is currently selected. To do this, show a checkmark next to the selected one. Just as you adjust the Enabled property to True or False to turn options on and off, you switch the Checked property back and forth to display a checkmark next to a menu item. You can put this code in each Click event of items in a mutually exclusive group (like Small, Medium, or Large):

```
Private Sub mnuSmallFont_Click()
   MnuLargeFont.Checked = False
   MnuMediumFont.Checked = False
   MnuSmallFont.Checked = True
End Sub
```

10 Min. To Go

Providing Context Menus

One popular form of menu is the context menu. You right-click an application's editing window (or a toolbar or some other feature) and out pops a menu of frequently used features relevant to that item. To create a context menu feature for your VB application, use the PopupMenu command and put it into the Form_MouseDown event. MouseDown is similar to the Click event, but it also tells you which mouse button was clicked.

The context menu itself must first be created as if it were a normal menu (as described earlier in this session). Just create the context menu, but set its Visible property to False. It won't appear visible to the user, but you can use the hidden menu as the basis for your context menu.

If you have a menu named mnuFile defined for your VB project, this code will display that menu if the user right-clicks anywhere on the form (see Figure 10-6):

```
Private Sub Form_MouseDown(Button As Integer, Shift As Integer, X
As Single, Y As Single)

If Button = 2 Then
    PopupMenu mnuFile
End If

End Sub
```

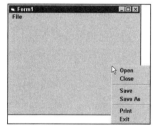

Figure 10-6
It's easy to provide a context menu for your users.

Understanding Parameters

Sometimes an event has *parameters* — items in parentheses like the Button, Shift, X, and Y in the MouseDown event in the previous example.

Parameters tell you, the programmer, information about the event. In this case, Button contains 1 for a left-button click, 2 for a right-button click, and 4 for a middle-button click. Shift tells you whether the user is pressing one or a combination of the Shift, Alt, or Ctrl keys during the click (some programs offer special features that are triggered by Shift+Click or Alt+Click or some other variation). The X and Y provide coordinates that tell you where on the form the user's mouse pointer is at the time of the click.

So, how do you know that 2 in the Button parameter represents a right-click? Just press F1 and click the Index tab in the VB Help window. Type **MouseDown** into the *Type in the keyword to find* field in Help and press Enter. The Help page for the MouseDown event describes each parameter in detail, and tells you, among many other things, that 2 means right-click.

I usually prefer the Help system when looking up parameters. It's quick, and it contains extra information. However, VB includes another feature called the Object Browser that defines parameters as well. Press F2. The Object Browser appears. In the left Classes pane, locate and click *MouseButtonConstants*. Then, in the right pane, click *vbRightButton* and you'll see the answer (= 2) in the bottom pane.

Figure 10-7
Some people like to use the Object Browser to look up parameters.

Using Constants

VB includes many *constants* — predefined values for such things as colors, keypresses (vbKeyF10 = 121, for example), and other elements used in programming. You can either use the value as we did above (If Button = 2) or you can actually use the constant name itself (If Button = vbRightButton) in your programming. Some programmers think that using constant names makes their programs easier to read and understand.

The Object Browser is sometimes harder to use than Help because you might not know which word to look up in the Browser. Should you look up Button, Mouse, or what? I find that pressing F1 often gets me the answer to the meanings of parameters and other questions faster than pressing F2. However, there is one additional approach you can try. It's the combination of the Auto List Members and Auto Quick Info features found in the Tools ⇨ Options menu. We'll look at these in the next session in the section on the InputBox.

Done!

Part II–Saturday Morning
Session 10

REVIEW

This session was mostly about menus — which ones to offer the user, and the easy way to create them. That easy way is to use the VB Application Wizard and let it provide the procedures that you later fill in with code. You also saw how to modify or create menus using VB's handy, built-in Menu Editor. Finally, you learned how to create context menus, and the uses of parameters and constants in programming.

QUIZ YOURSELF

1. Name a feature added to an application by the Application Wizard, in addition to menus. (See "Using the Application Wizard".)
2. For which menu item does the Application Wizard write the actual, usable source code? (See "Understanding Menu Code".)
3. What punctuation mark do you use to insert a separator bar into a menu? (See "Adding a Separator Bar"")
4. What programming command do you use to disable a menu item? (See "Some Tips for Using the Menu Editor".)
5. Why do some programmers like to use constants? (See "Using Constants".)

PART

II

Saturday Morning

1. What do the Auto Syntax Check and Auto List Members features do?
2. What does this line of code do?

   ```
   X = Shell("notepad.exe", 1)
   ```

3. How do you add a second form to a project, and why would you do this?
4. OptionButtons are often grouped on a Frame component. Why group them?
5. How do CheckBoxes differ from OptionButtons?
6. If you set a component's Enabled property to False, what happens?
7. The ToolTipText property does what?
8. What happens in the Properties Window if you drag your mouse to select several components at once on a form?
9. What is the purpose of a Label component?
10. Labels have an AutoSize property; what does it do and why would you use it?
11. Is it possible to superimpose the text in a Label on top of a background graphic in a form?
12. How do you request that a ListBox alphabetize its contents?
13. What command do you use to delete an item from a ListBox?
14. If you want to display data in multiple columns in a ListBox, how do you accomplish that?
15. List two ways that a ComboBox differs from a ListBox.

16. Name two ways that a PictureBox component differs from an Image component.

17. What does the following code do?

```
Picture1.Picture = LoadPicture()
```

18. There's a wizard in VB that automates the process of creating the standard menus. What's the wizard's name?

19. Sometimes a menu item makes no sense in the current state of the application. If the user hasn't typed any text into a TextBox yet, for example, Cut and Copy features on an Edit menu are useless. Typically, an application makes such inappropriate options unavailable to the user, and cues the user by making the text gray (disabled). What code do you write to disable a menu item named mnuCut?

20. What are built-in constants?

PART

III

Saturday Afternoon

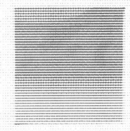

Talking to the User with Dialog Boxes

Session Checklist

✔ Working with the MsgBox feature

✔ How to use arguments

✔ Adding buttons and icons

✔ Getting back information from the user

✔ Text responses from an InputBox

✔ Using Auto Quick Info and Auto List Members

**30 Min.
To Go**

V B offers many ways for you to communicate with the user. You can display text in Labels, TextBoxes, or the Captions properties of other components. You can display pictures in Image or PictureBox components, or as wallpaper in the background of a form. You can ask the user to respond to CheckBoxes or to fill in TextBoxes.

But how do you display **temporary messages**? Brief warnings, for example, that alert the user that he has entered a zip code instead of a telephone number or some such thing?

Communicating via Message Box

The most common approach is to use a MsgBox to display information or an InputBox to get an answer back from the user. (You can get back some kinds of information from a MsgBox — such as which button the user clicked — but the InputBox sends back a text answer typed in by the user.)

You've seen them hundreds of times. The simplest version is a basic message box that says "Printing" or "File Not Found", and there's an OK button the user can click to close the box. Sometimes these little informational windows are called dialog boxes (see Figure 11-1).

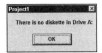

Figure 11-1
Message boxes are common Windows tools you can use to inform the user of something.

The message box shown in Figure 11-1 is created with this code:

```
Private Sub Form_Load()
    MsgBox "There is no diskette in Drive A:"
End Sub
```

When you're practicing or testing programming, it's sometimes a good idea to put your code into the Form_Load **event just temporarily. The** Form_Load **event is triggered when the form first appears, so it automatically executes its code when you press F5 to test your project.**

The MsgBox command has several arguments you can specify: the message, the buttons and icons, the title, and a help file. Help files are rarely used with message boxes, but you may want to define the other arguments.

Understanding arguments

This is the first time we've used the term *argument*. An argument is information that you provide to a Sub or its close cousin, the function. Often there is more than one argument. In such a case, commas separate the two or more arguments, and the group of them is referred to as the *argument list*. In the phrase *Bring food, put it on the table, wrap it*, the sub or function is the action *Bring* and the argument list is *table, wrap*. We'll discuss arguments in more detail in Session 13.

For now, just note that Visual Basic reads arguments *in order*. You must be careful to ensure that the arguments are in the proper order. The first argument for a message box is the message, and all the other arguments are optional so you can leave them off if you wish.

Pay attention now. All hands on deck. Because arguments are separated by commas, even if you want to use only the first and third arguments — but ignore the second argument — *you must still include the extra comma*. That's how VB knows that you're specifying 1st and 3rd rather than 1st and 2nd arguments. The third argument for a message box is the title. So if you want to add a title to the message box we used above, you would do it like this (*notice the placeholder comma for the missing second argument*):

```
MsgBox "There is no diskette in Drive A:", ,"Please Check"
```

This results in the dialog box shown in Figure 11-2.

Figure 11-2
Add a title to the title bar, if you wish.

Unless you specify otherwise, the title bar of the message box will default to the name of your VB project. Often, that's just fine.

**20 Min.
To Go**

Adding buttons and icons

Sometimes an argument can contain multiple specifications. The second argument of the MsgBox command is a multiple-meaning argument. You can use it to define several qualities: the kind of buttons and icons it has, which button is the default, and whether the message box halts only your VB program — or all running applications — until the user closes the message box. (This program-halting behavior is called *modality*.)

How can one argument describe several conditions? Perhaps we should start with *why*. It would be easier to read and maintain programs if each specified condition (button, icon, default, and modality) were a separate argument. This would add three arguments to the MsgBox's argument list, but so what?

The answer is the same as the reason for all the Y2K problems — in the early days of computing, memory was expensive and scarce. So various ways of conserving memory — shortcuts like using a single argument to define several conditions — were popular.

How does it work? Let's not get into binary arithmetic. All you have to know is that each condition you want to use is simply *added* to the other conditions. So, once you know the value (or constant) for each condition you want to use, just add them together in your program. Take a look at Table 11-1. It shows you all the buttons, icons, defaults, and modalities available. Use the items in this table to build the second argument in a MsgBox.

Table 11-1
MsgBox Buttons, Icons, Defaults, and Modalities

Constant	Value	Description
vbOKOnly	0	OK button only
vbOKCancel	1	OK and Cancel buttons
vbAbortRetryIgnore	2	Abort, Retry, and Ignore buttons
vbYesNoCancel	3	Yes, No, and Cancel buttons
vbYesNo	4	Yes and No buttons
vbRetryCancel	5	Retry and Cancel buttons
vbCritical	16	Critical Message icon
vbQuestion	32	Warning Query icon
vbExclamation	48	Warning Message icon
vbInformation	64	Information Message icon
vbDefaultButton1	0	First button is default.
vbDefaultButton2	256	Second button is default.
vbDefaultButton3	512	Third button is default.

Constant	Value	Description
VbDefaultButton	4768	Fourth button is default.
vbApplicationModal	0	Application modal — the VB application will not respond until the user reacts to the message box by clicking one of its buttons, or closing it by pressing the X button at the top right.
vbSystemModal	4096	System modal — no application will respond until the user reacts to the message box by clicking one of its buttons, or closing it by pressing the X button at the top right.

If you specify nothing for the second argument in a MsgBox, there will only be an OK button — no icon. The OK button will be the default (the one activated if the user presses the Enter key), and the modality will be Application modal.

Remember that you can pick one option from each of the four categories shown in Table 11-1. Let's say that you want Yes, No, and Cancel buttons on your message box, and you also want the Warning Message icon. You can add them together, like this:

```
Private Sub Form_Load()
MsgBox "There is no diskette in Drive A: Do you want to put one in
and try saving again?",vbYesNoCancel + vbExclamation
End Sub
```

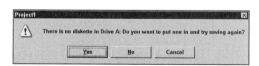

Figure 11-3
You can add icons and extra buttons to your message boxes.

You can also use the values rather than the constants, like this:

```
MsgBox "There is no diskette in Drive A:",3 + 48
```

(As you can see, VB can do math, like this addition, within an argument list.) Or if you wish, just add the numbers in your head and write 51.

Getting information back

So far so good. But if you're using several buttons, it usually means that you want to know *which* button the user clicked. Your program will respond to the user's selection. If he or she clicks the Cancel or No buttons, your program won't do anything (see Figure 11-3), but if he or she clicks the Yes button, the user wants your program to retry saving something to Drive A:. Therefore, your program needs to know which button was clicked.

To do this, you must create a *function*. A function is punctuated differently than a sub (subroutine). You must use parentheses to enclose the arguments, and you must also provide a variable in which the function can store the value it gives back. Unlike subs, a function returns a value (an answer). You don't always make use of the returned value, but in the case we're talking about, you do. You want to know if the user clicked the Yes button. Here's how to cast a MsgBox as a function. We'll use the variable name *Reply*, though you can use any word that's not in VB's vocabulary (it can't be a VB command, such as For or MsgBox — these words are reserved for VB's own use and cannot be used as names for your variables).

```
Reply = MsgBox ("There is no diskette in Drive A:",3 + 48)
```

Now you can test the value in the Reply variable, and if it's Yes, you execute a subroutine somewhere else in your program that saves the contents of the TextBox to Drive A. Use the following code to accomplish this:

```
Reply = MsgBox("There is no diskette in Drive A:", 3 + 48)

If Reply = vbYes Then

    SaveTxt      ' the sub that attempts to resave the text
    MsgBox "We are trying to resave it for you."

End If
```

Table 11-2 shows the constants and values that the MsgBox function returns for the various buttons that can be displayed.

Table 11-2
The MsgBox Return Values for Clicked Buttons

Constant	Value	Button Description
vbOK	1	OK
vbCancel	2	Cancel
vbAbort	3	Abort
vbRetry	4	Retry
vbIgnore	5	Ignore
vbYes	6	Yes
vbNo	7	No

**10 Min.
To Go**

Displaying the InputBox to Get Text Back

There is a variation on the MsgBox called the InputBox, and you can use it pretty much the same way as the MsgBox. InputBoxes are built to return information from the user — their primary value is that they include a built-in TextBox so that the information your program gets back is a piece of text rather than information that tells you which button was clicked (as happens with a MsgBox).

This offers you more flexibility when getting information — the user types in his or her response, so there can be many different responses — not just the limited number of buttons they can click in a message box. Also note that an InputBox has an OK and a Cancel button only. If the user clicks Cancel, an empty text string is returned "". You can find out if an empty string was returned by using programming such as this:

```
Result = InputBox("What is your Area Code?")
If Result = "" Then
   MsgBox "You pressed Cancel or refused to type anything in."
End If
```

The InputBox function requires a prompt, but the rest of its arguments — Title, Default, X, and Y — are optional. The Default argument is text that you can display in the InputBox, if you have a good guess regarding what the user will likely type. This saves the user time. If they agree with your default text, they just click OK. They don't have to type anything because you displayed what they would have typed. The X and Y coordinates enable you to enter numbers to specify where on your form you want the InputBox to appear. Just leave that alone and let the box appear in the middle of the screen — that's the usual Windows behavior. In rare cases, you might want to move it to expose something on the form the user should see while responding, but those *are* rare cases.

Here's an example. We'll leave out the title, but we will provide a default, the contents of Text3, a TextBox. Let's say that the user typed a two-letter last name into Text3:

```
Private Sub Form_Click()
Result = InputBox("Please retype your last name...you entered only
two letters and few last names are that short.", , Text3.Text)
Text3.Text = Result
End Sub
```

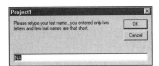

Figure 11-4
An InputBox is similar to a MsgBox, but the InputBox returns text.

Exploiting Auto Quick Info and Auto List Members

Some people find the Auto Quick Info and Auto List Members features of VB's help system quite useful. I still prefer the regular F1 Help when trying to remember a function's arguments or the values you can use with those arguments. But I promised in the last session that I'd introduce you to these features in case you like them. You've actually seen Auto List Members before, in Session 5, but it's worth another look here in conjunction with Auto Quick Info.

Select Tools ⇨ Options and make sure that both the Auto List Members and Auto Quick Info boxes are both checked in the Editor tab of the VB Options dialog box.

I'll use the MsgBox function to illustrate these features. Go to the VB code window and type this:

```
Result = MsgBox("You left the Quantity field empty.", vbOKCancel)
```

As soon as you type `result = msgbox` and then press the spacebar, Auto Quick Info does its job — a box pops out listing all of the parameters that can be used with the MsgBox command. The Auto Quick Info box is shown on the left in Figure 11-5.

Then, as soon as you continue on and type the comma and press the spacebar, out pops a drop-down listbox, allowing you to select a constant. The Auto List Members feature is shown on the right in Figure 11-5.

Figure 11-5
You can view both the list of members and the constants for the MsgBox function.

Done!

You might find these features helpful. The drop-down box of constants is pretty intelligent. If you double-click on a constant, then type a +, the drop-down box reappears, because it understands that you want to add additional conditions to the MsgBox's second argument.

REVIEW

This session is all about communicating with the user via dialog boxes. You saw how to display a MsgBox and the arguments you can use to create variations on the standard MsgBox. Then you saw how to use a variable to get information back from the user. Finally, you worked with the MsgBox's cousin, the InputBox, and also experimented with VB's Auto Quick Info and Auto List Members options.

Quiz Yourself

1. Why use the Form_Load event to test parts of your program? What's the advantage? (See "Communicating via Message Box".)

2. What is an argument in VB programming? (See "Understanding Arguments".)

3. If you have more than one argument, what punctuation do you use to separate them? (See "Understanding Arguments".)

4. What's the main reason you would use an InputBox rather than a MsgBox? (See "Displaying the InputBox to Get Text Back".)

5. Describe the difference between Auto Quick Info and Auto List Members (See "Exploiting Auto Quick Info and Auto List Members".)

Using the Common Dialog Component

Session Checklist

✔ Understanding the CommonDialog's purpose

✔ Adding a CommonDialog to your Toolbox

✔ Using CommonDialog properties

✔ The five common dialogs

✔ Offering file access to the user

✔ Changing colors

✔ Selecting font properties

✔ Working with the printer dialog box

**30 Min.
To Go**

In several previous sessions, you've worked briefly with the CommonDialog component. In this session, you'll explore this important component fully.

The main purpose of the CommonDialog is to provide predictable, standardized dialog boxes. The user shouldn't have to interact with a different File Open dialog box for each application. All Windows applications should use the same dialog box for some regular jobs (printing, file access) and regular customizations (choosing fonts and colors).

As a side benefit, your Visual Basic programs will look more professional and polished.

Microsoft has standard dialogs established for five tasks: Open, Save As, Color, Font, and Print. Everyone except a novice will already know how to work Common Dialogs — where the buttons are, and so on. And the bonus for you is that you can avoid a lot of programming by simply using the handy Common Dialog control.

Note that these commands are *modal* like a MsgBox. In other words, once you display one of these dialog boxes, it halts your VB program until the user responds and shuts the dialog box. After the user closes the dialog box, your program gets back information about what the user did, perhaps which file was selected, or which color. In each case, your program can query a property of the CommonDialog to find out what the user wants to happen.

For example, let's say you want to allow your user to choose a graphics file to display in a PictureBox. First, you display the CommonDialog ShowOpen window, then after the user closes the window, you query the CommonDialog object by using its FileName property. Here's the simplest version of this process:

1. Press Ctrl+T. You have to add a CommonDialog to your Toolbox; it's not part of the default set of components.

2. In the Components dialog box, locate Microsoft Common Dialog 6.0 and click the checkbox next to it. (It might be listed instead as Microsoft Common Dialog 6.0 (SP 3).)

3. Click the OK button to close the dialog box, and you'll see the CommonDialog icon appear on your Toolbox.

4. Double-click the CommonDialog icon to add it to your form. The icon is visible to you, but not to the user.

5. Add a PictureBox to the form, then type the following code into the PictureBox's Click event:

```
Private Sub Picture1_Click()

CommonDialog1.ShowOpen    ' display the Open dialog

Set Picture1 = LoadPicture(CommonDialog1.FileName)

End Sub
```

When you press F5 to run this code and then click the PictureBox, you see the dialog box shown in Figure 12-1.

Figure 12-1
The Open dialog box looks as it does in all other contemporary Windows applications.

Of course, this example is bare-bones. You would want to include some error-trapping code in case the user makes an error (like trying to load a .DOC file instead of a .BMP file or one of the other graphics files that VB can handle (.ICO, .GIF, .JPG, or .WMF files)). Error trapping is covered in Session 20, so we'll leave it alone for now.

Using CommonDialog Properties

You might also want to set some CommonDialog properties to make the behavior of a dialog box more helpful to the user, before you display it.

Notice that many properties can be used two ways:

1. You can *read* properties to get information, such as which filename the user double-clicked in the Open CommonDialog. (See the code just above for an example.)

2. Or you can *set* a property in your code to change that property while the program is running to modify the behavior, appearance, or some other quality of an object. (This is the same as adjusting a property in the Properties Window, except that you do it with code, while the program runs, rather than during design time.)

Let's try setting the Filter property of the CommonDialog so that the dialog box only displays graphics files that a PictureBox can accept. The following Filter property has two features. First, you provide a text description that the user sees in the dialog's Files of Type: listbox. These descriptions can be phrases such as "Bitmap Files" or "GIF Files" or whatever description you decide to provide. The user can click one of these descriptions to see only those kinds of files displayed in the dialog box. The second element is the actual file extension, such as ".EXE" or ".GIF". You pair these elements, separating them with the | symbol.

Change the code in Step 5 above to:

```
Private Sub Picture1_Click()

CommonDialog1.Filter = "Bitmap Files|*.BMP|JPEG
Files|*.JPG|Icons|*.ICO|GIF Files|*.GIF"

CommonDialog1.ShowOpen   ' display the Open dialog

Set Picture1 = LoadPicture(CommonDialog1.FileName)

End Sub
```

Now the user will see only graphics files in each folder.

There are many properties you can set for the various CommonDialog windows, prior to showing a dialog box to the user.

The Available CommonDialogs

**20 Min.
To Go**

Depending on which of the CommonDialog commands you use, a different dialog window is displayed, waiting for user input:

```
CommonDialog1.ShowOpen    'Open Disk File
CommonDialog1.ShowSave    'Save or Save As
CommonDialog1.ShowColor   'Select a color

CommonDialog1.Flags = 259 '(You must set this flags property,
because of a bizarre requirement, before you can use the ShowFont
version of the CommonDialog.)
CommonDialog1.ShowFont    'Select a font (and other font
properties)

CommonDialog1.ShowPrinter 'Print (and Printer Setup.)
```

To title a Dialog Box with the word *FILE*:

```
CommonDialog1.DialogTitle = "FILE"
```

Or to trigger an "error" if the user selects the Cancel button on a dialog box, use the following code:

```
CommonDialog1.CancelError = True '(the default is false)
```

Every one of the several CommonDialog variations has a `CancelError`, `DialogTitle`, `Flags`, `HelpCommand`, `HelpContext`, `HelpFile`, and `HelpKey` property. But they differ in which other properties they have. For instance, the Font Dialog Box has a `FontSize` property, which tells your VB program the size the user selected.

The Font Dialog Box also has `Max` and `Min` properties to allow you to set upper and lower font-size limits beyond which the user cannot choose. On the other hand, the two file-access dialog boxes have no font properties, but do have an `InitDir` property, which allows you to specify which disk directory will be displayed as the default. Each dialog box has its own appropriate properties, as do all objects in VB.

Tip

The `Flags` **property is *combinatorial*, a fancy way of saying that you can set more than a single flag in one line of code. Recall from Session 11 that some properties are multiple. Remember that you can specify buttons and icons for a MsgBox by *adding* their values (**`vbYesNoCancel` + `vbExclamation`**). This same multiplicity option is available with the** `Flags` **property. You can set more than one flag at a time by using the + symbol in your code to add the flag settings together. Here's an example of combining (by addition) more than one flag:**

```
CommonDialog1.Flags = 3
CommonDialog1.ShowColor
```

This displays the Color Dialog Box. Before activating the dialog box with the `ShowColor` method, we first set *two* flags (3 represents two conditions: 1 + 2). If you set the Color Box `Flag` property to 1, whatever is specified in the `Color` property will be shown as the default color when the dialog box first appears to the user. If you set the Color Box `Flag` property to 2, the Define Custom Colors window will be displayed along with the smaller Colors Box. Because we want *to do both of these things*, we add 1 + 2 and set the `Flags` property to 3.

Saving Files with ShowSave

The ShowSave version of the CommonDialog works nearly the same way as ShowOpen. The primary difference is that the user is saving a file rather than loading one.

```
Private Sub Picture1_Click()

    CommonDialog1.FileName = "Test.Txt"

    CommonDialog1.ShowSave    ' display the Save dialog

    Open CommonDialog1.FileName For Output As #1
    Write #1, Text1.Text 'put it into a TextBox
    Close #1

End Sub
```

Before you use ShowSave, you can set the FileName property to optionally contain a suggested default filename (as we did in the above example, displaying Test.Txt to the user as a suggested filename). The user always has the option of changing that suggestion in the dialog box. However, after ShowSave executes, the CommonDialog's FileName property automatically contains the full path of where the file was actually saved, such as C:\MyFolder\Trips.Txt. You then use that information to write the code that actually accomplishes the filesaving (using the Open, Write or Print, and Close commands). The Open command is covered in detail in Session 24.

File Access Dialog Box Properties

Here's an overview of the most important CommonDialog properties used with file access. Some only apply to ShowOpen, some only to ShowSave, and some work with both. Some of this has already been described earlier, but this review is worth looking at. Perhaps taking this second look, from a different angle, will clarify some of these properties and their uses.

DefaultExt

This three-letter text (string) variable is added automatically to whatever the user types (if the user leaves off an extension). Typical extensions are .DOC, .BMP, and

.TXT. For example, if you set `DefaultExt` to ".txt" and the user types in **MyText** and presses Enter, the filename you get back in the `CommonDialog1.Filename` property is MyText.txt. This is used only with `ShowOpen`.

FileName

This property can be used with both Open and Save File dialog boxes. Before using `ShowOpen` or `ShowSave`, you can assign a default filename to be displayed in the dialog box's TextBox by setting the `FileName` property. After the `ShowOpen` or `ShowSave` command is used, the `FileName` property tells you the full path (C:\WINDOWS\FILENAME.EXT, for example) of the file the user wants to save or open. A list of filenames is displayed to the user, and if the user selects one and clicks the OK button (or double-clicks on the filename, or types in a filename), the `FileName` property of the CommonDialog component then contains the full path for that file (`CommonDialog.Filename`). You can then write code that loads or saves the file.

Filter

The `Filter` property can be used with both Save and Open File dialog boxes. The `Filter` property is a text variable that you can employ to display only a subset of the files in a Windows directory. If you want to show only those files with a .DOC extension, you would program this:

```
CommonDialog1.Filter = "WORD Files|*.DOC"
```

Note that the description of the filter comes first, then a pipe symbol, and then the actual filter. You can also concatenate several filters, and they will be displayed for the user to select from:

```
CommonDialog1.Filter = "WORD Files|*.DOC|Text Files|*.TXT|Letters
to Karen|K*.*"
```

Flags

The `Flags` property is a collection of several "switches" that control how the dialog box looks, which options are checked, and so forth. Remember, you can add these numbers together if you want to set more than one flag, like this:

```
CommonDialog1.Flags = 1 + 8
```

Let's take a closer look at what all the possible values of Flags mean for this example.

Flags = 1   When the dialog box is displayed, the Read Only CheckBox is displayed with a checkmark.

If you want to find out afterward whether the user checked this box, you have to do a flag (*bitwise* they call it) test. To do this, use the And **command:**

```
If CommonDialog1.Flags And 1 Then
' put code here because yes it is checked
End If
```

Please don't ask for an explanation of the And **command. Just remember that you can test any flag using** And 4 **or** And 1024 **or** And **plus the number of whatever flag you're testing. The explanation of** And **is too complicated, and learning it isn't of much inherent value. Just trust that the** And **command works this way. (If you're madly curious, notice how the flag numbers are strangely discontinuous, jumping from, for instance, 512 to 1024, rather than being consecutive, like 1, 2, 3, 4 . . . . The reason is that each of these numbers represents a *position* within a binary number. It's similar to the positions in our familiar decimal arithmetic: 1's, 10's, 100's, 1000's, and so on. The** And **command tests these positions rather than the actual numbers per se.)**

Flags = 2   If the user saves with a filename that already exists on the disk, a message box will appear asking the user to confirm that he or she wants to overwrite the existing file.

Flags = 4   Eliminates the Read Only CheckBox.

Flags = 8   Causes the current directory to be retained. (In other words, even if the dialog box displays a different directory, the directory that was current when the dialog box was displayed will remain the current directory. The *current directory* is the one displayed by default when an Open or Save dialog box is first displayed, or when Explorer is run. It's usually the last directory the user looked at in some previous operation.)

Flags = 16   A Help button is displayed.

Flags = 256	Invalid characters will be permitted in the filename the user selects or types (normally such characters as * cannot be part of a filename).
Flags = 512	Allows the user to select a group of files rather than a single file (by holding down the Shift key and using the arrow keys to expand the selection). You can detect which files the user selected by looking at the FileName property. All the selected files are listed in a text (string) variable, separated by spaces.
Flags = 1024	You can check the Flags Property when the user closes the dialog box. If this flag is set, it means that the user specified a file extension (like .TXT) that differs from the default file extension used in the dialog box.
Flags = 2048	The user is permitted to type in valid file paths only. If the user enters an invalid path, the dialog box displays a warning message.
Flags = 4096	Prevents the user from typing in a filename that is not listed in the dialog box. Setting this Flag will also automatically set the 2048 Flag.
Flags = 8192	The user will be asked if he or she wants to create a new file. Setting Flags to 8192 also sets the Flags property to include the values 4096 and 2048, described previously.
Flags = 16384	The dialog box will ignore network-sharing violations.
Flags = 32768	The selected file will not be read-only and will not be in a write-protected directory.

InitDir

InitDir determines the initial directory that is displayed when the dialog box is shown to the user. If InitDir isn't specified, the current directory is displayed.

MaxFileSize

MaxFileSize defines how large the FileName property can be in bytes. The default is 256 bytes, but the permissible range is from 1 byte to 32,767 bytes.

**10 Min.
To Go**

Changing Colors with the Color Dialog Box

The ShowColor CommonDialog command is quite simple. Here's an example that shows how to use it:

```
Private Sub Picture1_Click()

    CommonDialog1.ShowColor
    Form1.BackColor = CommonDialog1.Color

End Sub
```

The user sees the standard Windows color picker dialog box, shown in Figure 12-2.

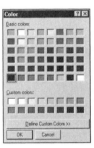

Figure 12-2
The Color dialog box is another of the familiar Windows common dialogs.

Here are some Flags properties of the Color dialog box you might want to set (remember, you can combine them by adding the numbers together, if you wish):

Flags = 1   Causes the color defined by the Color property to be displayed when the dialog box is first displayed to the user. You can also set CommonDialog1.Color to a different default color, like this:

```
CommonDialog1.Flags = 1
CommonDialog1.Color = vbBlue
```

Flags = 2   Opens the full Color Dialog Box (includes the Define Custom Colors window).

Flags = 4   Prevents the user from selecting the Define Custom Colors button.

Selecting Fonts

The Fonts dialog box is a bit different from the others because you *must* set the
Flags property prior to using the ShowFont command.

Use this example:

```
Private Sub Picture1_Click()
    CommonDialog1.FontName = Text1.Font
    CommonDialog1.Flags = 259
    CommonDialog1.ShowFont
    Text1.Font = CommonDialog1.FontName
End Sub
```

First, you should set the FontName property to the font of the component you're
letting the user choose a new font for. This gives the user a default when the dialog
box is displayed. Then set the Flags property to 3 + 256 so the user can choose
features such as strikethrough and colors, as well as seeing all of the fonts available
on your system. Finally, show the Fonts dialog box. After that, you can adjust the
component's font properties as shown in the final line of code in the above example. Note that there are several font-related properties of the CommonDialog component that the user might have selected in the dialog box: FontBold, FontItalic,
FontName, FontSize, FontStrikeThru, and FontUnderline. These properties can
either be set by your program prior to displaying the dialog box (so they are the
defaults), or queried after the user closes the dialog box. Your code can also query
the CommonDialog1.Color property to see if the user chose a color.

Flags

Here's a rundown of the things that the Flags property controls when used with
ShowFont:

Flags = 1	Displays only screen fonts.
Flags = 2	Lists only printer fonts.
Flags = 3	Lists both printer and screen fonts.
Flags = 4	Displays a Help button.
Flags = 256	Strikethrough, underline, and colors are permitted.
Flags = 512	The Apply button is enabled.
Flags = 1024	Only those fonts that use the Windows Character Set are allowed (no symbols fonts).

Flags = 2048	No vector fonts are permitted.
Flags = 4096	No Graphic Device Interface font simulations are permitted.
Flags = 8192	Displays only those font sizes between the range specified in the Min and Max properties (see them described below).
Flags = 16384	Displays only fixed-pitch (not scalable) fonts.
Flags = 32768	Allows the user to choose only fonts that can work on the screen and the printer. If you set this flag, you should also set the 131072 and 3 flags.
Flags = 65536	If the user tries to select a font or style that doesn't exist, an error message is displayed.
Flags = 131072	Displays only scalable fonts.
Flags = 262144	Displays only TrueType fonts.

Max and Min

Although font sizes can be as small as 1 point (a character will be 1/72 of an inch tall) and as large as 2048 points (and anywhere in between), you can set the Max and Min properties of the Font dialog box to specify a more limited range of permitted font sizes from which the user can select. For example, if you allow the user to customize the FontSize for a Label control, you want to limit the size so that the text isn't clipped off when displayed within the Label. You specify the limits with an integer that describes the largest or smallest permitted point size you will allow. Before you can specify this range, however, you must set the Flags property to 8192.

Printer Dialog Box

This option displays the usual Print dialog box, letting the user choose between printers, copies, which pages to print, and so forth:

```
CommonDialog1.ShowPrinter
```

Here are the main properties you can set or query with ShowPrinter:

Copies

Your VB program or the user can specify the number of copies of a document to be printed. (The Copies property will always be 1 if the Flags property is set to 262144.)

Flags

Following are the Flags values when used with the Print dialog box:

Flags = 0	Allows you to set (or query) the All Pages OptionButton.
Flags = 1	Allows you to set (or query) the Selection OptionButton.
Flags = 2	Allows you to set (or query) the Pages OptionButton.
Flags = 4	Disables the Selection OptionButton.
Flags = 8	Disables the Pages OptionButton.
Flags = 16	Allows you to set (or query) the Collate CheckBox.
Flags = 32	Allows you to set (or query) the Print To File CheckBox.
Flags = 64	Displays the Print Setup dialog box (instead of the normal Print dialog box).
Flags = 128	Even if there is no default printer, no warning message is displayed.
Flags = 256	Causes a device context to be returned in the CommonDialog's hDC property, which points to the printer selection made by the user. (Don't ask.)
Flags = 512	Causes an "Information Context" message to be returned in the CommonDialog's hDC property, which points to the printer selection made by the user. (Again — don't ask.)
Flags = 2048	Displays a Help button.
Flags = 262144	Disables the Copies control if the selected printer doesn't allow multiple copies of documents. If the printer *does* allow multiple copies, the requested number of copies is listed in the Copies property.
Flags = 524288	Hides the Print To File CheckBox.

FromPage, ToPage

Your VB program, or the user, can specify a range of pages to be printed within a document. For these properties to have any effect, you must first set the Flags property to 2.

Max, Min

Your VB program can limit the range of the FromPage and ToPage boundaries. Set Min to specify the earliest permitted starting page number, and set Max to specify the last page number permitted.

PrinterDefault

Done!

This property is normally True, and in this state, VB will make appropriate changes to the Registry if the user selects a different printer setup (a different page orientation, switching to a FAX device as the default printer, etc.). If you set this property to False, the user's changes will not be saved in the Registry and therefore will not become the default setup for the printer.

REVIEW

In this session, you zeroed in on the CommonDialog control — perhaps the single most useful user-interaction component. Why so useful? Because it does many things, and is also very easy to program. You also learned how to work with file-access, color, fonts, and printer dialogs, and how to deal with their various properties.

QUIZ YOURSELF

---

1. What does the DefaultExt property do? (See "DefaultExt".)
2. In which of the CommonDialogs must you first set the Flags property before you can use it? (See "The Available CommonDialogs".)
3. What does the InitDir property do? (See "InitDir".)
4. Name three of the available CommonDialogs. (See "The Available CommonDialogs".)
5. Describe what the following code does: CommonDialog1.FontName = Text1.Font. (See "Selecting Fonts".)

SESSION

13

Making the Most of Procedures

Session Checklist

✔ Understanding procedures

✔ Passing parameters to procedures

✔ Understanding functions (they pass information back)

✔ Knowing when to use the argument-passing modes

✔ Single-stepping to see how code executes

✔ How to remove redundancies, if you really want to

**30 Min.
To Go**

I n previous sessions, you wrote your programming code in VB's events. This is an excellent way to organize a program into manageable subdivisions. Relatively small units of programming are more easily written, tested, fixed, and are, in general, easier to understand. It's just natural that a program does things in events — responding to mouse clicks, keypresses, and other stimuli.

So, most of your program's code can usually go into these events. In some VB programs, *all* code can go into events.

But sometimes you want to create separate procedures of your own. We'll see why shortly. First, let's understand the term *procedure*.

Understanding Procedures

What's a procedure? It's a relatively small unit of programming that accomplishes some specific job. Events are procedures.

There are two kinds of procedures: subroutines and functions. Events are subroutines. That's why they begin with the word Sub and end with End Sub. Between the Sub and End Sub lies your programming code, if you choose to write some for that event.

You can also just type in a plain sub of your own that's not part of an event. The reason to create your own sub is that your program might need to accomplish the same task in several events. There's no reason to type in the same code in each of those events. You only need to write it once, in a sub of your own, then *call* that sub from all of the events that need it.

Let's say that your program needs to display a message box from several different events. You can repeat the code that displays the message box in each of those events. Or you can write a single, standalone sub to do the job.

To see how to make this work, let's give it a try now. Start a new VB project. Put two CheckBoxes on the form. Now double-click the form to open the code window. Press the down-arrow key and hold it until you're in a blank area in the code window. You don't want to be in the Form_Load procedure. You want to type in your own procedure.

Type:

```
Sub ShowThem()
```

Press Enter. Notice that VB understands that you're writing a new sub, so it automatically and intelligently adds this code to complete the procedure structure:

```
End Sub
```

Now, in between the Sub and End Sub, type the following lines of code to display a message box:

```
Sub ShowThem()

Msg = "Please be sure you meant to click this."
Style = vbYesNo + vbInformation + vbDefaultButton2
Title = "My Program's Warning"
```

```
MsgBox Msg, Style, Title

End Sub
```

If you get an error message when you run this example saying, "Compile Error: Variable not defined", it means that you have `Option Explicit` **at the top of the code window. Please delete** `Option Explicit` **and the above code will run fine. The** `Option Explicit` **feature is discussed at the end of Session 14.**

You want to use this code in several different events. You wouldn't want to have to put that same code over and over into each of those events, would you? It would waste time, waste space, and make your program harder to read and maintain.

Now, when the user clicks a CheckBox (or any other component), that component's `Click` event automatically executes any code it holds. But how do you trigger this new `ShowThem` procedure you wrote? It's not part of any event. The answer is — *you put a reference to it into all the events that need to use your procedure.* You just use its name to trigger it from an event or other procedure.

Locate the `Check1_Click` event and type the following code into it:

```
Private Sub Check1_Click()
ShowThem
End Sub
```

And then locate Check2_Click and do it again:

```
Private Sub Check2_Click()
ShowThem
End Sub
```

Now press F5 and try clicking either of the CheckBoxes.

Great! Your `ShowThem` procedure works. Wherever in this form that you want `ShowThem` to do its job, just name it, type `ShowThem`, and your little procedure will happily oblige and do its thing, displaying a message.

Some programmers like to use the optional `Call` **command whenever they call a sub or function. This helps remind them of what the line does:**

```
Call ShowThem
```

Customizing the Behavior of a Procedure

So far so good, but how about a little customization? What if you want to display a different message, depending on what the user clicks?

That's easy. You just *pass* the message as a parameter. Have you wondered why every procedure's name always has a pair of parentheses following it, even if the parentheses are usually empty?

They can be used to enclose passed parameters. Let's change the ShowThem procedure to make it more flexible. We'll remove the fixed (hard-coded) message that is stored inside the procedure, and let the caller (the procedure that triggers ShowThem) pass whatever message it wants. The ShowThem sub will display that passed message, rather than a canned one that's already pre-written in the ShowThem sub. You have to change two lines. Delete this line:

```
Msg = "Please be sure you meant to click this."
```

And change the title line to this:

```
Sub ShowThem(msg As String)
```

I'll explain what that As String **code means in the next session. (Hint: It tells VB to expect text, rather than a number or some other kind of variable.)**

So now your ShowThem procedure looks like this:

```
Sub ShowThem(msg As String)

Style = vbYesNo + vbInformation + vbDefaultButton2
Title = "My Program's Warning"
MsgBox msg, Style, Title

End Sub
```

You can use any name that you wish instead of *msg*. Take your choice (but remember that you cannot use a VB command such as If or Sub, or a name you've already used as a variable or procedure name elsewhere in the program).

If you *do* change the name in the parameter list (between the parentheses), remember to also change it in the second-to-last line where you display the message box. Replace the *msg* that I'm using with your new word.

OK, now the message gets passed to the ShowThem procedure. To pass it, you want to change the calls. Change the CheckBoxes' code to the following:

```
Private Sub Check1_Click()
ShowThem "This is Check1. Thanks for clicking me!"
End Sub

Private Sub Check2_Click()
ShowThem "This is Check2. Thanks for clicking me!"
End Sub
```

The only thing you do to pass a parameter is press the spacebar after typing the name of the procedure, then type in the passed parameter. If it's text you're sending, you must enclose it in quotes, as illustrated in the above code.

Press F5 and see what happens when you click either CheckBox. Sure enough, the caller passed information to the procedure.

Do you think it's possible to go the other way? That is, for a procedure to pass information back to the caller? That would be handy in some situations. The procedure could send back an OK code (perhaps the number 1) if all went well, but send back an error code (perhaps 0) if the procedure had a problem carrying out its task. Maybe the procedure was supposed to save some information to the floppy drive, but when it tried, it found that there was no diskette in Drive A.

Sending information back would also come in handy when the procedure does some transforming. Maybe various events in your program need to round off numbers. You could write a procedure that accepts (gets passed) a number, rounds it off, and then passes it back.

**20 Min.
To Go**

Understanding Functions

There are two kinds of procedures. One kind of procedure gives feedback, and the other does not. A sub doesn't give any feedback. However, the second kind of procedure, the *function*, does provide feedback. It gives feedback to the caller, the location in your program that triggered the function.

Often, your code doesn't need feedback. If you write a sub that plays a note of music to alert the user that they made an error, that sub doesn't need to provide any feedback to the caller code. It just plays its note and that's the end of it.

Sending information back

However, other times a caller *does* want information back. That's why there are two kinds of procedures: Functions send back information; subs do not. Let's see how this works. Let's translate the ShowThem sub into a function. It will pass back to any caller the name of the button that the user clicks to close the message box. Some callers might be simply displaying a warning to the user and won't care which button was pressed. They can just ignore the button code that gets passed back. Other callers might want to react one way if the user presses Cancel and a different way if the user presses OK. For instance, the message "If you want this data saved, press the OK button" requires feedback.

Change your ShowThem sub into a function. All you have to do is replace the word Sub with the word Function, and replace End Sub with End Function, like this:

```
Function ShowThem(msg As String)



End Function
```

However, we need to find out which button the user clicked in the message box. (Do you remember from Session 11 how you can get this information back? If you don't remember, press F1 and look at the Help information about the MsgBox command.) Here's one way to rewrite the sub so that it will send back the information:

```
Function ShowThem(msg As String)

Style = vbOKCancel
Title = "My Program's Warning"

response = MsgBox(msg, Style, Title)

ShowThem = response

End Function
```

There are two things to notice in this code. The MsgBox command is rearranged to add a variable (we chose the name response, but choose your own word if you wish). That variable gets information about which button the user clicked back from the MsgBox. Whenever you send information back into a variable, you must also put *parentheses* around the arguments (msg, Style, Title). So, we changed the MsgBox from the following style, which returns no information:

```
MsgBox msg, Style, Title
```

to this style, which does return information:

```
response = MsgBox(msg, Style, Title)
```

Let's consider what happened here. The first style, which returns no information, is a *sub*. It's not named Sub, but it behaves like one: no variable, no = symbol, no parentheses around the arguments.

Then we changed it into a *function* because we wanted information back from it. We added a variable, an =, and put parentheses around the arguments.

The second thing to notice in the code is that we used *the name of the function*, ShowThem, to pass back to the caller the information about which button was clicked:

```
ShowThem = response
```

Pause here until you memorize this: To pass information from your function back to the caller, assign that information to the name of your function.

You don't have to worry about assigning information to a variable when using the MsgBox function. It's not a function you wrote. It's built into Visual Basic — so the code that makes a MsgBox work is hidden from you. It's hard-wired into VB itself. Does VB offer other built-in functions? You betcha. Many of them. So many that we're going to spend all of Sessions 16 exploring them — so you know they're available if you need them. You don't want to reinvent the wheel, if VB has already done the job for you.

How to call a function

You probably suspect that because we've changed ShowThem from a sub to a function, we have to change how we call it from elsewhere in the program. We called the sub like this:

```
Private Sub Check1_Click()

ShowThem "This is Check1. Thanks for clicking me!"

End Sub
```

Do you know what to change to transform this from a sub call to a function call? Take the following steps:

- Add a variable (to get back the information the function sends).
- Add an = sign to copy the value returned into the variable.

- Put the arguments in parentheses, like this:

```
ButtonClicked = ShowThem("This is Check1. Thanks for
clicking me!")
```

Now let's add a little code that will display the results when we test this program. This is how `Check1_Click` should be changed:

```
Private Sub Check1_Click()

ButtonClicked = ShowThem("This is Check1. Thanks for clicking me!")
If ButtonClicked = vbOK Then MsgBox "They clicked OK"
If ButtonClicked = vbCancel Then MsgBox "They clicked Cancel"

End Sub
```

Press F5, then click `CheckBox1` to trigger the code.

Watching and Stepping

**10 Min.
To Go**

Single-stepping is a technique you can use to see your program execute in slow motion. This technique will let you watch as your program moves from line to line in your code. You'll also see the effect of calling, then returning from, a function.

Single-stepping is a good way to see your program *flow*, as its path of execution is sometimes called. Single-stepping is also often the best way to figure out why things are not working as you hoped they would.

If your program is still running, select Run ⇨ End to stop it. Now, instead of pressing F5 to run it at normal speed, press F8.

Things look normal — the form is displayed as usual. Click the Check1 CheckBox to trigger the code. Ha! Rather than seeing the message box, as you did before, you see the code window instead. And the line `Private Sub Check1_Click()` has been highlighted (in yellow, by default), as you can see in Figure 13-1. There's also an arrow pointing to this line. What happened?

You are using VB's single-step feature. Every time you press F8, one line of code is executed. Press F8 a second time. (If you had itchy fingers and already pressed it, choose Run ⇨ End, then press F8 to restart the program. This is a controlled experiment. You have to maintain self-control.)

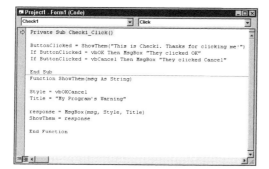

Figure 13-1
Pressing F8 allows you to step through your program one line at a time.

You now go to the second line of code in the Click event. This line triggers your ShowThem function. What do you think will happen next?

Press F8 a third time. The program jumps out of the Click event and lands at the ShowThem event. Much of the time, a program executes a line, goes to the next line, executes it, goes to the next line, and so on — moving down through a procedure in a linear fashion. Sometimes, however, the program jumps somewhere else, as is happening now.

Press F8 again. You're on the line that defines the Style variable. Press F8 again. You're on the line that defines the Title variable. Now try something new: Move your mouse pointer until it rests on the word *Style*. A small window opens and displays the contents of the variable Style, as is shown in Figure 13-2.

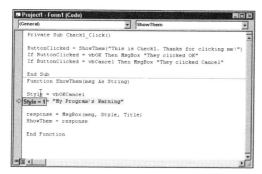

Figure 13-2
Move your mouse pointer onto any variable or constant and you can see its current contents.

Try moving your mouse pointer over to the constant `vbOKCancel`. You're shown that its value is 1. So, that 1 was transferred from the constant to the `Style` variable as you expected. Press F8 twice until you execute the `MsgBox` command. The message box appears as always. Click Cancel. You're back in the code window.

Move your mouse pointer to see what the variable `response` contains (that's the code for what button the user clicked). Press F8 to assign the value from `response` to `ShowThem`. Press F8 again and now you're back up in the `Click` event. Program execution picks up right after the line that called the `ShowThem` function. Press F8 until you see what happens in the line that detects the correct button code. When the `If` command is True, the execution moves to the second part of the line and displays another message box.

A Couple of Efficiencies

Some programmers like to write code that is as compact as possible. It's not really necessary any more (it was 20 years ago, though, when programmers tried to conserve every little byte of memory — hence the concern over Y2K glitches).

But if you do like sleek code, and want to show off your prowess, there are a couple of ways to shorten the code examples in this chapter.

You don't really need to use the `response` variable in this next example. (In order to focus on the technique being illustrated here, I'll leave out some of the arguments, such as Style and Title, that were used in this Sub in the examples earlier in this session.)

```
Function ShowThem(msg As String)

response = MsgBox(msg)
ShowThem = response


End Function
```

Instead, you can directly assign the message box's return value to `ShowThem`, like this:

```
ShowThem = MsgBox(msg)
```

If that seems to you to be more readable code, or preferable because it's shorter, go ahead and take that approach.

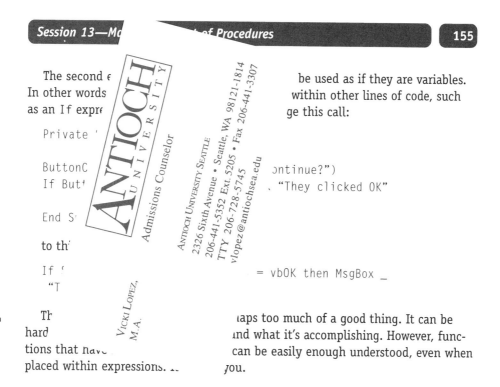

The second ε
In other words
as an If expre

```
Private '

ButtonC
If But'

End S'
```

to th'

```
If '
    "T
```

Tr
hard
tions that nave
placed within expressions. ᵢᵤ jou.

be used as if they are variables.
within other lines of code, such
ge this call:

```
ontinue?")
, "They clicked OK"
```

```
= vbOK then MsgBox _
```

ιaps too much of a good thing. It can be
ınd what it's accomplishing. However, func-
can be easily enough understood, even when

Done!

REVIEW

By now, you know all (well *a lot*) about the mysteries of procedures — those little
programlettes within a large program. You saw that putting small, individual tasks
into small packages called procedures makes your program easier to read, test,
maintain, and debug. The techniques for passing information to, and back from,
procedures became part of your programmer's arsenal in this session. You also
found out when to use functions and when to use subs. Finally, the great single-
stepping feature of VB showed you in slow motion just exactly how your program's
execution flowed from line to line, but sometimes jumped to a different procedure.

QUIZ YOURSELF

1. What are the two kinds of procedures? (See "Understanding Procedures".)
2. How do you pass information to a procedure? (See "Customizing the
    Behavior of a Procedure".)

3. Can you send information from a procedure back to the line of code that called the procedure? (See "Sending Information Back".)

4. Do you call a function the same way you call a subroutine? (See "How to Call a Function".)

5. What key do you press when you want to single-step through your program? (See "Watching and Stepping".)

Understanding Variables and Scope

Session Checklist

✔ Visualizing the two kinds of data: text and numeric

✔ How to name and create variables

✔ Manipulating variables and their values

✔ Understanding data types

✔ Working with scope (the range of influence)

✔ Using Option Explicit to discipline yourself

**30 Min.
To Go**

C omputers process information in much the same sense that a Cuisinart processes food: You put some carrots, cabbage, and mayo in — they get transformed, chopped up — then you take the result out and yell SLAW! at the top of your voice.

Likewise, with a database program, you type in a list of names and phone numbers. Then the program processes them to give you a list, say, of all the people located in one area code.

The Two Kinds of Data

It's called data processing, or information processing. But no matter how huge the database program, or how sophisticated the graphics program, all computer programs process only two categories of information: strings or numbers.

A string is characters strung together: "Don Wilson", "b", and "454-5001 ext. 23" are all strings. When you assign some literal text to a string variable, the text is enclosed in quotation marks. If there's enough memory in your computer and an application permits large strings, you can hold the entire phone book in a single string if you wish. By contrast, this: "" is an empty string.

As you see from the example above, a string can be a single character, really huge, empty, or anything in between. It can contain letters of the alphabet, symbols like * or @, and even digits like "2".

Note, however, that a *digit* is *not* the same as a number. It is just a character (string) representation. You cannot do math with strings. You can *concatenate* strings: `Print` "fluor" + "ide" will display `fluoride`. `Print` "2" + "3" displays 23. You cannot multiply or subtract or do other math on strings. (Actually, VB prefers that you use the & symbol to concatenate and reserves + for adding numbers. It will usually accept +, but it doesn't like it.)

I like the `Print` command. If you use the `Print` command all by itself, the result will print on the form itself. `Print` can also print to a PictureBox (this is rarely useful). The `Print` command when used with a form is an alternative way of testing things. In this book, I've mostly used the `MsgBox` to show you a result or demonstrate how a technique works. But sometimes I use `Print`. `MsgBox` has a drawback: You must click its button to close it after you've seen the message. My favorite way to test commands is to use the `Form_Load` event (that way you don't have to click anything — the result is automatically displayed when you press F5). If you do use the `Print` technique, remember to also type in `Form1.Show` (by default, the commands in a `Form_Load` event take place before the form is displayed to the user, so anything involving the `Print` command doesn't show up when the form is finally displayed). So here's my very favorite way to experiment with a VB command — you need do nothing other than simply press F5:

```
Private Sub Form_Load()
Form1.Show
Print 2 * 5
End Sub
```

You understand strings now. Numbers are the other kind of data, and they operate inside the computer just as they do in real life: You can do all kinds of math with them. Programmers sometimes store numbers as strings, though, if they don't expect that they'll be doing math with them. Your area code "27244" and phone number "336-555-0123" make better sense stored as strings. You can't store a phone number as a number if you want to include those hyphens in it, anyway. Symbols like that must be stored in a string. If you left the quotation marks off of 336-555-0123, Visual Basic would think you wanted to subtract real numbers, and would store the value, -342, in your variable. Always remember to enclose strings in quotation marks.

Understanding Variables

We've been talking about *storing* data. Here's how it works. The computer asks you to type in how much you're willing to pay for a new TV. You oblige and type in **299**. What happens then? The computer must store that information. It puts the information into a *variable*.

Each variable has a name that the programmer gave it. Usually, programmers like to use memorable variable names, something easily recognized, like `TopTvPrice`. Underscore characters are allowed, so some programmers make the name even more readable: `Top_Tv_Price`. After the user types in 299 (called a *value*), the program assigns the value to the variable:

```
TopTvPrice = 299
```

In our example, the user types **299**; let's assume he or she types it into a TextBox. So the code that assigns the value to the variable would look like this:

```
TopTvPrice = Text1.Text
```

The contents of the TextBox are copied into the variable `TopTvPrice`.

How to name variables

You must observe several rules when making up a name for a variable (otherwise, Visual Basic will protest):

- It must start with a letter, not a digit.
- It cannot be one of Visual Basic's own command words, like `For` or `Height`.
- It cannot be larger than 255 characters.
- It cannot contain any punctuation marks or spaces.

How to create a variable

When you need to use a variable in a program, you can simply type in a name for it, and voila, the variable will come into existence. Let's say that your program displays an InputBox that asks the user how old he or she is. The variable you want to put his or her answer (the value) in can be named UsersAge (I know, I know; it should be User'sAge, but you can't use punctuation in variable names):

```
UsersAge = InputBox ("How old are you?")
```

As soon as the user types **44,** or whatever, and closes the InputBox, the value 44 is assigned to the variable UsersAge. The value is stored. When your program later wants to process that data, it knows where to look. It merely uses the variable name. Let's say you want to find out if the user is eligible for AARP:

```
If UsersAge < 50 Then MsgBox _
"You're too young to join AARP. Sorry."
```

(The < symbol means *less than*.) Notice that you use the variable name as you would any other number in this programming. When the program executes, whatever number the user typed in is compared to 50.

There's a second way to create a variable, and many programmers swear by it. Use the Dim command to explicitly declare the variable:

```
Dim UsersAge
UsersAge = InputBox ("How old are you?")
```

If you're going to use several variables in the procedure, Dim each of them:

```
Dim UsersAge, UsersName, UsersHeight, Nickname
```

You only need to use Dim at the start of the line, and then just separate the variable names by commas. (Now do you see one reason why you can't use punctuation in variable names? Visual Basic uses various kinds of punctuation to mean various things in a line of code. Recall that the single-quote symbol (') means that you're making an annotation, and VB should ignore everything following the ' on that line. The * means multiply, & means concatenate, and so on.)

One reason that using Dim is so highly regarded is that when you later look at the code you wrote and you're trying to figure it out, you can see a list of all the variables right there at the top of the procedure. (There's a second reason for using Dim that we'll get to in the section about Option Explicit at the end of this session.)

Many programmers go even further and define the variable *type* when they declare the variable:

```
Dim UsersAge As Integer, UsersName As String
Dim UsersHeight as Integer, Nickname as String
```

There are nine variable types in VB. We'll get to them later in this session. For now, just note that each of these variables is explicitly typed (*typed* here means given a data type, not pressing keys on the keyboard), rather than letting them default to the Variant type (also explained shortly).

**20 Min.
To Go**

Manipulating Variables

Variables hold only one value at a time. But the value can change as necessary (hence the name *variable*). For example, if you write the following code (it would be crazy to do so):

```
TVShow = "Barney"
TVShow = "Five-0"
```

when it executes, VB assigns Barney to the variable TVShow, but immediately dumps that value and replaces it with Five-0. When a new value is assigned to a variable, the previous contents of that variable simply no longer exist.

You can assign literal values ("Barney" or 299, as illustrated several places above), but you can also assign one variable to another. When you assign a variable to another variable, the variable on the left of the = sign gets the value held in the variable to the right of the = sign. At this point, both variables contain the same value. This is like making a copy of the value. In this next example, the contents of the variable PopularShow are copied into the variable MyTVShow:

```
MyTVShow = PopularShow
```

One practical and common use of copying one variable into another was illustrated earlier in this chapter with this line:

```
TopTvPrice = Text1.Text
```

Properties are a kind of variable

What do I mean by this? Am I saying that the `Text` property of a TextBox is a variable? Sure. *Properties are variables*. True, they're a bit different from ordinary variables: They're predefined by the people who created the component, and they usually have a default value. However, you can assign a new value to them, either during design time in the Properties Window, or at run time in code, or both: `Command1.Height = 55`. Their values can vary.

Communicating across forms

You can also assign variables to other forms in your project. Many programs use more than one form. If you need to write code in, say, Form1 that modifies a Label in Form3, just attach Form3's name to the front of the component's name, like this:

```
Form3.Label1.Caption = "Press this button to see the list"
```

Some more efficiencies

Sometimes you want to concatenate or otherwise combine two variables. Let's say you want to personalize your program, so first ask the user to type in his or her name, then use that variable along with another variable to create a complete sentence:

```
Result = InputBox("Please type your first name.")
Msg = "Thank you, " & Result
MsgBox Msg
```

Or if you're one of those people who is always looking to conserve variable names, you can reuse `Result` like this, without even needing that second variable `Msg`:

```
Result = "Thank you, " & Result
MsgBox Result
```

Or if you're one of those people who always want to save space and condense code, you can do it like this:

```
Msgbox "Thank you, " & Result
```

As this illustrates, a variable can be part of what's assigned to *itself*. One use
for this technique is illustrated in the previous example: You want to preserve the
contents of the variable (Result), but add something to the contents ("Thank
you"). To illustrate this same principle with a numeric variable, perform the following math equations using the variable name:

```
A = 233
A = A + 1
```

Now A holds 234.

There are usually several ways to code, and your personal style will emerge over
time. Notice how I always seem to use `Result` or `Response` as the variable names
with the `InputBox` command? It's just a little habit of mine — you can use
`Reaction`, `Retort`, `Reply`, or `Rejoinder`, just as long as it begins with an *r*. Just
kidding! You know the rules for thinking up variable names — you can use pretty
much any word, or even a nonsense word like `jaaaaakaa`. But it's best to make
your variable names descriptive of what the variable holds.

A note on arrays

Recall that I said that a variable can hold only one value at a time. Sometimes,
though, it's useful to collect a whole group of values together in one package.
There is a special way to group values: You give them one name, but each is given
a unique *index number*. This collection of values is called an *array*. An important
feature of arrays is that you can use their index numbers as a way of working with
the values in sequence. This is particularly useful in loops like `For...Next` where
you keep incrementing a counter variable each time through the loop. That
counter can access each value in the array by using the index numbers. (The term
counter variable is merely a description of what that variable is doing in the code.
It's still just another ordinary variable. There's nothing odd about it.)

For example, if we want to manipulate the names of people coming to dinner
this Friday, we can create an array of their names:

```
Dim guests(1 To 5)
```

This creates five "empty boxes" in the computer's memory, which serve as
spaces for five values. However, instead of five unique individual variable names,
the values share the same name, "guests", and each value is identified by a unique
index number from 1 to 5:

```
guests(3) = "Bill Hitch"
MsgBox guests(3)
```

Arrays *must* be declared (Dim). You cannot implicitly create an array the way you can with an ordinary variable. We'll discuss arrays more thoroughly in Session 17. Now let's consider the various numeric data types.

Data Types and the Variant

Text variables (strings) are pretty simple. However, there are several sub-varieties of numeric variables. The reason for these different numeric data *types* is that you can speed up your applications with some of them, or achieve greater precision with others. But you can actually ignore this issue if you want because VB can handle data types for you. It just makes all data the *variant* type, which is a generic, all-purpose type.

By default, unless you specifically define them as something else with Dim, VB makes all variables the variant type. It's very convenient because that means you don't have to worry about saying: ThisVariable will hold strings, but ThisOther Variable will hold only whole numbers (no fractions). Instead, you let VB decide which type to use based on the value you assign it.

Here's an example that shows how variants achieve their chameleon changes:

```
A = 12
B = 12.4
```

When it assigns the 12 to A, VB figures that 12 can be an integer type, but when it assigns 12.4 to B, VB knows that this number has to be the floating-point (decimal) type because it is a fraction. So VB types the variables for you. It can even convert some kinds of data:

```
A = "12"
B = 14
B = B + A
MsgBox B
```

You get the correct mathematical answer of 26 because when you assigned 14 to B, it became an integer variable type, and then you assigned a string to it, which converted the string into an integer. However, don't take this too far. It's best to not mix types if you can avoid it.

The interpreting that VB must do when it works with Variants is said to slow program execution down some, though I've never noticed it. If you are interested in speeding up your program, go ahead and explicitly type your variables, particularly those used inside For...Next or other kinds of loops, as discussed in Session 17. Then see if *you* notice any difference in execution speed. I doubt you will.

The simplest variable type is `Boolean`. It can only hold two states: True and False (it defaults to False). Use this when you want a toggle variable (something that switches off and on like a light switch). To create a `Boolean` variable, use the following code:

```
Dim MyToggle As Boolean
```

Another simple data type is the `Integer`. It holds numbers between -32,768 and 32,767. You'd be surprised at how often the only thing you need is an integer. No fractions are allowed. If your non-fractional number is larger or smaller than an integer can hold, make it a long data type.

```
Dim MyLittleNumber As Integer
Dim MyBigNumber As Long
```

The other major numeric type is called floating point. It has similar small and large versions called `Single` and `Double`, respectively. It's used when a number involves a fraction:

```
Dim MyFraction As Single, MyBiggerNumber As Double
```

I suggest you not worry too much about data types. In future sessions, I'll suggest you type a variable a couple of times, but in general, the `Variant` system works very well indeed. For the most part, I just leave variable typing up to VB.

Following is a table that lists all of the various data types, their symbols, if any, and the range of values they can contain. (It's now out of fashion, but people used to type data by using symbols rather than `Dim`. `A$` = "`Hello`" ensured that the variable *A$* was typed as a string. The $ becomes part of the variable name. If you decide you must type a variable, forget about the symbols and use the `Dim...As` commands.)

Table 14-1
The VB Data Types

Name	Symbol	Range
Boolean	None	True or False
Byte	None	0 to 255
Integer	%	−32,768 to 32,767

Continued

Table 14-1 *Continued*

Name	Symbol	Range
Long Integer (or Long)	&	–2,147,483,648 to 2,147,483,647
Single (Single-precision floating-point)	!	From -3.402823E38 to -1.401298E-45 (for negative values). From 1.401298E-45 to 3.402823E38 (for positive values).
Double (Double-precision floating-point)	#	From -1.79769313486232E308 to -4.94065645841247E-324 (for negative values). From 4.94065645841247E-324 to 1.79769313486232E308 (for positive values).
Currency (scaled integer)	@	–922,337,203,685,477.5808 to 922,337,203,685,477.5807
Decimal	None	+/-79,228,162,514,264,337,593,543, 950,335 if no decimal point; +/- 7.9228162514264337593543950335 with 28 places to the right of the decimal; the smallest number other than zero is +/-0.0000000000000000000000000001.
Date	None	January 1, 100 to December 31, 9999
Object	None	Any Object
Text (string) (a string of variable length)	$	Up to roughly 2 billion (2^{31})
Text (string) (a string of fixed length)	$	Up to roughly 64 thousand (2^{16})
Variant (when holding a number)	None	Any number
Variant (when holding text)	None	1 to roughly 2 billion

**10 Min.
To Go**

The fixed-length string can be defined, if you want to limit the number of characters. This example limits the string to 22 characters, and discards any characters beyond the 22nd:

```
Dim MyText As String * 22
```

There isn't much use for this feature.

Scope: The Range of Influence

So far we've been using variables inside procedures. When you declare a variable inside a procedure, *the variable only works within that procedure*. When the program executes the procedure or event, the variable comes to life, does its thing, but then dies (disappears) as soon as the End Sub line is executed. Variables that live only within a single procedure are called *local* variables.

Local variables have two qualities that you should understand:

1. No programming outside their own procedure can interact with them, either to read their value or to change their value. Their *scope* is limited to their own procedure.

2. When VB finishes executing the procedure in which they reside, their value evaporates. If that procedure is executed a second time, whatever value the local variable once contained is no longer there. One execution of the procedure is their *lifetime*. There are some situations in which you do want a local variable's value to be preserved. In those cases, use the Static command rather than the Dim command:

```
Private Sub Form_Load()
   Dim n
   Static x
End Sub
```

In this example, the variable n loses its value when the End Sub is executed. However, the variable x retains its value until the program is shut down. Another way of putting it is: When you use the Static command with a local variable, the value of that variable is preserved for the lifetime of your application.

What do you think would happen if you clicked Command1, and then clicked Command2, in this next program?

```
Private Sub Command1_Click()
X = 12
```

```
X = X + 5
End Sub

Private Sub Command2_Click()
MsgBox X
End Sub
```

The message box would display nothing. The variable X in Command1's Click event *is a completely different variable* from the X in Command2's Click event.

What if you want both of these procedures to be able to access and manipulate the same variable? To do this, move your insertion cursor to the very top of the code window — above any procedures. When you do this (press the up arrow until you move the cursor to the top, or click your mouse at the top), you'll notice that the two listboxes at the top of the code window now say (General) and (Declarations), as you can seen in Figure 14-1.

Figure 14-1
Declare a variable up here in the General Declarations zone if you want it usable anywhere — in all the procedures — in this form.

Now if you run the same program, click Command1, and then click Command2, you will see the result shown in Figure 14-2.

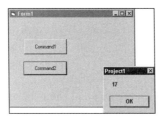

Figure 14-2
The Click events of these two CommandButtons share the same variable.

When a variable has form-wide scope, it's then available to all of the procedures in that form. It's not available, however, to the procedures in any other forms in the project. (Sometimes people call form-wide variables *module variables* because the term *module* is sometimes used as a synonym for form.)

What if you want to make a variable available to all of the procedures in all of your forms? In such a case, you have to use the `Public` command rather than `Dim`. What's more, you have to put the declaration into a *module*. A module is similar to a form, but it doesn't have a user interface. It is never made visible to the user. It also contains no events. It's just a code window — a location where you put public declarations (program-wide in scope). Most programmers also put any custom subs or functions they write into modules. That makes them available to the entire program, too.

To add a module to your program, choose Project ⇨ Add Module. The Add Module dialog box opens. Double-click the Module icon and a new module (named Module1) appears in your Project Explorer window. You also see the module's code window, as shown in Figure 14-3. Notice that I typed in a variable *x* that is declared Public, thereby making *x* available to any procedure in the entire project.

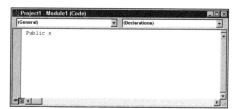

Figure 14-3
Put Public variables and your own procedures in a module to make them available to all of your forms.

Both form-wide and program-wide variables are preserved for the lifetime of your application. They never lose their value, as does a local variable declared with the `Dim` command.

It's considered good programming practice to try to avoid using `Public` variables. Variables with that much scope make your programming harder to debug. Looking at the status of variables is one of the primary ways to find out where a problem is located in a program. If you use a local variable, a problem with that variable will be found only in its procedure. That really narrows your search for a bug. You have more code to search if there's a bug involving a form-wide variable, but at least this kind of variable limits the problem to a single form, rather than the entire program.

You may have noticed that procedures also have scope. By default, VB makes all events `Private` (`Private Sub Command1_Click`). `Private` events can be triggered only from within the form in which they reside. However, you can change the default *Private* to `Public Sub Command1_Click`. When it's Public, you can trigger the procedure from another form, like this: `Form1.Command2_Click`. I've rarely seen an occasion when it was useful to trigger an event from within another procedure (generally the user triggers events). And I've never heard of anyone wanting to trigger one form's events from another form, but you never know.

There are five commands that define scope: `Public`, `Private`, `Dim`, `ReDim`, and `Static`. We've discussed all but the `ReDim` command. It is not often used, and it works only with arrays. So we'll postpone discussing it until Session 17.

Forcing Yourself to Declare Variables

In this book, I don't explicitly declare all of the variables. I'm trying to get you to see the main point of each example, without adding extra code that's not absolutely necessary. However, be warned that many programming teachers insist that all variables be officially declared. They do this so that you can easily see which variables are in use — without having to search the code for them. Another reason to require the declaration of variables is that it prevents a common source of error. Consider this code:

```
Private Sub Form_Load()

TempString = "Tex"
TempString = TemString + "as"
MsgBox TempString

End Sub
```

You probably think that the above code displays a message box with the word *Texas* in it. No, it only displays *as*. Can you see why? One of those variable names is misspelled. That's very easy to do. (*TemString*, the typo made when this code was typed in, contains nothing. So when you add nothing to "as", you're left with "as".) However, there's a way to get VB to alert you if you make this common kind of mistake. Type the following into the General Declarations section of the form:

```
Option Explicit
```

Then try running the above example code. VB responds by highlighting the first instance of TempString and telling you Variable Not Defined. So go ahead and declare it:

```
Private Sub Form_Load()
Dim TempString

TempString = "Tex"
TempString = TemString + "as"
MsgBox TempString

End Sub
```

Now when you run this code, VB shows you the typo, as you can see in Figure 14-4.

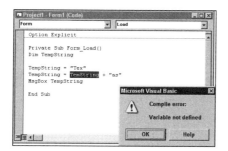

Figure 14-4
When you use the Option Explicit feature, VB will point out any typos.

Done!

You never intended to have a variable named TemString, and with Option Explicit turned on, VB shows you the typo. VB flags any undeclared variables. You must put Option Explicit in General Declarations for each form in your program. However, you can automate this. VB will insert the command in every form for you if you choose Tools ➪ Options and then click the Require Variable Declaration checkbox. (If you already have some forms in your project when you turn on this option, you must go back and type in Option Explicit for them.)

REVIEW

This session was all about variables — one of the most important tools in a programmer's arsenal. You saw that variables are divided into two primary categories:

1. Strings that can be alphabetized and concatenated, but are not numbers and can't be manipulated mathematically (even if the string holds a series of digits that *look* like real numbers).
2. Real numbers that can be manipulated mathematically.

You also discovered the naming conventions and the various ways that variables can be copied and typed. Then you saw how to use the `Dim`, `Public`, and `Private` commands to specify a variable's scope. Finally, the `Option Explicit` command was introduced.

QUIZ YOURSELF

1. Which kind of variable uses quotation marks around its value? (See "The Two Kinds of Data".)
2. Would the word *Function* make a good variable name? (See "How to Name Variables".)
3. Why can properties be considered variables? (See "Manipulating Variables".)
4. If you don't specify a data type, what type does VB use as the default? (See "Data Types and the Variant".)
5. What is the General Declarations section of a code window — and what happens when you declare a variable there? (See "Scope: The Range of Influence".)

Exploring VB's Built-in Functions

Session Checklist

✔ Learning to use literals, constants, and expressions

✔ Using the string functions

✔ Working with numeric functions

✔ Converting data and querying data types

✔ Formatting numbers

✔ Using the financial functions

✔ Programming with date and time functions

**30 Min.
To Go**

I n Session 13, you saw how to work with event procedures, as well as subs and functions that you yourself create. In this session, you'll see how to tap into several collections of built-in functions that are provided by VB. This session doesn't cover *every* built-in function, but it does survey the ones you're most likely to need.

This session is something of a reference — so we'll leave out figures. You should come away from this session with a sense of the variety of tools VB contains to help you get things done in your own applications.

You perhaps suspected that the `InputBox` and `MsgBox` commands were, in fact, functions. Both can return information to your program. (Recall that the key distinction between a function and a sub is that a sub doesn't return anything.) You were correct in your suspicions.

VB has many other built-in functions. Knowing they exist will save you the trouble of writing them yourself when you want to get a particular job done.

VB's functions fall into six categories: string; numeric; data conversion and data-testing; formatting; financial; and date and time. Let's survey them in order.

Understanding Literals, Constants, and Expressions

Before plunging into the various built-in functions, let's pause for a bit to deepen your understanding of variables. Sometimes you provide a variable to a function, like this:

```
Msg = "Hello"
Response = MsgBox(Msg)
```

Literals

Other times you might use a *literal* (you type the actual value itself instead of using a value stored in a variable):

```
Response = MsgBox("Hello")
```

Literals can be strings or numeric. String literals are enclosed in quotation marks.

Constants

A *constant* is a number that doesn't change while your program runs, like pi or the address of the White House. You may recall that VB contains many built-in constants (`vbBlue` is a built-in constant), but you can also define your own, like this:

```
Const WHITEHOUSE = "1600 Pennsylvania Ave."
```

Constants can hold strings or numbers. To give a constant enough scope so that it's available to your entire program, define it in the General Declarations section of a module. By convention, constant names use all uppercase letters. VB doesn't care if you use upper- or lowercase, but it helps programmers to recognize a constant.

Some programmers like to use constants. They argue that one good candidate to be a constant is something like the state sales tax. Let's say it's 7 percent. Rather than putting 1.07 several places in their program, they define a constant instead:

```
Const STATESALESTAX = 1.07
```

This accomplishes a couple of things. It makes the program easier to understand:

```
GrandTotal = TotalPurchases * STATESALESTAX
```

Rather than:

```
GrandTotal = TotalPurchases * 1.07
```

But it also makes it easier to modify your program later. If the sales tax changes in the future, you don't have to go through your entire program looking for 1.07 and adjusting it to 1.08 or whatever. Instead, you only have to modify that single line in the General Declarations section of a module where the constant is defined.

To me, whether you use constants or not depends on your situation. If you write lengthy programs that can benefit from them, go ahead. If you write programs that might need to be maintained later by you or by other people, constants are yet another way to clarify the meaning of your code.

Expressions

Usually, you can also use an *expression* as part of the argument list for a function. An expression is a compound entity that VB evaluates at run time. An expression can be made up of literals, variables, or a combination of the two:

```
Response = MsgBox ("Hello" + MyVariable)
```

If someone tells you she has a coupon for $1 off a $15 Bach CD, you immediately think $14. In the same way, at run time, VB reduces the items in an expression into its simplest form. A *numeric expression* results in a single number (after the expression is evaluated). When an intelligent entity hears an expression, the entity collapses that expression into its simplest form. In other words, if you type 15 – 1 into one of your programs, when the program runs, Visual Basic reduces that group of symbols, that expression, to a single number: 14. Visual Basic simply evaluates what you've said and uses it in the program as the essence of what you are trying to say.

Here is a list of numeric entities you can use in an expression:

- A numeric or string variable
- A variable in an array
- A literal (numeric or string)
- A function that returns a number or string
- A numeric constant, like `Const Pi = 3.14159265358979`
- Any combination of the above

**20 Min.
To Go**

The String Functions

The various string functions can manipulate text in many ways. Some of them take more than one argument. Arguments can include string variables, string literals, or expressions.

Chr (number)

This function returns the ASCII code for the character. In computer languages, all characters (which include the uppercase and lowercase letters of the alphabet, punctuation marks, digits, and special symbols) have a numeric code — from 0 to 255 (though this is changing to a larger set of numbers to accommodate most of the world's languages).

The computer works exclusively with numbers. The only purpose of text, from the computer's point of view, is to facilitate communication with humans. When you type in the letter *a*, the computer "remembers" it as the number 97. When that character is printed on the screen or on paper, the computer translates 97 back into the visual symbol we recognize as *a*. Although we think of text as information, to the computer the text characters are merely graphic images that, when strung together, have meaning for humans. It will be an important step toward artificial intelligence when text has as much meaning to the computer as mathematical and numeric data already does.

`Chr` can be useful when encrypting messages, or to solve specialized character-displaying problems, as the example below illustrates.

You cannot put quotes around words in MsgBoxes because the " (quote mark) tells the MsgBox that the message has ended. However, there is a way around this problem. Define a variable containing the code for the quotation mark, which is 34:

```
quot = Chr(34)
MsgBox ("We're selling " & quot & "wood." & quot)
```

Another common use of Chr is to force a carriage return/linefeed; in other words, to simulate pressing the Enter key to move down to the next line in a TextBox. There is no way to type Enter into a string, so you must define the two character codes that simulate it, like this:

```
cr = Chr(13) & Chr(10)
Text1.Text = "Hi" & cr & "How are you all!"
```

The format is: InStr([start,], string1, string2).

InStr tells you where (which character position) string2 is located within string1. Optionally, you can specify a starting character position.

This is a remarkably handy function when you need to *parse* (to locate or extract a piece of text within a larger body of text) some text. InStr can enable you to see if a particular word, for example, exists within a file or within some text that the user has typed into a TextBox. Perhaps you need to search a TextBox to see if the user typed in the words *New Jersey*, and if so, to tell them that your product is not available in that state.

InStr is case-sensitive; it makes a distinction between *Upper* and *upper*.

What if you want to know whether there is more than one instance of the search string within the larger text? You can easily find additional instances by using the result of a previous InStr search. InStr, when it finds a match, reports the location and the character position within the larger text where the search string was found.

```
Private Sub Form_Load()

quot = Chr(34)

MainText = "Masterpieces are built of pieces."
SearchWord = "pieces"

Do
    X = Y + 1
    Z = Z + 1
    Y = InStr(X, MainText, SearchWord)

Loop Until Y = 0

MsgBox "We found " & SearchWord & " " & Z - 1 &  _
```

```
" times inside " & quot & MainText & quot

End Sub
```

Don't worry about the Do...Loop structure. It's covered in a future session. In this example, the loop continues to look through the MainText until the InStr function returns a zero (which indicates that the SearchWord isn't found any more). The variable Z is used to count the number of times there's a successful hit. The variable X moves the pointer one character further into the MainText (X = Y + 1). You can use this example as a template any time you need to count the number of occurrences of a string within another, larger string.

To merely see if, in the above code, a string appears within another one, use this:

```
If InStr("Masterpiece", "piece") Then MsgBox "Yep!"
```

Which translates: If "piece" is found within "Masterpiece", then display "Yep!"

There's also an InStrRev function that works in a similar way, but it starts looking at the last character and searches backward to the first.

LCase(String)

This function removes any uppercase letters from a string, reducing it to all lowercase characters. AfterWord becomes afterword. Likewise, there's also a UCase function that raises all of the characters in a string to uppercase.

These functions are used when you want to ignore the case — when you want to be case-insensitive. Usually, LCase or UCase are valuable when the user is providing input and you cannot know (and don't care) how he or she might capitalize the input. Comparisons *are* case-sensitive:

```
If "Larry" = "larry" Then MsgBox "They are the same."
```

This message box will never be displayed. The *L* is not the same. You can see the problem. You often just don't care how the user typed in the capitalization. If you don't care, just use LCase or UCase to force all the characters to be lowercase or uppercase.

```
Private Sub Form_Load()
reply = UCase(InputBox("Shall we proceed?"))
If InStr(reply, "YES") Then
  MsgBox ("Ok. We'll proceed.")
End If
End Sub
```

Notice that it now does not matter how the user capitalized *yes*. Any capitalization will be forced into uppercase letters, and we in turn compare it to a literal that is also all uppercase.

Left(String,Number)

The Left function returns a portion of the string, the number of characters defined by the Number argument.

```
N = Left("More to the point.", 4)
MsgBox N
```

This code results in More. There's also a Right function.

Len(String)

This function tells you how many characters are in a string. You might want to let the user know that their response is too wordy for your database's allotted space for a particular entry. Or perhaps you want to see if they entered the full telephone number, including their area code. If they have, the number will have to be at least ten characters long. You can use the less-than symbol (<) to test their entry:

```
If Len(Text1.Text) < 10 then MsgBox _
"You must enter your area code."
```

LTrim(String)

LTrim (and its brother RTrim) remove any leading (or trailing) space characters from a string. The uses for this function are similar to those for UCase or LCase: Sometimes people accidentally add extra spaces at the beginning or end of their typing. Those space characters will cause a comparison to fail because computers can be quite literal. " This" is not the same thing as "This", and if you write code If " This" = "This", and the user types in " This ", the answer will be no.

Mid(String, StartCharacter, number of characters)

The format is: Mid(String, StartCharacter [, NumberOfCharacters])

I find myself using this function surprisingly often. It's a little like the Left or Right functions, except Mid can extract a *substring* (a string within a string) from anywhere within a string. Left and Right are limited to getting characters on one end of a string or the other.

The `Mid` function works like this:

```
MsgBox Mid("1234567", 3, 4)
```

This results in 3456. You asked `Mid` to begin at the third character and extract 4 characters, and that's exactly what you got.

Use `Mid` with the `InStr` command to find, then extract, a substring. Recall that `InStr` searches for a matching letter, word, or phrase. If `InStr` finds what you've asked it to look for, it tells you the character *position*, within the larger text, where it found the match. You can then feed this information to `Mid` as the position at which it should begin extracting text.

You can also use `Mid` to *replace* a piece of text within a larger body of text rather than extracting it. Here's how it works:

```
B = "Down by the old mill stream."
Mid(B, 13, 3) = "new"
MsgBox B
```

This results in: `Down by the new mill stream.`

StrReverse(string)

This function turns, for example, `Mandy` into `ydnaM`. I can't, off the top of my head, think of a use for this, but it's there if you think of one:

```
MsgBox StrReverse("Mandy")
```

Numeric Functions

Most of the numeric functions have to do with trigonometry. If you need them, you know where to look. Press F1, then use the Index tab to search VB Help for `Atn`, `Cos`, `Exp`, `Len`, `Log`, `Sin`, or `Tan`.

The only numeric function I've ever found a use for is `Abs`. It strips off a minus sign, if there is one. In other words, -88 becomes 88, and 88 stays 88.

Use `Abs` when you want to find out the *difference* between two numbers but don't know which is the smaller number (in other words, which to subtract from the other). For example, let's say the user types in **25** as his age and **44** as the age of his sister:

```
MyAge = 25
HerAge = 44
```

```
MsgBox "The difference in age between you and your sister is " _
    & Abs(MyAge - HerAge)
```

The point is that you don't know, when programming, which number should be subtracted from the other. You want to know the *difference* between them. When you use Abs, it doesn't matter which variable you subtract from the other.

```
Abs(MyAge - HerAge)
```

produces the exact same result as:

```
Abs(HerAge - MyAge)
```

You get the same result even if you reverse the order. (Without Abs, the result would not be the same in both versions.)

Data Conversion Functions

10 Min. To Go

Sometimes, but not often, you want to force a variable to be a certain type, usually because you want to achieve a high level of precision. A string can be coerced into a numeric type, or an integer can be made into a floating-point type — any type can be converted into any other type.

As you'll see in the following example, when you add two integers (whole numbers smaller than about 30,000), VB is smart enough to choose an Integer variable type. If you then do math that results in a fraction, VB chooses a precise variable type, called the Double.

```
Private Sub Form_Load()

x = 1 + 2
MsgBox TypeName(x)
x = 1 / 3
MsgBox TypeName(x) & x


End Sub
```

The TypeName function tells you which variable type a variable is.

The "C . . ." functions

These functions force variables to become particular types using these functions: CCur (currency), CDbl (double), CInt (integer), CLng (long), CSng (single), CStr (string), CVar (variant), Fix (removes the fractional part of a number), Int (rounds down to the next lowest integer — even 1.9 becomes 1), Hex (changes to hexadecimal base), and Oct (changes to octal base).

Here are the primary uses for these "C . . ." functions:

- For the greatest possible precision and the greatest possible range, use the Decimal type. The special Decimal numeric type provides this enormous range: plus or minus 79,228,162,514,264,337,593,543,950,335 for numbers with no decimal places. For numbers with a decimal, the Decimal type provides this enormous precision: plus or minus 7.9228162514264337593543950335. The smallest possible fraction is 0.0000000000000000000000000001. Note that unlike the other subtypes, you can't declare a variable to be of the Decimal subtype (using Dim, Static, or Public). You can't, in other words, do this: Dim X as Decimal. You can only coerce an existing subtype into a Decimal subtype, for example: MsgBox CDec(2) / 3.

- Use Cint (for simple integers) or CDbl (for large numbers with fractions) if you want to change a string variable type into a numeric variable. Use cStr to force real numbers to become text digits (characters rather than computable numbers).

- The CDate command might seem to duplicate the behavior of the DateValue or TimeValue commands (we'll get to them later in this session), but there is a difference. DateValue converts a number to the date format; TimeValue converts to the time format. CDate converts *both* date and time.

Data-testing

There is a small set of "Is . . . " functions that tell you the status of variables: IsArray, IsDate, IsError, IsEmpty, IsMissing, IsNull, IsNumeric, and IsObject. Note that there is no IsString function, but you can use the VarType or TypeName functions to find that out. Also, the IsNull and IsEmpty functions aren't identical: *Empty* and *null* have special meanings. Null is what you typically think of as an "empty" variable (A = "" makes A Null). Empty, by contrast, means that the variable has so far *never been used in the program at all*; it has never even been initialized or referred to in any fashion. Also, when testing for null, you can't use something like this code: `If Var = Null`. If an expression includes the null command, *the whole expression* automatically becomes null. Therefore, you'll always get False as an answer to the query `If Var = Null`. The solution: You must use the `IsNull` command to test for nullness.

The Formatting Function

The `Format` function is a multipurpose tool. It's most useful for adding commas to numbers to separate the thousands, displaying a number in scientific notation, displaying percents, displaying time in 12-hour or 24-hour formats, or for making your own custom formats.

The `Format` command's job is to format and display numeric data as text characters (digits) according to your needs — as percentages, fractions, and/or words. It can specify a specific number of digits to the right of the decimal point. For dates, it can display the day's month's full name, an abbreviation of them, or only digits. With displays of time, it can format with AM, PM, and so forth.

Use `Format` for accounting, scientific, or other purposes where you need to present numbers in a particular format for readability, consistency, or conformity to accepted syntax and punctuation.

You can use `Format` in this fashion:

```
MsgBox Format("22222", "currency")
MsgBox Format("22222", "scientific")
```

This code results in $22,222.00 and 2.22E+04. The most useful predefined formats in addition to currency and scientific are: *fixed* (0.00) — at least one digit to the left, and two to the right of the decimal; *standard* (1,000.00) — same as fixed, but includes thousands punctuation; and *percent* (56.00%) — multiplies the number by 100 and adds a % symbol.

Or if you don't find a predefined format you like, you can define your own using various symbols:

```
X = 12000000
Print Format(X, "###,###,###")
```

This code results in 12,000,000 (without `Format`, this number would print as 12000000).

You can also define date formats, like this:

```
Print Format(Now, "dddd, mmmm dd, yyyy")
```

This code results in: Thursday, December 12, 1992

There are many possible formats. See VB's Help if you need to work out a custom format for a special job.

The Financial Functions

If you're an accountant, or otherwise heavily into the mathematics of business, you should know that VB includes a generous supply of functions for you. It can do what financial calculators can do. Here is a sample of three of the 13 financial functions available:

DDB Calculates depreciation based on the double-declining balance method.
`X = DDB(Cost, Salvage, Life, Period)`

FV Calculates the future value of an annuity (like a home mortgage). Payments and interest rate remain constant. `X = FV(irate, nperiods, payment, presentvalue, whendue)`

IPmt Calculates the interest payment for a given period of an annuity. Payments and interest rate remain constant. `X = IPmt(irate, paymentrange, totalperiods, presentvalue, futurevalue,> whendue)`

Date and Time Functions

After all of the generosity you've noticed in the other categories in this session, do you think VB is stingy with functions that manipulate and display dates and time? Of course not. Here are the main date/time functions you'll likely want to use in your programming.

Date Gives you the current date.

Time Gives you the current time.

Now Gives you both the date and time: `MsgBox Date & " " & Time & " " & Now`. (The spaces enclosed in quotes add a space character between each item.)

Although they are technically functions, they don't require any arguments, so the parentheses are not used.

The Day function gives you the day of the month from a date serial number:

```
MsgBox Day(Now)
```

This code results in 5 (if it's the fifth of the month).

There are also Hour, Minute, Month, Second, Weekday, and Year functions that work the same way.

Several date/time functions permit you to work *mathematically* with dates or time. The DateSerial function transforms dates (such as *1995*) into numbers in a series so you can manipulate the dates using addition and subtraction.

Suppose you arbitrarily decide that January 1, 100 A.D., will be day 1 of a huge list that includes a serial number for every day thereafter (through the year 9999). Then you give a date such as November 14, 1992, to your assistant and ask him to find a serial number for that date. He discovers that November 14, 1992, is day 33,922 on the list, so the serial number for that date is 33922. You then ask him to find the serial number for another date. With both serial numbers, you can now perform math on the dates. For example, you can easily add 8 hours to 11 PM and not have to worry that you'll go past midnight. We'll get to how you code this shortly.

Astonishing as it seems, Visual Basic can provide and manipulate individual serial numbers for *every second of every day* between January 1, 100, and December 31, 9999. These serial numbers also include coded representations of all the hours, days, months, and years between 100 and 9999. You can see a serial number for a date with this code:

```
Dim x As Double
'  arguments: (year, month, day)
x = DateSerial(1999, 12, 5)
MsgBox x
```

One obvious problem when working with dates or time is moving past midnight, or from December to January. For example, let's say that you display a scroll bar component for the user to slide as a way of selecting a date when they promise to pay a bill. Without the serial number, you would have problems doing the math. For instance, how would you handle adding five hours to 10 PM? You have to go past midnight, so simple addition (5+10) doesn't give the correct hour, which is 3 AM. Similar problems occur when you slide from December into January, or the reverse. However, with DateSerial, you can do these kinds of things easily. Here's some math that not only goes past a year marker (December to January) but also goes past a century marker (1999 to 2000). We simply add two months to this date:

```
n = DateSerial(1999, 12 + 2, 5)
MsgBox n
```

And the correct result, 2/5/00, is returned to you. Don't even try to imagine how to accomplish this without using the `DateSerial` function.

The number of seconds in a span of 9,899 years is obviously quite large. There are 31,536,000 seconds in a single year. VB date/time serial numbers contain the day, month, and year to the left of the decimal point and the hour, minute, and second to the right of the decimal point. However, the meaning of the serial number is encoded. There is no direct way to examine the serial number and write some code to extract the information contained therein. That is why VB provides various functions — such as Second, Minute, Hour, Day, Month, and Year — to decode that information for you.

There's a comparable `TimeSerial` function that provides the serial number for time.

The `DateValue` function is similar to `DateSerial`, but `DateValue` translates a *text* representation of a date (such as Jan 1, 1992) into a VB date/time serial number that can be computed and manipulated mathematically. `DateSerial`'s job is to translate a *numeric* expression (such as 1992, 1, 1) into a date/time serial number. There's a comparable `TimeSerial` function.

The `Dateadd` function allows you to add a time or date interval to a date. This way, you can find out what date it will be 200 days from now, what date it was 200 days ago, and so on.

```
Private Sub Form_Load()
Show 'show the form

whatinterval = "d" 'use day as the interval
numberofintervals = 200
startdate = Date 'today's date

Print "Today is: "; startdate
Print "200 days from now will be: ";

Print DateAdd(whatinterval, numberofintervals, startdate)

End Sub
```

DateDiff is the opposite of DateAdd. DateDiff tells you how many days (d) between two dates, how many hours (h) between two years, or how many weeks (w) between now and the end of the year. In other words, it tells you how many of a particular time/date interval fall between two times or dates:

```
Private Sub Form_Load()
Show 'show the form
    whatinterval = "w" 'weeks
    firstdate = Date 'today
    secondate = "31-Dec-02"

    Print "Today is: "; firstdate
    Print "The number of weeks left until the end of 2002 are: ";
    Print DateDiff(whatinterval, firstdate, secondate)
End Sub
```

Done!

REVIEW

This session introduced you to the close cousins of variables: literals and constants. Then you were introduced to a compound structure known as an *expression*. You then went on a cook's tour of all the major built-in functions that VB generously offers. There's no point in reinventing the wheel if VB itself already contains the solution.

QUIZ YOURSELF

1. How does a literal differ from a variable? (See "Literals".)
2. Name two benefits of using constants. (See "Constants".)
3. What is the LCase function useful for? (See "LCase(String)".)
4. If you want to get the current date and time, what function do you use? (See "Date and Time Functions".)
5. How do the DateValue and DateSerial functions differ? (See "Date and Time Functions".)

The Big Operators: Comparison, Math, and Logical

Session Checklist

✔ Understanding what operators do

✔ Using comparison operators

✔ Working with arithmetic operators

✔ Learning about the specialized logical operators

✔ Solving the problem of operator precedence

30 Min.
To Go

This session shows you how to use *operators*. Operators are used in expressions to compare two elements (like two variables), to do math on them, or to perform a "logical" operation on them. The plus sign (+), for example, is an operator in the following example: 2 + 4. The greater-than symbol (>) is an operator in this example that says n is greater than z: n > z.

Recall that expressions are not limited only to variables. Expressions can also be built out of literal numbers, literal strings, numeric variables, string variables, numeric variables in an array, a function that returns a number or string, a constant, or any combination of the above.

An expression is looked at and evaluated by VB during run time. This evaluation produces a result (it might be that the expression is True, or it might produce the number 6, or some other result that the expression yields, such as the expression "A" & "sk", which produces the result "Ask").

An expression must contain at least two elements, separated by an operator: "A" > "B" (this expression asks if the literal letter *A* is greater alphabetically than *B*, which is untrue, so this expression evaluates to False).

However, an expression can contain more than two elements: 1 < 2 And 3 < 4 uses three elements and evaluates to True because the number 1 is less than 2 and the number 4 is greater than 3. However, if any part of a compound expression is false, the whole expression evaluates to False. For example, the following expression is false: 1 < 2 And 3 > 4. (We'll get to the And operator later; it's one of the so-called "logical" operators.)

Comparison Operators

Often, you need to compare two values, and then your program reacts based on the result of the comparison. Let's say the user types in his or her age:

```
If UsersAge < 50 Then
    MsgBox "You qualify for reduced term insurance."
Else
    MsgBox "You do not qualify for reduced term insurance."
End If
```

The expression in the above code is UsersAge < 50. This particular expression uses one of the comparison (relational) operators, the less-than symbol (<). That line of code means: If the value in the UsersAge variable is less than 50, then show the "You qualify..." message. Otherwise (Else), show the "You do not qualify..." message.

The eight comparison operators

Here is a table of the comparison operators:

Table 16-1
The Comparison Operators

Operator	Description
<	Less than
<=	Less than or equal to

>	Greater than
>=	Greater than or equal to
<>	Not equal
=	Equal
Is	Do two object Variables refer to the same object?
Like	Pattern matching

It's easy to remember the meaning of the < and > symbols. The large end of the symbol is the greater, so A > B means A greater than B. A < B means A less than B.

You can use the relational operators with text as well. When used with literal text (or text variables), the operators refer to the *alphabetic* qualities of the text, with the value of *Andy* being less than *Anne*.

The Is operator is highly specialized. It tells you if two object variable names refer to the same object (more on this in Session 30). It can be used with arrays that keep track of controls or forms.

The Like operator lets you compare a string to a pattern, using wildcards. This operator is similar to the wildcards you can use when searching, using the symbols * or **?**. In Windows's search utility or Explorer, for instance, you can see all files ending with .DOC by typing *.DOC.

Working with the Like operator

Use Like to compare strings, as follows:

```
A = "Rudolpho"
If A Like "Ru*" Then MsgBox "Close Enough"
```

This results in the message box being displayed. The Like operator can be used to forgive user typos. When testing for Pennsylvania, you could accept Like Pen* since no other state starts with those characters; any misspellings the user makes further on in this word can be ignored.

Following are some ways to use Like.

To compare against a *single* character in a particular position, use the following code. (And notice that we're putting two logical lines on a single physical line here, separated by a colon. You can use a separate line for Print X, but it's so short I just stuck it onto the end of the other code. If you do put two or more logical lines together, remember that the colon is necessary to separate them.)

```
X = "Nora" Like "?ora": Print X
```

results in: True.

```
X = "Nora" Like "F?ora": Print X
```

results in: False (the first letter in *Nora* isn't *F*, the third letter isn't *o*, and so on).

Or use Like to compare when you don't care about a match between a series of characters:

```
If "David" Like "*d" Then
Print "Match"
Else
Print "No Match"
End If
```

This code results in: Match. "D*" or "**D*d" or "*i*" will all match "David".

Or you can use the following to match a single character in the text against a single character or range of characters in the list enclosed by brackets:

```
If "Empire" Like "??[n-q]*" Then
```

This code results in: Match, because the third character in *Empire*, *p*, falls within the range *n-q*. You can also use multiple ranges such as: "[n-rt-w]".

Or you can use the following to match if a single character in the text is not in the list:

```
If "Empire" Like "??[!n-q]*" Then
```

This code results in: No Match (! means "not").

**20 Min.
To Go**

Using Arithmetic Operators

Arithmetic operators work pretty much as you would expect them to. They do some math and provide a result.

Table 16-2
The Arithmetic Operators

Operator	Description
^	Exponentiation (the number multiplied by itself: 5 ^ 2 is 25 and 5 ^ 3 is 125)
-	Negation (negative numbers, such as –25)
*	Multiplication
/	Division
\	Integer division (Division with no remainder, no fraction, no decimal point: 8 \ 6 results in the answer 1. Use this if you don't need the remainder.)
Mod	Modulo arithmetic (see Tip below)
+	Addition
-	Subtraction
&	String concatenation

Use the + operator only with arithmetic operations (to add numbers). To concatenate text, use the & operator: MsgBox A$ & B$.

Use the arithmetic operators like this:

```
If B + A > 12 Then
```

The modulo (Mod) operator gives you any remainder after a division — but not the results of the division itself. You just get the remainder. This is useful when you want to know if some number divides evenly into another number. That way, you can do things at intervals. For instance, say you wanted to print the page number in bold on every fifth page. Here's how you could code that:

```
If PageNumber Mod 5 = 0 Then
    FontBold = True
Else
    FontBold = 0
End If
```

Here are some examples:

15 Mod 5 results in 0.

16 Mod 5 results in 1.

17 Mod 5 results in 2.

20 Mod 5 results in 0 again.

The Logical Operators

The logical operators are most often used to create a compound expression. The logical operators you'll use frequently are And, Or, and Not. They allow you to construct expressions like this:

```
If BettysAge > 55 And JohnsAge > 50 Then
```

The And operator means that both comparisons must be true for the entire expression to be true.

Similarly, Or allows you to create an expression where only one comparison must be true for the entire expression to be true:

```
If TomsMother = Visiting Or SandysMothersAge > 78 Then
```

The Not operator is good for switching a toggle back and forth:

```
Private Sub Form_Click()
Static Toggle As Boolean
Toggle = Not Toggle
If Toggle Then MsgBox _
 "See this message every other time you click."
End Sub
```

The Static command preserves the contents of the variable Toggle (Dim would not). The Boolean variable type is the simplest one: It has only two states: True and False. It can be flipped back and forth like a light switch. This line, Toggle = Not Toggle, means: If Toggle's value is False, make it now True. If it's True, make it False. You'll be surprised how often you use this technique.

Here is a complete list of all the logical operators, some of which have esoteric uses in cryptography and such.

Table 16-3
The Logical Operators

Operator	Description
Not	Logical negation
And	And
Or	Inclusive Or
Xor	Either but not Both
Eqv	Equivalent
Imp	Implication — first item False or second item True

Here are some examples:

```
If 5 + 2 = 4 Or 6 + 6 = 12 Then Print "One of them is true."
```

One of these expressions is true, so the comment will be printed. Only one *or* the other needs to be true.

If 5 + 2 = 4 And 6 + 6 = 12 Then Print "Both of them are true."

This is false, so nothing is printed. Both expressions, the first *and* the second, must be true for the printing to take place.

How to read or flip bits

Xor can be used to change an individual *bit* within a number, without affecting the other bits. This technique can be useful when encrypting. Here's how to use And to test (query) a bit, and how to use Xor to change a bit. As you may recall from the session on the CommonDialog component, sometimes information is stored in bits (remember the flags?).

Files on your hard drive have attributes, and these attributes are "packed" into a single byte. Any single number from 0 to 255 can be held in a byte. There are 8 bits in a byte. Each bit can be only on or off, but that's enough information if you want to know whether or not, say, a file is hidden. If it is hidden, bit 2 will be on. If not, bit 2 will be off. Here are the values of each of the 8 bits: 1, 2, 4, 8, 16, 32, 64, 128 (these add up to 255, so if each bit is on, the number is 255).

When you get an attribute value (or a flag with the CommonDialog), you can check to see if a particular bit is on or off using the And command. Here are the attributes for a disk file:

    0 = "Normal"

    2 = "Hidden"

    4 = "System"

    8 = "Volume Label"

    16 ="Directory"

    32 ="Archive"

Notice that the numbers follow the bit values described above. Use the GetAttr command to find out the attribute(s) of a file, like this:

```
FAttribute = GetAttr ("C:\Bootlog.Txt")
```

If you run this, you'll find that the Bootlog.Txt file returns a value of 6, telling you that the file is both Hidden and System (2 + 4).

You can use the following code to test all of the attributes:

```
If FAttribute And 0 Then f = "Normal"
If FAttribute And 1 Then f = f & " " & "Read-Only"
If FAttribute And 2 Then f = f & " " & "Hidden"
If FAttribute And 4 Then f = f & " " & "System"
If FAttribute And 8 Then f = f & " " & "Volume Label"
If FAttribute And 16 Then f = f & " " & "Directory"
If FAttribute And 32 Then f = f & " " & "Archive"
MsgBox f
```

You can change a file's attributes, too. This next example illustrates how to flip a bit (if it's on, the bit goes off; if it's off, it goes on). Say that you found out that the Hidden bit is set (on), and you want to turn it off. You can use the SetAttr command to change the entire byte, along with Xor to flip the Hidden bit (bit 2).

The Xor command will flip an individual bit without disturbing the other bits in the number. More than one attribute can be on, but they are all stored in a single byte — so you don't want to change more than the bit representing the attribute you are interested in. Here's how we flip the Hidden bit:

```
Private Sub Form_Load()
Fattribute = GetAttr("C:\Bootlog.Txt")
Fattribute = Fattribute Xor 2
```

```
SetAttr "C:\Bootlog.Txt", Fattribute
End Sub
```

Each time you run this little program, the second bit in the attribute byte will flip. The first time I ran it, GetAttr returned a 6, and the Xor changed it to 4 (removing the 2 bit). Then SetAttr changed the actual attribute on the hard drive. Then I ran it again, and this time Xor change the 4 back into a 6. You can imagine why this flipping back and forth behavior makes Xor so useful when encrypting and decrypting text. It's like putting text into a black box and flipping it one way to encrypt it. Then, when it needs to be restored back to plain text, you run it again through that same black box to restore it to the original.

The concatenation operator

The & operator adds pieces of text together (concatenates them):

```
N = "Lois"
N1 = "Lane"
J = N & " " & N1
Print J
```

This code prints Lois Lane.

Operator Precedence

**10 Min.
To Go**

When you use more than one operator in an expression, which operator should be evaluated first? Clearly, a simple expression is unambiguous: 2 + 3 can only result in 5. But sometimes a complex expression can be solved more than one way, like this one:

```
3 * 10 + 5
```

Does this mean first multiply 3 times 10, resulting in 30, and then add 5 to the result? Should VB evaluate this expression as 35?

Or, does it mean add 10 to 5, resulting in 15, and then multiply the result by 3? *This* alternative evaluation would result in 45.

Expressions are not necessarily evaluated by the computer from left to right. Left to right evaluation in the above example would result in 35 because 3 would be multiplied by 10 before the 5 was added to that result. But remember that complex expressions can be evaluated backwards sometimes.

Visual Basic enforces an *order of precedence*, a hierarchy by which various relationships are resolved between numbers in an expression. For instance, multiplication is always carried out before addition.

Fortunately, you don't have to memorize the order of precedence. Instead — to make sure that you get the results you intend when using more than one operator — just use parentheses to enclose the items you want evaluated first. In the above example, if you want 3 * 10 and then add 5, write it like this:

```
(3 * 10) + 5
```

By enclosing an operator and its two surrounding values in parentheses, you tell VB that you want the enclosed items to be considered as a single value and to be evaluated before anything else happens. If you intended to say 10 + 5 and then multiply by 3, move the parentheses here instead:

```
3 * (10 + 5)
```

In longer expressions, you can even *nest* parentheses to make clear which items are to be calculated in which order:

```
3 * ((9 + 1) + 5)
```

If you work with these kinds of expressions a great deal, you might want to memorize Table 16-4. But most people just use parentheses and forget about this problem. If you're interested, here's the order in which VB will evaluate an expression, from first evaluated to last.

Table 16-4
Arithmetic Operators in Order of Precedence

Operator	Description
^	Exponents (6 ^ 2 is 36. The number is multiplied by itself *X* number of times.)
–	Negation (Negative numbers like –33)
* /	Multiplication and division
\	Integer division (Division with no remainder, no fraction)
Mod	Modulo arithmetic
+ –	Addition and subtraction
The relational operators	Evaluated left to right as found
The logical operators	Evaluated left to right as found

Done!

Given that multiplication has precedence over addition, our ambiguous example that started this discussion would be evaluated in the following way:

```
3 * 10 + 5
```

results in: 35.

REVIEW

This session is all about operators — ways to take two elements (like two variables) and combine, modify, compare, or otherwise manipulate them. You saw how you can compare numbers in various ways (greater-than, equal) or text (alphabetically, or similarity with the Like command). Then you explored all the various arithmetic operators. Finally, you experimented with logical operators such as And, Not, and Or to create longer, more complex expressions: with Not to toggle a value; with And to read a bit; with Xor to toggle a bit. Finally, you saw how to use parentheses to specify the order in which the parts of a complex expression should be evaluated.

QUIZ YOURSELF

---

1. What operator would you use if you wanted to ask, is A less-than or equal-to B? (See "The Eight Comparison Operators".)

2. What does the code If N Like "T*" mean in plain English? (See "Working with the Like Operator".)

3. Which arithmetic operator allows you to specify intervals? (See "Using Arithmetic Operators".)

4. What is concatenation and what operator do you use to accomplish it? (See "The Concatenation Operator".)

5. Why does operator precedence matter, and what's the easy way to solve the precedence problem? (See "Operator Precedence".)

PART

III

Saturday Afternoon

1. Define the purpose of an *argument*.
2. Can you leave out an argument in an argument list?
3. What is the difference between a subroutine and a function?
4. Name four of the five CommonDialog boxes.
5. Which of the CommonDialog boxes requires that you set the Flags property before displaying the dialog box to the user?
6. How do you send information back from a function?
7. What is *stepping* and what is it good for?
8. Do you call a function the same way you call a subroutine?
9. What are the two fundamental kinds of variables?
10. What does the term *value* mean when used with variables?
11. Name two rules you must observe when making up a variable's name.
12. What does "implicit" variable creation mean?
13. Name three of the five commands that explicitly create a variable.
14. How many values can a variable hold at one time?
15. Are properties variables?
16. What is the default variable type in Visual Basic?
17. What is unique about the Boolean data type?
18. Define the concept of *scope*.

19. What is an *expression*?

20. What is an *operator*?

PART

IV

Saturday
Evening

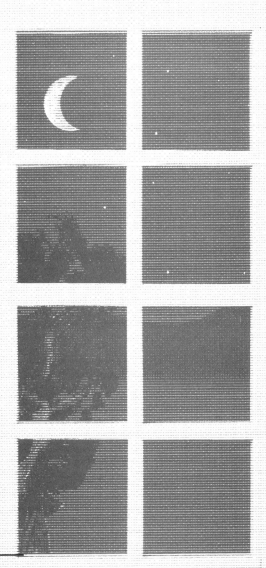

Arrays and Looping

Session Checklist

✔ How to create and manipulate arrays

✔ Understanding For...Next loops

✔ Learning to use Do...Loops

✔ While...Wend, the simplest loop structure

**30 Min.
To Go**

Now for some heavy-duty programming. By that, I don't mean to imply that it's hard to learn, it's just that looping is a common and important programming technique.

Because we often use arrays within loops, we'll take a look at arrays first.

Understanding Arrays

An array is a set of variable values that have been grouped together. Once inside an array structure, the variables share the same text name, and are individually identified by an *index number*.

Since numbers can be manipulated mathematically (and text names cannot), putting a group of variables into an array allows you to easily and efficiently work with the entire group. You can manipulate the items in the array by using loops, such as `For...Next` and `Do...Loop` structures.

Numbers and names

Arrays can be extremely useful to a programmer. For example, if you want to remember all of the trips you have taken, you can create an array to hold the names of each place you visit:

```
Dim PlacesVisited(1 to 500) As String
```

This creates 500 "empty boxes" in the computer's memory, which serve as spaces for text (`String`) variables that name the trips taken. However, instead of 500 unique individual variable names for each of these 500 variables, the variables in this cluster share the single name `PlacesVisited`, and each box is identified by a unique index number from 1 to 500. (We decided that 500 is probably large enough for our purposes, vacation-mad though we are.)

To fill this array with the names of the places you've visited, assign the names just as you would assign them to normal variables, but then use the index number to distinguish them. (You can tell an array from a regular variable because arrays always have parentheses following the array name. The index number goes between these parentheses, like this: `MyArray(122)`. Also, arrays must always be formally declared with `Dim`, `Private`, `Public`, or `Static` commands. You cannot implicitly just start using an array. You must use one of those four commands to declare the array. It's not possible to just use code like this: `PlacesVisited(1) = "St. Louis"`, with no previous declaration of the `PlacesVisited` array.

Here's one way to put the names of places you visit into an array:

```
PlacesVisited(1) = "St. Louis"
PlacesVisited(2) = "San Diego"
PlacesVisited(3) = "Richmond"
PlacesVisited(4) = "Jordon"
PlacesVisited(5) = "Montana State Park"
```

Now the array is partly filled with data. The process of filling an array can be accomplished in several ways: by having the user type in the array items, by reading the data from a disk file, or as we did, by directly filling the array with pieces of information (literals) from within the program.

Now that we have the array filled, we can manipulate it in ways that are much more efficient than when using ordinary variables. What if we wanted to know if a particular place had been visited? We could loop through the array.

```
For I = 1 To 500
If PlacesVisited(I) = "Toronto" Then MsgBox "Yes, " _
    & PlacesVisited(I) & " has been visited."
Next I
```

Using line breaks

Notice how that line in the above example ends with a space character followed by an underscore (_). This is how you can force a line break in VB. VB executes lines of code one at a time, so you must never press the Enter key until you have completed the line of code, *or used the _ space-underscore to indicate that the line continues below.* Also, you cannot put a line break within a string (between quotation marks). You cannot do the following, for instance, and break the text *Toronto* in two:

```
"Toron _
to" Then
```

To return to the subject at hand: The key to the utility of arrays is that you can search them, sort them, delete from them, or add to them *using numbers to identify each value,* instead of using individual text variable names. Index numbers are much easier to access and manipulate — for groups of data — than text labels.

Why arrays are efficient

Still not convinced? Here's another example. Suppose you want to figure out your average electric bill for the year. You can go the cumbersome route, using an individual text variable name for each month:

```
JanElect = 90
FebElect = 122
MarElect = 125
AprElect = 78
MayElect = 144
JneElect = 89
JulyElect = 90
AugElect = 140
SeptElect = 167
OctElect = 123
NovElect = 133
DecElect = 125
```

```
YearElectBill = JanElect+FebElect+MarElect+AprElect _
   +MayElect+JneElect+JulyElect+AugElect+SeptElect+ _
   OctElect+ NovElect+DecElect
```

Or, you could use an array to simplify the process:

```
Dim MonthElectBill(1 To 12)
MonthElectBill(1) = 90
MonthElectBill(2) = 122
MonthElectBill(3) = 125
MonthElectBill(4) = 78
MonthElectBill(5) = 144
MonthElectBill(6) = 89
MonthElectBill(7) = 90
MonthElectBill(8) = 140
MonthElectBill(9) = 167
MonthElectBill(10) = 123
MonthElectBill(11) = 133
MonthElectBill(12) = 125


For I = 1 to 12
Total = Total + MonthElectBill(I)
Next I
```

By grouping all of the variables under the same name, you can manipulate the variables by individual index number. This might look like a small savings of effort, but remember that your program will perhaps have to use and manipulate these variables in several different ways. You'll also have to save them to disk. If they're in an array, you can save them like this with a loop:

```
Open "Ebills" For Output As 1
For I = 1 to 12
Print #1, MonthElectBill(I)
Next I
```

If they're not in an array, you need to do this:

```
Print #1, JanElect
Print #1, FebElect
Print #1, MarElect
Print #1, AprElect
Print #1, MayElect
```

```
Print #1, JneElect
Print #1, JulyElect
Print #1, AugElect
Print #1, SeptElect
Print #1, OctElect
Print #1, NovElect
Print #1, DecElect
```

Unless you have put this group of variables into an array, you'll have to access each by its text name every time you deal with the group in your program. That's quite inefficient.

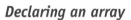

Declaring an array

20 Min.
To Go

Arrays must be formally declared and can be created by using one of five declaration commands: `Public`, `Private`, `Dim`, `ReDim`, or `Static`. All five of these commands create arrays in the same way: by dimensioning the new array. This means that the computer is told how much space to set aside for the new array (how many values it will contain). We'll use the `Public` command in the following examples, but the `Private`, `Dim`, `ReDim`, and `Static` commands follow the same rules.

To create space for 51 text variables that share the label `Names` and are uniquely identified by index numbers ranging from 0 to 50, type the following in a module:

```
Public Names(50)
```

Notice that unless you use the `Option Base 1` command, or use something like `Public Names (1 to 50)`, an array defaults to 0 as the lowest index number. I prefer the `1 to 50` technique, but if you use `Option Base 1`, you must put it at the very top of a form or module in the General Declarations section, and above any declarations such as `Public`. The `Option Base 1` command makes all of your arrays default to 1 as the lowest index number — so the first value in the array is `ArrayName(1)`, rather than `ArrayName(0)`.

Multi-dimensional arrays

Arrays can be more complex. You can create arrays that you might visualize as similar to a spreadsheet with multiple columns and rows. You could use this as a way to associate related information such as places visited, plus length of the trip, plus the date of the trip. (VB allows you to create as many as 60 dimensions for a single array! But few programmers can visualize, or effectively work with, more than two or three dimensions.)

A two-dimensional array is like a graph, a crossword puzzle, or a spreadsheet: cells of information related in an *x,y* coordinate system. A three-dimensional array is like a honeycomb — it not only has height and width, it also has *depth*. Most of us check out at this point — we cannot visualize or imagine a 3-D array.

A four-dimensional array cannot be physically constructed, so there simply is no example of one to try to visualize. (You might think of it as a *set* of several honeycombs, if you're brave.) Go beyond four dimensions, and you've gone past physics into an abstract domain that would challenge Leonardo.

Anyway, to make a two-dimensional array, program something like this:

```
Public PlacesVisited (1 To 500, 1 To 3)
```

This means that there will be potentially 500 `PlacesVisited`, and each of them can have three associated additional values.

Here's how to retrieve the data about the fourth trip. Its name would be stored in `PlacesVisited(4,1)`, its length, let's say, would be in `PlacesVisited(4,2)`, and its date would be in `PlacesVisited(4,3)`. So, you can display the information about the date of the fourth trip using the following code: `MsgBox Places Visited(4,3)`.

Note that arrays default to the `Variant` type unless you specify otherwise. With a `Variant` array, you can mix text, numbers, and date/time data within the same array.

Understanding ReDim

The `ReDim` command works only with arrays. It sets aside space in the computer's memory to *temporarily* hold an array. `ReDim` works within a procedure, and cannot be used in the General Declarations section of a form or module. As soon as your program has moved on out of the procedure, the array is collapsed, and it evaporates. So, the `ReDim` command is useful when you only need an array temporarily within a procedure. It embodies the same principle as a local variable — here today, gone when the `End Sub` (or `End Function`) command is executed. Arrays that bloom and fade like this within a single procedure are called *dynamic* arrays, as opposed to *static* or *public* arrays.

The benefit of temporary arrays is that they don't use up the computer's memory by taking space that can be otherwise used while a program is running. Normally, space isn't much of an issue, but some programs are data-intensive and need to manipulate large amounts of information. In such cases, being able to create and then destroy dynamic arrays can be of value.

You *can* preserve the data within a dynamic array (one created with `ReDim`**) by using the** `Preserve` **command. You can also change the size of a dynamic array, but preserve its contents, using this code:**

```
ReDim Preserve MyArray(60) As Integer
```

Going Round and Round in Loops

Often a job requires repetition until a result is achieved: Polish your boots until they shine, add spoonfuls of sugar one at a time until the lemonade tastes good.

Using For...Next

The same kind of repetition is often needed in computer programs. The most common loop structure is `For...Next`. Between the `For` and the `Next` are the instructions that get repeatedly carried out. The number of times the computer will execute the loop is defined by the two numbers listed right after the `For`:

```
Private Sub Form_Load()

For I = 1 To 4
    A = A + I
Next I

MsgBox A
End Sub
```

In this example, the loop's *counter variable* is named I. (There's something of a tradition to use the name I in For...Next loops in programs.) But the important thing to understand is that the counter variable is incremented (raised by 1) each time the program gets to the Next command. The Next command does three things: It adds one to the variable I; it checks to see if I has reached the limit we set in the For statement (4 in this example); and it checks to make sure the limit has not been exceeded. Then Next sends the program back up to the For statement to repeat the code one more time. Any code within the loop is executed each time the loop cycles.

The answer displayed by the MsgBox is 10. Try single-stepping through the execution of this loop (press F8 repeatedly) and pause your mouse cursor over the counter variable I and also over the variable A each time you go through the loop. You'll see that the first time through I is 1 (we said 1 To 4, so the counter starts with 1). The variable A is empty, but as soon as its line of code is executed, it contains the value of I (plus whatever was in A). The second time through the loop, A has a 1 in it, but the value of I is 2, so A then contains 3. The third time through the loop, 3 is added to 3, resulting in 6. Finally, the last time through the loop, I has a value of 4, which, added to 6, becomes 10. The program then exits the loop and displays the MsgBox.

You can use literal numbers to specify the start and count:

```
For I = 1 to 20 'literal
```

Or you can use a variable. Perhaps you want to allow the user to decide how many copies of a document should be printed.

```
Numberofcopies = InputBox("How many copies?")

For I = 1 To Numberofcopies
Printer.Print Text1.Text
Next I
```

Notice the convention of indenting the code inside a For...Next loop. This graphically illustrates the loop.

Using the Step command

There is an optional command that works with For...Next called Step. Step can be attached at the end of the For...Next structure to allow you to skip numbers, to *step* past them. When the Step command is used with For...Next, Step alters the way the loop counts.

By default, a loop counts by one:

```
For I = 1 to 12
    Print I;
Next I
```

results in: 1 2 3 4 5 6 7 8 9 10 11 12.

However, when you use the Step command, you change the way a For...Next loop counts. It can count every other number (Step 2):

```
For I = 1 to 12 Step 2
   Print I;
Next I
```

results in: 1 3 5 7 9 11.

Or you can `Step` every 73rd number (`Step 73`), count down backward (`For I = 10 to 1 Step -1`), and even count by fractions (`Step .25`).

Nesting loops

For...Next loops can be *nested*, one inside the other. At first this sort of structure seems confusing (and it often *is*). The inner loop interacts with the exterior loop in ways that are instantly clear only to the mathematically gifted. Essentially, the inner loop does its thing the number of times specified by its own counter variable multiplied by the counter variable of the outer loop. Got it?

Simply *hack* away, as programmers say, substituting counter numbers (and maybe moving code from one loop to the other) until things work the way they should. *Hacking* to a programmer means the same thing as adding spices means to a cook — messing around until the desired result emerges.

```
Private Sub Form_Load()
Show
cr = Chr(13)

For I = 1 To 2
   For J = 1 To 3
      Print I & " " & J & cr
   Next J
Next I

End Sub
```

Any *numeric expression* can be used with `For...Next`. However, the range you're counting must be *possible*. The following is not possible:

```
For i = -10 To -20 Step 2
   Print "loop"; i
Next
```

This loop does nothing. It cannot. You're asking it to count downward, but your `Step` command is positive. As any intelligent entity would when confronted with a senseless request, Visual Basic does nothing with these instructions. It ignores you. You have to make the `Step` negative with –2:

```
For i = -10 To -20 Step -2
   Print "loop"; i
Next
```

Early exits

If, for some reason, you want to exit the loop before the counter finishes, use the Exit For command:

```
If n > 500 Then Exit For
```

The Exit For command is rarely used, but perhaps you are filling an array that can only hold 500. You don't want to overflow it. So you make a provision for an early exit from the loop if necessary. If the Exit For is carried out, execution moves to the line of code following the Next command. There are Exit Do (for Do...Loops), Exit Function, Exit Property, and Exit Sub commands as well.

Working with Do...Loops

Sometimes, you might prefer the Do...While structure; in fact, some programmers favor it over For...Next. It can be a bit more flexible.

Do While

In its most common style, Do...While uses a comparison operator at the start of the loop to test something (is it = or =>, and so on). The first time the comparison fails, the loop is skipped and execution continues on the line following the Loop command. The Loop command signals the end of the Do...While structure just as the Next command signals the end of the For...Next loop structure.

```
Private Sub Form_Load()

Show

Do While Y < 11
   Y = Y + 1
   Print Y
Loop

End Sub
```

Remember that you must do something in the code within the loop that *changes the comparison value*. Otherwise, you have created an *endless loop* that will never stop looping. Also note that if Y already holds a value of 11 or more when the program reaches this loop, the loop will never execute. The comparison test will fail the very first time the loop is encountered and none of the code within the loop will execute at all.

Do Until

A version of Do While is Do Until. It's just another way of expressing the same idea, but you might find it a little clearer. Do While loops as long as the comparison is *true,* but Do Until loops until the comparison is *false*:

```
Do Until y = 11
    y = y + 1
    Print y
Loop
```

Loop While and Loop Until

If you want to put the comparison test at the *end* of the loop structure, there are two additional ways to construct a Do...Loop:

```
Do
    y = y + 1
    Print y
Loop While Y < 11
```

This works the same way as the Do...While example above. The difference is that when you put the test at the end, the loop will always execute at least once — no matter what value is in the variable *y* when you enter the loop.

```
Do
    y = y + 1
    Print y
Loop Until Y = 11
```

Which of these four structures should you use? Use Do While or Do Until if you don't want the loop to execute even once if the condition test fails at the start. As for the difference between the While and Until styles, it's often a matter of which one seems to you to be more readable, or which one works better with the comparison test. Many times, it's merely a semantic distinction: the difference between "do the dishes while any are still dirty" versus "do the dishes until all are clean".

While...Wend: A Simple Loop

Finally, there's the While...Wend structure, though it's little used. It's simple, but relatively inflexible:

```
Private Sub Form_Load()
Show

While X < 7
  X = X + 1
  Print X
Wend

End Sub
```

Done!

As you can see, this looping technique is comparatively simple. While...Wend has no Exit command (like the Exit Do command). While...Wend is limited to a comparison test at the start of the loop and it does not permit you to use the alternative command *Until*.

REVIEW

Having finished this session, you know how to store groups of values in arrays. You found out the ways you can access those values using an index number (mathematically), rather than accessing each value via a separate variable name. You saw how to associate more values to a given index number by adding a second index number — thereby creating a multi-dimensional array. Then you learned how to get the computer to do a repetitive job, and how to get it to stop. You worked with For...Next, and saw how to nest For...Next loops. You saw the distinction between putting your comparison test at the start or end of a loop structure. And you learned the difference between While and Until. Finally, we covered the simplest loop, While...Wend.

QUIZ YOURSELF

1. How do arrays differ from ordinary variables? (See "Understanding Arrays".)

2. What is the line-break character in VB and when is it useful? (See "Using Line Breaks".)

3. If you create a two-dimensional array and the first index is 1 To 100, can the second index be 1 To 2 or does it have to be at least 1 To 100 or larger? (See "Multi-dimensional Arrays".)

4. What does the `Step` command do? (See "Using the Step Command".)

5. What's the reason for sometimes putting a comparison test at the end of a loop structure? (See "Working with Do...Loops".)

Making Decisions (Branching)

Session Checklist

✔ Working with `For...Next`

✔ Using `Else` to branch to a second course of action

✔ Understanding the `Select...Case` structure

✔ Employing the `Is` command for comparison tests

✔ Using the `To` command to test ranges of values

30 Min. To Go

aking decisions is central to any intelligent behavior. The `If...Then` structure is one of the most important features in any computer language —
indeed, in any kind of language.

    `If...Then` is the most common way that decisions are made. After the decision
is made, actions are taken that respond to the decision. A program is said to
branch at this point, as if the path it was following splits into more than one trail.
The path the program follows is decided here at the `If...Then` junction. For each of
the paths, you write code appropriate to that path.

    Many times a day we do our own personal branching using a similar structure: If
you're hungry, you eat some breakfast. If it's nice weather, then you don't wear a
jacket. If the car windows are fogged up, then you wipe them off. This constant

cycle of testing conditions, and making decisions based on those conditions, is what makes our behavior intelligent and adaptive. This same kind of testing is what makes computer behavior intelligent.

You try to make your programs behave intelligently by giving them decision-making rules in the code. You put If...Then structures into a program so it reacts appropriately to various kinds of user input, as well as such additional events as incoming data from a disk file, the passage of time, or other conditions.

Understanding If...Then

In previous sessions you've experimented a little with If...Then. Here's a simple example:

```
Private Sub Form_Load()

Response = InputBox("How many calories did you take in today?")

If Response > 2200 Then
    M = "Keep that up and you'll have to buy new pants."
  Else
    M = "Good self-control on your part."
End If

MsgBox M

End Sub
```

The line of code starting with If tests to see if something is *true*. If it is true, then the code on the line or lines following the If are carried out. If the test fails (the test condition is not true), then your program skips the line(s) of code until it gets to an Else, ElseIf, or End If command. Then the program resumes execution. Put another way, the If test determines whether or not some lines of code will be executed.

Notice that if you are making a simple decision (either/or) with only two branches, you can use the Else command. In the above example, if the user's response is that he or she ate more than 2,200 calories, the first message is displayed. Or, if the opposite happened, the message following the Else command is displayed.

What if you want to branch into more than only two paths? You can use the ElseIf command, but it's fairly clumsy:

```
If X = "Bob" Then
    Print "Hello Bob"
ElseIf X = "Billy" Then
    Print "Hello Billy"
ElseIf X = "Ashley"
    Print "Hello Ashley"
End If
```

In a way, using ElseIf is like using several If...Thens in a row. But for situations in which you want to test multiple conditions, the better solution is to use the Select Case command, as you'll soon see.

As with loops, it's traditional to provide a visual cue by indenting all lines of code that will be carried out inside the If...Then **structure.**

There is a simple, one-line version of If...Then. If your test is simple enough (true/false) and short enough, just put it all on a single line. In that case, you do not use End If (the If...Then structure is assumed to be completed by the end of the line of code). The computer knows that this is a single-line If...Then because some additional code follows the Then command. (In a multiline If...Then structure, the Then command is the last word on the line, and the code to carry out should the test pass is on the following line(s).)

```
PassWord = "sue"

Reply = InputBox("What is the password?")

If Reply <> PassWord Then MsgBox ("Access Denied"): End

MsgBox "Password verified as correct. Please continue."
```

20 Min. To Go

Notice the colon that appears at the end of the If...Then line. This is a rarely used technique, but you should be aware of it. It's handy for single-line If...Then code, as this example illustrates. We want to do two things should the password fail the test:

1. Show a message box.

2. End the program.

Normally, the End command would have to be on a line of its own in the code. When you use the colon, VB reads the code that follows it as *a separate line of code*. Recall that you can use the space/underscore characters to break a single, long, logical line of code into two physical lines. (*Logical* here means, "what VB acts on," and *physical* means, "what you see onscreen.") Using a colon is the opposite of the space/underscore. A colon allows you to place two logical lines on the same physical line. (You can even cram more than two logical lines on one physical line: X=X+1:A=B:N="Hi.", for example.)

Remember that the condition you test with If is an *expression*, so it can involve variables, literals, constants, and any other valid combination of components that can make up an expression. For instance, you can use a function in an expression:

```
Private Sub Form_Load()

If InputBox("Enter your age, but it's optional") <> "" Then
MsgBox "Thank you for responding"
End If

End Sub
```

The InputBox function is executed, and its result is tested to see if it does not equal (<>) a blank, empty string (""), which would mean that the user failed to type anything into the InputBox.

Some programmers like to use optional parentheses around the comparison test in an If...Then structure. They feel that it makes the line more readable, isolating the test itself from surrounding code:

```
If (Reply <> PassWord) Then MsgBox ("Access Denied"): End
```

To me, though, it's easy enough to see that the test starts with the If command and ends with the Then command.

Multiple Choice: The Select Case Command

If...Then is great for simple, common testing and branching. But if you have more than two branches, If...Then becomes clumsy. Fortunately, there's an alternative

decision-making structure in VB that specializes in multiple-branching. Select
Case should be used when there are several possible outcomes.

The main distinction between If...Then and Select Case goes something
like this:

If CarStatus = burning, *Then* get out of the car.

But the Select Case structure tests many and various situations:

```
Select Case CarStatus
    Case Steaming
        Let radiator cool down.
    Case Wobbling
        Check tires.
    Case Skidding
        Steer into skid.
    Case Burning
        Leave the car.
End Select
```

Select Case works from a list of possible "answers". Your program can respond
to each of these answers differently. There can be one, or many, lines of code
within each case:

```
Private Sub Form_Load()
Response = InputBox("What's your favorite color?")

Select Case LCase(Response)
Case "blue"
    MsgBox "We have three varieties of blue"
Case "red"
    MsgBox "We have six varieties of red"
Case "green"
    MsgBox "We have one variety of green"
Case Else
    MsgBox "We don't have " & Response & ", sorry."
End Select

End Sub
```

This example illustrates that you can use any expression (variable, literal, function, compound expression, or other kind of expression) in the Select Case line.

In this example, we used the LCase command to reduce whatever the user typed in to all lowercase letters. Then VB goes down the list of cases and executes any lines in which the original expression on the first line matches one of the Case lines. Note that the final case is special: The optional Case Else command means that if there were no matches, execute the following code.

Using the Is command

You can use the special Is command with each case to run comparison tests on each case:

```
X = InputBox("Your weight, please?")

Select Case X
Case Is < 200
        '(put one or more commands here)
    MsgBox "Good for you"
Case Is < 300
        '(put one or more commands here)
MsgBox "Not too bad."
End Select
```

In the above example, if the number is lower than 200, the first block of code executes, then execution jumps to the line right after End Select. If the number is lower than 300, the second block of code executes (any code between Case Is < 300 and End Select). Note that as soon as one of the cases triggers a match, no further cases are even checked for a match. The Case structure is merely exited.

10 Min. To Go

Using the To command

If you want to check a range, use the To command. It can be a numeric range (Case 4 To 12) or an alphabetic range (based on the first letter of the string being tested):

```
Private Sub Form_Load()

Reply = LCase(InputBox("Type in your last name."))

Select Case Reply
Case "a" To "m"
    MsgBox "Please go to the left line."
```

```
Case "n" To "z"
    MsgBox "Please go to the right line."
End Select

End Sub
```

You can also combine several items in a Case, separating them by commas:

```
Case "a" To "l", "gene", NameOfUser
```

This combination is an Or type. It means display the following message box if the answer begins with a letter between *a* and *l*, or if it's *gene*, or if it matches the value in the variable NameOfUser.

Done!

REVIEW

This session is all about how to write code that makes choices during run time. You saw how to use an If...Then statement to evaluate an expression and to take one of two courses of action based on that evaluation. It's possible to extend If...Then to take more than two branches with a series of ElseIf commands, but that quickly becomes awkward. So it's better, as we saw, to use the Select Case statement for situations in which you want to offer multiple branches.

QUIZ YOURSELF

---

1. What is the purpose of the Else command? (See "Understanding If...Then".)
2. If you put a colon (:) in a line of code, what does it do? (See "Understanding If...Then".)
3. When using Select Case, is there a command that executes code if no match is found? (See "Multiple Choice: The Select...Case Command".)
4. The Is command accomplishes what? (See "Using the Is Command".)
5. How do you combine several different items in a Case statement? (See "Using the To Command".)

Using Timers and Control Arrays

Session Checklist

✔ Understanding what Timer controls do

✔ Gang-programming with control arrays

✔ Changing colors

✔ Reducing redundancy using the With...End With structure

30 Min.
To Go

There are three cool features in VB that you'll want to know about — Timers, control arrays, and the With...End With structure. In this session, you'll get to experiment with each of them.

The Timer component has several uses: It can make things happen at intervals (for instance, animation), remind people that it's time to do something, measure the passage of time, cause a delay, and several other things. It's versatile.

The second cool feature discussed in this session is the control array. Control arrays are useful in much the same way that ordinary arrays are: A group of components is given the same name, but a different index number. You can therefore manipulate the components using math to access their index numbers. In this session, you'll see how this works, and also how to bring components into existence during run time.

You use the third cool feature, With...End With, to avoid redundancy when changing several properties for the same component.

But let's start with the Timer component; it's one of the standard, classic components that is always on the VB Toolbox.

Getting a Grip on Timers

A Timer component is a sophisticated clock. It is accurate to a millisecond — 1/1,000th of a second. To specify a delay of 2 seconds, set a Timer's Interval property to 2,000, like this: `Timer1.Interval = 2000`.

Once started, a Timer works independently and constantly. No matter what else might be happening in your Visual Basic program — or indeed, in Windows itself — your Timer keeps ticking away.

A Timer's Interval property specifies a duration. The Interval determines how long the Timer waits before it executes any code you've put into that Timer's event. In other words, when a Timer's event is triggered, nothing happens — none of the code in that event is executed — until the Interval is finished counting down to zero.

The Timer event is quite different from the other events in VB. For one thing, the code within all other events is executed as soon as the event is triggered. The `Command1_Click` event is triggered the very moment the user clicks that CommandButton, for example.

But a Timer's event is different: When its event is triggered, it looks at its Interval property, *then it waits until that interval of time has passed before it carries out any instructions you've put into its event*. After all, that's the purpose of a Timer: to time things. Its whole reason for being is to be able to *delay* carrying out the code in its event.

I keep saying its *event*, as if the Timer has only one event. And, in fact, it *does* have only one event. This is another reason why Timers are different from other components you're used to. Most components have many events; for example, a CommandButton has 17 events.

How Timers differ from other components

As useful as they are, Timers are a little confusing when you first start to work with them. They're unlike other components in several ways. Here is a summary of the ways in which a Timer is a unique component:

- Most controls have more than a dozen properties; Timers have only seven. And two of those properties, `Left` and `Top`, are wacky. The Timer control is never visible when a program runs, so giving it those two properties to describe its position on a form is peculiar.

- Most controls have at least ten events they can respond to; Timers have only one event, awkwardly named `Timer1_Timer( )`.

- Most controls are visible and can be accessed and triggered by the user of the program; Timers work in the background, independent of the user. They are always invisible when a program runs.

- Most controls' events are triggered instantly; Timers don't carry out the instructions you've put into their events until their Interval (the duration) passes.

- Most controls' events are only triggered once; Timers will repeatedly trigger their event until you either set their `Interval` property to 0 or their `Enabled` property to False.

Think of a kitchen timer

It's best to think of a Timer as one of those kitchen timers that you wind to, say, 10 minutes, and then it starts ticking. Ten minutes later, it goes BING! The BING is whatever code you have put into the `Sub Timer1_Timer( )` event.

The 10 minutes is the value in the Timer's `Interval` property, the amount of time that you set the Timer to. (For a Timer to be active, its `Interval` property must contain something other than zero, and its `Enabled` property must be True. The `Interval` defaults to zero, but the `Enabled` property defaults to True. Therefore, to get a Timer going, the only thing you really have to do is assign some number to the Timer's `Interval` property.)

There's just one way that the kitchen timer analogy breaks down. Unlike a kitchen timer, a VB Timer *resets itself after going BING*. Then it starts counting down from 10 again (or whatever `Interval` it's set to). After 10 more minutes pass — BING! Reset. Count down. BING! And on and on.

This resetting/countdown repetition will continue forever unless the program stops, or somewhere in your code you deliberately turn off the Timer by setting the `Interval` to 0 or the `Enabled` property to False. If you need the Timer again, put some number other than 0 in the `Interval` (and if necessary, set `Timer1.Enabled = True`).

The theory of Timers

What do they *do* for you? When you put a Timer onto one of your forms, you can make it repeatedly interrupt whatever else might be going on in the computer — even if the user is doing something outside your VB program, like working within another application. You can make a Timer do pretty much anything you want that involves duration, timing, clock effects, delay, or repetition by using the Interval and Enabled properties in various ways.

Once turned on, a Timer becomes an automaton, a relentless robotic agent that's loose in Windows. It has its instructions, and it knows how often you want the job repeated. Let's try it out.

1. Start a new VB project and double-click the Timer icon on the Toolbox (it looks just like a stopwatch). It doesn't matter where on your form you put it. The icon turns invisible at run time. Also add a Label to your form.

2. Double-click the Timer to get to the code window, and in the Timer's Timer event, type this:

```
Private Sub Timer1_Timer()
Label1.Caption = Time
End Sub
```

3. Press F5. The program runs, but nothing happens. Why? Because you haven't provided an interval. In the Form_Load event, type this:

```
Private Sub Form_Load()
Timer1.Interval = 1000
End Sub
```

The Interval property is expressed in milliseconds, so 1000 means *one second*. We'll shortly see how to specify minutes, hours, or whatever interval you want.

4. Press F5 and now you see a little digital clock that changes every second, as shown in Figure 19-1.

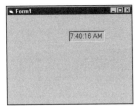

Figure 19-1
You can create a digital clock with only two little lines of code.

Attention: Using Default Properties

This is an important tip — we'll use the technique I describe next for the rest of this book. Each component has a *default property*. This means that if you're using that property in your code, *you need not specify it.*

The default property is always the most commonly used property. For a TextBox, it's the Text property; for a Label, it's the Caption property. Unfortunately, there are slip-ups. The Interval is not the default for a Timer. Nonetheless, you can often simplify your code by stripping off the reference to the default property, like this:

```
Label1 = Time
```

```
Text1 = "Rasmati"
```

So, in future examples in this book, if you see a value being assigned directly to a component, remember that it's really being assigned to the implied default property.

**20 Min.
To Go**

Turning a Timer off

If you want a Timer to do its job only once, include this code, Timer1.Interval = 0, within the Timer event. That will turn off the Timer as soon as it carries out the instructions one time:

```
Sub Timer1_Timer ()
MsgBox ("This Timer has done its job. Now it will be turned off.")
Timer1.Interval = 0
End Sub
```

You can alternatively just set the Timer's Enabled property to False, but I find it easier to ignore the Enabled property and just manipulate the Interval property. Remember that a Timer only starts counting if *both* the Enabled property is True and there is a value larger than zero in its Interval property.

Note that you cannot use the Timer event to hold the code that turns the Timer on (that *sets* an Interval property to something other than zero: Timer1.Interval = 4000, for example). For one thing, the Timer event will never execute unless the Interval is set from some *other* event, such as Form_Load or Command1_Click.

Setting longer Intervals

A Timer's Interval property can range from 0 to 65,535 milliseconds. This means that the longest time an Interval can be set for is 1.092 minutes. You can, however, easily extend the amount of time that a Timer will delay. You can make it wait until next Labor Day if that's what you want.

One way to measure time in longer intervals than the one-minute limit of a Timer's Interval property is to use a Static variable within the Timer event, and increment it (raise it) by 1 each time the Timer event is triggered.

Recall that a Timer *keeps going off, repeatedly triggering its Timer event,* until it's turned off (with Timer1.Enabled = False or Timer1.Interval = 0). To wait two hours, set the Interval property to 60000 (one minute), and then enter the following code:

```
Sub Timer1_Timer
Static Counter as Integer
Counter = Counter + 1
If Counter >= 120 Then
    MsgBox "TIME'S UP!"
    Timer1.Enabled = 0
End If
End Sub
```

Setting a specific future time

In personal information managers (PIMs) and other reminder programs, the idea is that you specify a specific date or time when you want a message to be displayed. Instead of saying, *delay 10 minutes*, you say, *show the message at 4:00 PM.*

The job of the Timer in this example is to take a look at the computer's clock at regular intervals, independently of what the user might be doing or what else is going on in Windows. When the specified time is matched (or exceeded), the Timer will remind us to feed the puppies or whatever.

To do that, just set the Interval to 60000 so that the Timer checks the time every minute. Then, put code into the Timer event that sees if the built-in Time function is equal to or greater than the specified time:

```
Private Sub Form_Load()
Timer1.Interval = 60000
End Sub

Private Sub Timer1_Timer()
```

```
SpecifiedTime = TimeValue("8:44:00 AM")

If Time >= SpecifiedTime Then
    MsgBox ("It's time to feed the pups.")
    Timer1.Interval = 0
End If


End Sub
```

This example uses the `TimeValue` function to provide a value that VB can compare to the `Time` function. Use the greater-than or equal operator (>=) in these situations rather than equals (=);otherwise, your code might skip right over the comparison value. In other words, the time might be checked at 8:43:33 and again a minute later at 8:44:33 and, therefore, *would never equal* 8:44:00. Seconds are required in both the `Time` and `TimeValue` functions — so they do matter.

Suggested uses for the Timer

As the previous examples have illustrated, a Timer can do various jobs for a programmer. Here is a summary of the main ways in which you can employ a Timer:

- It can act like *a traditional kitchen timer* — counting down from a preset time and then ringing a bell (or doing whatever you want) after the preset interval has elapsed.

- It can *cause a delay* so that, for example, your program displays a message in a small window (a form), but the user doesn't have to click any buttons to make the window go away. Instead, the form appears onscreen for maybe four seconds and then disappears automatically.

- It can cause events to *repeat at prescribed intervals,* like a digital clock changing its readout every second. Or it can save the user's work to a disk file every 10 or 20 minutes or whatever backup interval the user selected in an Options Menu in your program. Another use for this repetition is to animate something, as we'll discuss at the end of this session.

- It can repeatedly check the computer's built-in battery-powered clock to *see if it is time to do something*. In this way, you can build reminder programs that display a message or take some other action based on a predefined time or date. The Timer looks at the computer's clock at regular intervals, independent of what the user might be doing or what is going on in Windows.

● It can measure the passage of time, acting like a stopwatch and reporting how long it took for something to finish what it was doing.

Manipulating Control Arrays

A control array is a group of components that share the same name (they must be the same kind of component, such as an array of TextBoxes). A control array offers two major benefits:

1. When you have several controls of the same type performing similar functions, grouping them into a control array can be a valuable feature, allowing you to work with them more efficiently.

2. Using a control array is the only way you can create a new control (such as a brand-new TextBox) during run time.

Recall that an array groups items under the same name, but each item has its own unique index number. This way, you can manipulate the entire collection more quickly, without having to provide a different name for each item — you just increment the index number instead.

For example, when boxes are identified by index numbers, you can say, "Empty all the boxes from #4 to #15." That's much easier than working with individual names and saying, "Empty Mr. DeLillo's Box. Empty Ms. Philips's Box. Empty Dr. Sandringham's Box.", and so on.

Arrays work with the For...Next statement. You can quickly loop through an array to empty it, or search for a particular item, or put something new into each item, and so on. If we created a control array of TextBoxes, we could "empty" the text in all of them easily with a For...Next statement:

```
For I = 1 to 15
    Text1.Text(I) = ""
Next I
```

Create control arrays three ways

There are three ways to create a control array.

● Give more than one Label (or other component) *the same Name property*.

● Set the Index property of a control during design time. If you set a TextBox's Index to 0, it becomes the first TextBox in a potential array of

TextBoxes (you could also create the array during run time with the Load command, discussed shortly).

● Click a component to select it in the form's design window, and then press Ctrl+C to copy the component. Next press Ctrl+V to paste a copy of that component onto the form. At this point, VB asks you if you want to create a control array. Answer yes to create the array. Repeatedly pressing Ctrl+V will add more new members to your new control array.

Control array behaviors

In addition to sharing a name, all the members of a control array also share a single set of events. In other words, clicking on one of these three buttons — Command1(0), Command1(1), or Command1(2) (three members of the control array called Command1()) — triggers the same Click event.

You can tell which button was clicked by its index number. A triggered event provides the index number of the component in the array that triggered the event, like this:

```
Sub Command1_Click (Index as Integer)
    If index = 1 Then...
End Sub
```

Note how an array's Click event differs from a normal Click event. A normal Click event does not have Index as Integer:

```
Sub Command2_Click ( )
```

When new members of a control array are created (either during design time or run time), each new member initially inherits the values in *nearly* all the properties of the original member of the array. If the original TextBox had a Width of 500, so will all its clones as you build the array. Three properties, however, are not inherited from the parent component: Visible, Index, and TabIndex. After a new member of a control array has been created, you can adjust its properties individually as you wish.

If you use the Load command to create new members of a control array during run time, the new components in the array will be invisible unless you explicitly set their Visible property to True.

If you use the Load command with the index number of an existing member of a control array, VB will display an error message. Each newly created member of a control array must have a unique index number.

If you are working on your program and have already put some code into a component's events, you cannot then use that particular component as the parent to create a control array. The solution is to remove any programming from within a component that you intend to use to create a new control array.

Using a Control Array

**10 Min.
To Go**

Now for an example. Our goal is to create a gentle animation — nothing jerky or rude. Just a mild change in color from blue to black in the caption of a group of Labels. We'll use a control array so the Labels' ForeColor properties can be manipulated easily, and we'll also use a Timer to pace the animation effect.

Start a new project and put a Timer and a Label on the form. Since all its clones will inherit most of its properties, let's change the Label's Font and ForeColor properties now. Double-click the Label's Font property in the Properties Window. Change it to size 12. Double-click the ForeColor property, and click the Palette button in the pop-out color picker. Click the third blue down from the top (&H00FF0000& should appear in the Properties Window).

Now click the Label so that it's selected, then press Ctrl+C followed by Ctrl+V to copy, then paste, a new clone of the parent Label. VB displays a message box pointing out that you *already have* a control named Label1, and asks if you want to create a control array. Click Yes. Repeat this twice more so you have a total of four Labels in your control array. Their names are: Label1(0), Label1(1), Label1(2), and Label1(3). Line them up in order vertically from number 0 to number 3.

Now double-click the form to open the code window. In the General Declarations section at the top, type this:

```
Const BlackColor = vbBlack    'the animation color
Const DarkBlue = &HFF0000     'the normal color
```

Picking colors in Visual Basic

For black, you can use the ordinary vbBlack (there are 16 simple built-in color constants), but to get the number code (it's a "hex" number and starts with the & symbol) for more complex colors, use the palette feature in the Properties Window. Or, you can create a small VB program that uses the CommonDialog to display the complete custom color dialog box, and then displays the color's hex code in a message box. Here's how to do it:

```
Private Sub Form_Load()
CommonDialog1.Flags = 2 'show complete dialog
CommonDialog1.ShowColor
chosen = Hex(CommonDialog1.Color)
MsgBox chosen
End Sub
```

Note that in the custom color window you must move the slider on the far right up from its default bottom position, or all you'll get is black. That slider is intended to adjust the shade of the color, but it's a bit confusing.

Anyway, back to our animation example. Type in the rest of this code:

```
Private Sub Form_Load()
Timer1.Interval = 1000 'set a one second interval
End Sub

Private Sub Timer1_Timer()
Static counter

Select Case counter

Case 0
    Label1(counter).ForeColor = BlackColor 'animate
    Label1(3).ForeColor = DarkBlue 'restore original color
Case 1
    Label1(counter).ForeColor = BlackColor
    Label1(counter - 1).ForeColor = DarkBlue
Case 2
    Label1(counter).ForeColor = BlackColor
    Label1(counter - 1).ForeColor = DarkBlue
Case 3
    Label1(counter).ForeColor = BlackColor
    Label1(counter - 1).ForeColor = DarkBlue
End Select

counter = counter + 1
If counter = 4 Then counter = 0 'reset

End Sub
```

The main behavior produced by this code is that each Label's text color is set to black for one second, then it's restored to blue when the next lower Label is set to black (see Figure 19-2). When we reset and go back up to the first Label again, we have to do something other than merely subtract 1 from the current index number of the array. So we specifically state that index number 3 is to be returned to the original blue color.

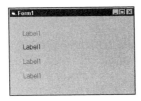

Figure 19-2
Each of these labels changes colors in turn, thanks to a Timer governing the animation.

This code can be written in a more condensed, but less readable fashion, like this:

```
Private Sub Timer1_Timer()
Static counter

If counter = 0 Then
    Label1(counter).ForeColor = BlackColor 'animate
    Label1(3).ForeColor = DarkBlue 'restore original color
Else
    Label1(counter).ForeColor = BlackColor
    Label1(counter - 1).ForeColor = DarkBlue
End If

counter = counter + 1

If counter = 4 Then counter = 0 'reset

End Sub
```

You can always write code in different ways; which way you choose depends on your personal style and preferences, such as whether you favor readability over concision.

If you're letting the user click on these labels to select options, here's how you use the labels' collective `Click` event to respond to the user's choices:

```
Private Sub Label1_Click(Index As Integer)

Select Case Index
Case 0
    MsgBox "You chose the first label"
Case 1
    MsgBox "You chose the second label"
Case 2
    MsgBox "You chose the third label"
Case 3
    MsgBox "You chose the bottom label"
End Select

End Sub
```

Creating a component during run time

You can always set a component's `Visible` property to False in the Properties Window, and then turn it to True at run time to make it appear that the component was just "created". But sometimes you want to *really* create them during run time. In the following example, you want to create enough clone Image components to fill the form with a tiled wallpaper.

Start a new VB project and put an Image component on the form. Set the Image control's `Index` property to 0. That's how you prepare a component to be the parent of clones. Now you have your seed: Giving a component an index number of 0 creates the basis for a control array.

Now, in the Properties Window, use the Image's `Picture` property to put a graphic into the seed Image control. Move the Image so it is flush against the upper left-hand corner of the form. If you want to resize the Image, change its `Stretch` property to True.

Now type the following code into the `Form_Load` event:

```
Private Sub Form_Load()
Rows = 7
Columns = 8
Movedown = Image1(0).Height
Moveacross = Image1(0).Width
```

```
Image1(0).Visible = False
For I = 0 To Rows - 1
  For J = 0 To Columns - 1
    x = x + 1
    Load Image1(x)
    Image1(x).Top = Movedown * I
    Image1(x).Left = Moveacross * J
    Image1(x).Visible = True
  Next J
Next I
End Sub
```

Press F5 and fill your form with clones of the original image, as shown in Figure 19-3.

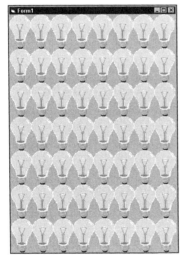

Figure 19-3
Only one of these Images is the original component; all others are created as clones at run time.

The above code took me the better part of an afternoon to figure out. I kept trying different ways to nest the two loops and to figure out the variables and how they interrelated to create the tiling effect. Sometimes you come up against a tough one, and you just have to keep hacking away, trying different approaches until you get the result you're after. Other days, programming goes as smoothly as sailing on a summer day. But not for me, with this, on that day. It was a toughie.

Notice the Load command. That's how a clone is created and added to a control array during run time. The variable *x* in this example gives the new clone its index number within the array: Load Image1(x).

Using With...End With

The With...End With feature can simplify your programming. Use it to avoid having to repeat a component's name over and over if you're adjusting it in several ways at once. With...End With can also be used with other objects (such as forms or objects you create, as is described in Session 30).

Let's say you want to change six properties of a TextBox. You can type the six changes in, like this:

```
Text1.Text = ""
Text1.Left = 12
Text1.Top = 100
Text1.FontBold = False
Text1.FontSize = 12
Text1.Width = Text2.Width
```

Or, you can use the With...End With structure, like this:

```
With Text1
   .Text = ""
   .Left = 12
   .Top = 100
   .FontBold = False
   .FontSize = 12
   .Width = Text2.Width
End With
```

Done!

Part IV—Saturday Evening
Session 19

REVIEW

This session exposed you to what I think are two of the more interesting features in VB: the Timer and the control array. You saw all of the ways that Timers can be used, and how to use them for any length of interval you need. The concept of default properties was also introduced. Then you explored control arrays — learning to group components or other objects into an array, or to create new members of the array during run time. Finally, you saw how to simplify code when assigning values to multiple properties of the same component by using the With...End With command.

QUIZ YOURSELF

1. Name two ways that a Timer is unlike any other component. (See "How Timers Differ from Other Components".)

2. How do you turn off a Timer? (See "Turning a Timer Off".)

3. How many minutes can you set the Interval property to? (See "Setting Longer Intervals".)

4. Do the clone components in a control array inherit all of the properties of the original parent component? (See "Control Array Behaviors".)

5. What command do you use to create components dynamically during run time? (See "Creating a Component during Run Time".)

Tracking Down Bugs (and Smashing Them Dead)

Session Checklist

✔ Typos and bad punctuation are easy to fix

✔ How to deal with run-time errors

✔ Understanding techniques for locating logic bugs

✔ Using alternative debugging tools

30 Min. To Go

Bugs — errors in a computer program — are inevitable. You can be enormously painstaking, tidy, and thoughtful, but if your program is more than 50 lines long, errors are likely to occur. If it's longer than 100 lines, errors are virtually certain.

Errors in computer programming fall into three primary categories:

- Typos
- Run-time errors
- Logic errors

We'll deal with each in turn, from easiest to toughest. Logic errors are the toughest.

Fortunately for us programmers, Visual Basic provides a powerful suite of tools to help you track down and eliminate bugs — we're the envy of programmers using other languages.

Wiping Out Typos

Typos are the easiest errors to locate and deal with. Visual Basic knows at once that you've mistakenly typed `Prjnt` instead of `Print`. If it doesn't recognize the word, it can detect that kind of error and will alert you.

When you give VB impossible commands like that, VB realizes that it cannot do anything with that line of code because some of the words are not in the language's vocabulary.

Or perhaps you didn't mistype; you merely mistakenly thought VB knew a command that it doesn't know. For example, if you type in the command `Pass the Salt`:

```
Private Sub Form_Load( )
Pass the Salt
End Sub
```

as soon as you press the Enter key after typing *Salt*, that line of code turns red (or another color if you've changed the Syntax Error Text color setting in the Tools ⇨ Options menu, Editor Format tab). The point here is that by changing the line's color, VB immediately alerts you that it cannot understand what you've typed — that something's wrong with the line of code. Also, if you have the Auto Syntax Check option selected in Tools ⇨ Options, an error message box is displayed, identifying the problem here as a "Syntax Error".

Punctuation counts, too

If you press F5 to run the code, VB displays that same "Syntax Error" message. Typos and false commands result in this error message. VB expects to see a command at the start of that line, and *Pass* is not part of the list of commands that VB understands. VB also expects correct punctuation, so this — `Form1...Show` — would trigger a syntax error. There's no double-period punctuation in VB's little book of correct punctuation.

Related to typos are errors you make when you don't provide the right type of information, or enough information, for VB to carry out a command:

```
Line (10,20)
```

This information is incomplete; you've given only the upper-left starting point of the line. The Line command wants four parameters, not two. To this code, VB will also reply with a "Syntax Error" message.

A third variety of easily detected, easily fixed error is an inconsistency of some kind between parts of your program. If you have a procedure that expects three arguments:

```
Sub Transf(a, b, c)
End Sub
```

and you try to call it, but give only two arguments:

Transf a, b

VB will not catch the error right away when you press Enter (these lines of code are both syntactically correct), but it *will* catch the inconsistency when you try to run the program. It will then provide as much help as it can by specifying what it thinks is causing the error. In response to the above code, VB replies "Argument not optional", as you can see in Figure 20-1:

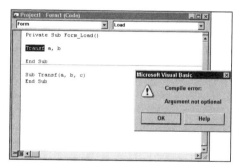

Figure 20-1
Notice that when VB locates an error, it highlights the word in your code where it thinks the error is located.

VB always attempts to highlight the command that caused the error, but is often off by one word.

If you have the Auto Quick Info option selected in Tools ⇨ Options, VB will display the argument list for any procedure you're trying to call. This happens as soon as you type the procedure's name and press the space bar to prepare to list the arguments.

Keep your finger near F1

If the explanation that VB provides in an error message isn't sufficient to point you to the problem, press F1. VB's online Help feature will pop up and give you the possible reasons for this kind of error in greater detail.

Handling Run-time Errors

The second major category of errors only shows up during run time. Perhaps the user does something wrong; perhaps the problem arises from your programming.

Imagine, for example, that you plan to tell the user the result of Text1 divided by Text2:

```
Private Sub Form_Click()
MsgBox "Your result is: " & Text1 / Text2
End Sub
```

If the user types a 0 into Text2 or both text boxes, that causes a run-time error because it causes a mathematical problem for the computer. You see a different kind of error message box, like the one shown in Figure 20-2:

Figure 20-2
A run-time error message gives you four choices: Continue, End, Debug, or Help.

If you click the Debug button, the line in your source code where the error occurred will be highlighted (in yellow by default).

You need to prevent, or at least gracefully handle, run-time errors. It's no good having a smoothly running program that suddenly crashes if the user has, say, forgotten to put a disk into Drive A:, or failed to close the drive door.

How run-time errors occur

Run-time errors include all of those unexpected situations that can come up when the program is running. The user might type in a 0, causing a division by 0 error. Also, there are a number of things you cannot know about the user's system. For example, how large is the disk drive? Is it already so full that when your program tries to save a file, there won't be enough room? Are you creating an array so large that it exceeds the computer's available memory? Is the printer turned off, but the user tries to print anyway?

Whenever your program is attempting to interact with an entity outside the program — the user's input, disk drives, Clipboard, RAM — you need to take precautions by using the On Error structure. This structure enables your program to deal effectively with the unexpected while it runs.

Visual Basic keeps track of any problems that occur, putting the error code of the problem into an internal VB variable called Err. There is also an Error function that can translate the Err code into text that you can show the user.

Unfortunately, your program cannot correct many run-time errors. For instance, you can only let the user know that his or her disk drive is nearly full. The user will have to remedy this kind of problem; you cannot fix it with your code.

Using On Error Resume Next

So if it is possible for a run-time error to occur, you should use the On Error command to *trap* the error. If you don't use On Error, Visual Basic will provide an error message to the user, *but VB will then shut down your VB program.*

Because there is no Drive Z:, the following input will cause an error:

```
Private Sub Form_Load()
Open "Z:\MYFILE" For Output As #1
Print #1, x
Close #1
End Sub
```

When this program runs, the message in Figure 20-3 will appear; then, as soon as the user clicks the OK button on the dialog box, the program will be shut down by VB. No second chances in this situation! To users, this kind of message can be obscure, confusing, and, sometimes, frightening.

Figure 20-3
*This kind of error message simply puzzles most users. And they are really
puzzled when they click OK because your whole program shuts itself down.*

If you insert an error-handling structure, you can provide a more helpful
message of your own, and also make the program continue to run, as shown
in Figure 20-4.

```
Private Sub Form_Load()
On Error Resume Next

Open "Z:\MYFILE" For Output As #1

If Err Then
MsgBox (Error(Err)) & " There was a problem with the disk drive"
Close
Exit Sub
End If

Print #1, x
Close #1

End Sub
```

Figure 20-4
You can provide a custom error message, if you trap errors.

Notice in the above code that you put an On Error Resume Next command at
the start of a procedure where you suspect that a run-time error might occur. This
command tells VB not to shut down the program if an error occurs. Rather, it
should *resume* execution of the *next* line of code following the error.

You then place the line that starts handling the error (If Err Then) just following the possible error (Open Z:). This is sometimes called an error handler or an error trap. The point is that you are saying: If the Err variable contains some value other than 0, there is an error. Consequently, you must do something about that error in your code between the If Err and the End If commands, as we did in the above example. The Error(Err) command feeds the error code (Err) to the Error function — and you get back a text description of the error.

Tracking Down Logic Errors

**20 Min.
To Go**

The third major category of programming bugs — logic errors — is usually the most difficult of all to find and fix. Some can be so sinister, so well concealed, that you might think you will be driven mad trying to find the source of the problem within your code. VB devotes most of its debugging features and resources to assisting you in locating logic errors.

A logic error occurs even though you have followed all of the rules of syntax, made no typos, and otherwise satisfied Visual Basic so that your commands can be carried out. You and VB think everything is shipshape. However, when you run the program, things go wrong: Say, the entire screen turns black, or every time the user enters $10, your program changes it into $1,000.

Visual Basic's set of debugging tools help you track down the problem. The key to fixing logic errors is finding out *where* in your program the problem is located. Which line of code (or lines interacting) causes the problem?

Some computer languages have an elaborate debugging apparatus, sometimes even including the use of two computer monitors — one shows the program as the user sees it, the other shows the lines of programming that match the running program. Using two computers is a good approach because, when you are debugging logic errors, you often want to see the code that's currently causing the effects in the application.

It's not that you don't notice the *symptoms*: Every time the user enters a number, the results are way, way off. You know that somewhere your program is mangling the numbers — but until you X-ray the program, you often can't find out where the problem is located.

The watchful voyeur technique

Many logic errors are best tracked down by watching the contents of a variable (or variables). Something is going wrong somewhere, and you want to keep an eye on a variable to find out just where its value changes and goes bad.

Three of VB's best debugging tools help you keep an eye on the status of the variables. We'll take a look at them in the following examples. Type in a simple program, like this:

```
Private Sub Form_Load()
Dim a, b

a = 112
b = a / 2
b = b + 6

End Sub
```

Now press F8 *once* to take your first step into the program. *After* (it must be after) you've pressed F8 to take that first step, make two of the debugging windows visible: Click the View menu and select Locals Window and Watch Window (the Immediate Window automatically appears). (Recall that each time you press F8 to execute the next line of code, the program again goes into Break mode. On the Debug menu, the single-stepping feature is called *Step Into*.) If you don't see the Locals Window and Watch Window options on your View menu, right-click a toolbar, then select Debug to display the Debug toolbar. Open the Locals and Watch windows by clicking their buttons on the Debug toolbar. For now, look at the Locals Window. It displays the contents of all variables that have been declared (they must have been declared) within the current procedure. Watch the variables in the Locals Window change as you press F8 to execute each line in this example code, as shown in Figure 20-5.

Also take a look at the Immediate Window. In this window, you can directly query or modify variables. To find out the value in B, for instance, just type the following into the Immediate Window, and then press Enter:

```
? B
```

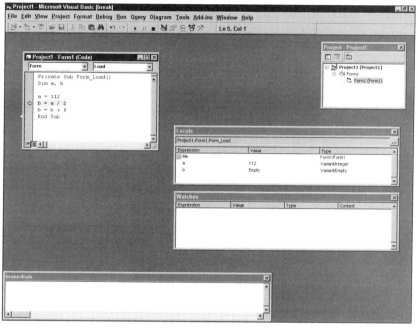

Figure 20-5
The Locals Window displays the contents of all local variables in the currently executing procedure.

The answer — whatever value B currently holds — will be printed in the Immediate Window. (The ? command is shorthand for the Print command.) You can also use the Immediate Window to *change* the contents in a variable. Type the following into the Immediate Window, and then press Enter:

```
B = 20
```

This assigns 20 to B. Try it, and watch what happens in the Locals Window. You can also launch procedures (events, subs, or functions) by typing their names and pressing the Enter key. VB will execute the procedure and then halt again. This is a good way to feed variables to a suspect procedure and watch it (and it alone) absorb those variables to see if things are going awry within that procedure.

Using Debug.Print

Some programmers like to insert `Debug.Print B` commands at different locations within their code (I don't). This also has the effect of displaying the contents of the variable B in the Immediate Window. But in this case, you're causing the values in the variables that you choose to `Debug.Print` to be displayed via code within your program. Try inserting some `Debug.Print MyVariableName` lines here and there in a VB program, and then run the program and watch the results appear in the Immediate Window.

Actually, you can type any executable commands *that can be expressed on a single line* into the Immediate Window to watch their effects. Notice that this is all done while the VB program is halted during a run — you can test conditions from within the living program while it's in Break (pause) mode. You can get into Break mode several ways: by inserting a `Stop` command into your code, by setting a breakpoint (discussed later in this session) in the code, by single-stepping (F8), by choosing Break from the Run menu (or the Toolbar), or by pressing Ctrl+Break.

The flexible Add Watch technique

The Locals Window is fine for local variables, but what about undeclared, form-wide, or program-wide variables? They don't show up in the Locals Window. To watch one of these other kinds of variables, choose Debug ➪ Add Watch, as shown in Figure 20-6.

Figure 20-6
The Add Watch feature is highly flexible.

When you add a watch (using Add Watch), VB keeps an eye on whatever *expression(s)* you have asked it to watch. You can watch a single variable, an expression, a property, or a procedure call. The Watch Window shows the current status of any watched expressions. To add a watch, select (highlight with the mouse) a variable or expression in the code window, click on the Add Watch option in the Debug menu, and VB will add it to the Watch Window.

Remember the example earlier in this session when $10 grew to $1,000 for no good reason? You would want to find out where that happened in your code. You could instruct the Add Watch feature to stop the program at the precise line of code when $10 grows larger than, say, $200. Then, when the $10 is transformed into $1,000 — our logic error — VB will halt the program and show us exactly where this problem is located. To do that, type `MoneyVariable > 200` into the textbox labeled Expression in the Add Watch dialog box (see Figure 20-6). Then click the OptionButton that says *Break When Value is True*. When you press F5 and run this program, as soon as the value in `MoneyVariable` becomes larger than 200, the program will halt and highlight the line where the value grew too large.

You can also specify the scope of a watch in the Add Watch dialog box (scope is called *Context* in the Add Watch dialog box).

An alternative way to use the Watches Window is to keep an eye on the watches you've defined as you single-step through your code. The Watches Window continually displays the value of all active watches.

A third option for the automatic halting of a running VB program is to tell the Add Watch dialog box that you want to use the Break When Value Changes option. In this case, you want to see *every* change in that variable, not just some specific change.

Another tool in the Debug Menu is the Quick Watch option. If you select (highlight) an expression or variable in your programming in the code window, and then choose Debug ➪ Quick Watch (or press Shift+F9), VB will show you at once the current contents or status of the highlighted expression or variable. VB also gives you the option of adding the item to the watched items in the Watches Window.

Setting Breakpoints

10 Min. To Go

Sometimes you have a good idea which form or module contains an error. Or you might even think you know the procedure where the error can be found. So instead of single-stepping through the entire code, press F5 to execute the program at normal speed, but then stop when execution enters the dubious form or procedure. After halting the program in a suspect region, you can slow down and press F8 to single-step.

Breakpoints can be one of the most useful debugging aids. As you know, you can press Ctrl+Break and stop a running program in its tracks. But what if it's moving too fast to stop just where you want to look and check on things? What if it's alphabetizing a large list, for example, and you can't see what's happening?

You can specify one or more breakpoints in your program. While running, the program will stop at a breakpoint just as if you had pressed Ctrl+Break. The code window will pop up, showing you where the break occurred, so you can see or change the code, or single-step, or look at the Watch Windows to see the values in variables.

You set a breakpoint by using the arrow keys to move your insert cursor to the line of code where you want to put the breakpoint. (The insert cursor is the vertical line indicating that anything you type will appear at this spot in the code.) You can also move the insert cursor by clicking your mouse pointer on a line of code.

Then, to set a breakpoint, select the Toggle Breakpoint option on the Debug Menu. Or, you can just press F9, or click in the margin of the code window to the left of the line of code where you want the break. The line of code turns a different color (red by default), and a dot is placed in the margin of the Code Window, indicating that this line is a breakpoint, as you can see in Figure 20-7.

Figure 20-7
A red dot and red background alert you that a line of code is a breakpoint. Execution will halt on this line, and VB's debugger will enter pause mode.

You can set as many breakpoints as you wish. You can turn off a breakpoint by again pressing F9 or selecting Toggle Breakpoint in the Debug Menu.

Another use for breakpoints is when you suspect that the program is *not running some lines of code*. Sometimes a logic error is caused because you think a subroutine, function, or event is getting executed, but, in fact, the program never reaches that procedure. Whatever condition is supposed to activate that area of the program never occurs. Perhaps you are trying to call a subroutine from a TextBox's Change **event. To activate the subroutine, you program the following commands to respond when the user presses the Enter key:**

```
Sub Text1_Change( )
If KEYASCII = 13 Then
    MySubroutine
End If
End Sub
```

The `MySubroutine` **will never be called. The** `Change` **event does not recognize the** `KeyASCII` **variable, and so the code inside the** `If` **structure will never execute. (These commands should have been put inside the** `Text1_KeyPress` **event, where they would work.) To find out if, as you suspect,** `Text1_Change` **is not executing properly, set a breakpoint on the first line of code within the** `MySubroutine` **procedure. Then, when you run your program — and the breakpoint never halts execution — you have proven that** `MySubroutine` **is never called.**

Sometimes you set several breakpoints here and there in your code, but then you want to delete all of them. If you've set a lot of breakpoints, the Clear All Breakpoints (Ctrl+Shift+F9) feature allows you to get rid of all of them at once without having to hunt them all down and toggle each one off individually by pressing F9.

Alternative Debugging Strategies

You likely noticed several other tools on the Debug menu. They're not as widely useful as breakpoints, single-stepping, or watches — but when you need these lesser tools, you are glad they're available. Here's a brief survey of the minor debuggers.

Step Over (Shift+F8)

Step Over is the same as single-stepping (F8), except that if you are about to single-step into a procedure, Step Over will ignore the procedure. No procedure calls will be carried out. All other commands will be executed. So, if you are single-stepping (pressing F8 repeatedly) and you come upon a procedure that you know is not the location of the bug, press Shift+F8 on that line, and you will step over the entire procedure. This option gets you past areas in your program that you know are free of bugs and would take a lot of single-stepping to get through.

Step Out (Ctrl+Shift+F8)

The Step Out feature was introduced in VB5. It executes the remaining lines of the procedure that you're currently in, but it stops on the next line in the program (following the current procedure). Use this to quickly get past a procedure that you don't want to single-step through.

Run to Cursor (Ctrl+F8)

To use the Run to Cursor option, click somewhere else in your code (thereby moving the insertion cursor). VB remembers the original, and new, locations of the insertion cursor. Press Ctrl+F8, and the code between the original and new locations is executed fast. This is a useful trick when you come upon, for example, a really large For...Next loop. You want to get past this loop quickly rather than waste all the time it would take to complete the loop by pressing F8 over and over. Just click on a program line past the loop, and then press Ctrl+F8. VB executes the loop at normal execution speed, and then halts at the code following the loop. You can now resume stepping from there.

Set Next Statement (Ctrl+F9)

With the Set Next Statement feature, you can move anywhere in the current procedure and restart execution from there (it's the inverse of the Run To Cursor feature described above). While the program is in Break mode, go to the new location you want to start execution from, and then click the new line of code where you want to resume execution. Now, pressing F8 will single-step from that new location forward in the program. This is the way you *skip over* a line or lines of code. Say that you know that things are fine for several lines, but you suspect other lines farther down. Move down using Set Next Statement and start single-stepping again.

Show Next Statement

If you've been moving around in your program, looking in various events, you may have forgotten where in the program the next single-step will take place. Pressing F8 would show you quickly enough, but you might want to get back there without actually executing the next line. Show Next Statement moves you in the code window to the next line in the program that will be executed, but doesn't execute it. You can look at the code before proceeding.

The Call Stack

Done!

The Call Stack feature is on the View menu rather than the Debug menu (don't ask). The Call Stack provides a list of still-active procedures if the running VB program went into Break mode while within a procedure that had been called (invoked) by another procedure. Procedures can be "nested" (one can call on the services of another, which, in turn, calls yet another). The Call Stack option shows you the name of the procedure that called the current procedure. And if that calling procedure was *itself* called by yet another procedure, the Call Stack shows you the complete history of what is calling what.

REVIEW

This session explored the topic of debugging — from fixing the easy culprits like typos to tracking down those tough logic errors. You learned how to use On Error to anticipate and handle problems that might come up when a user is running your program. You also learned how to use the impressive suite of debugging features built into Visual Basic, including watches, breakpoints, and single-stepping.

QUIZ YOURSELF

1. When you press Enter after typing a line of code that contains a syntax error, what does VB do? (See "Wiping Out Typos".)

2. What does On Error Resume Next mean? What happens if you use that line in your code? (See "Using On Error Resume Next".)

3. Can you use expressions with the Add Watch feature? (See "The flexible Add Watch Technique".)

4. What shift key do you press to insert a breakpoint on a line of code? (See "Setting Breakpoints".)

5. Which debugging feature should you use if you want to skip over a For...Next loop and resume single-stepping just after the loop? (See "Alternative Debugging Strategies".)

PART

IV

Saturday Evening

1. What is an *array*?

2. Can you beak a logical line of code into two physical lines of code?

3. How are arrays used? When are they more efficient than ordinary variables?

4. What is the `Step` command used for?

5. What does the `If...Then` structure do?

6. Parts of an `If...Then` structure are traditionally indented. Which parts, and why?

7. When is the `Select...Case` structure preferable to `If...Then`?

8. What is the purpose of the `Case Else` command?

9. Can you use `Select...Case` to test for any number lower than 200? If so, what is the code that accomplishes this?

10. Can you use `Select Case` to test for an alphabetic range, such as a name that begins with any letter between n and z? If so, what is the code that accomplishes this?

11. Name two things that a Timer control can accomplish.

12. Timers are unique components in several ways. Describe one way that a Timer is unlike any other component.

13. How do other applications running in Windows affect a Timer's behavior?

14. What measure of time is represented by the `Interval` property of a Timer?

15. What is a component's *default property*?

16. A control array allows you to manipulate components as a group, offering a similar efficiency to the benefits you get by using ordinary variable arrays (you can work with the components in a control array by using loops). However, there is a second, perhaps equally valuable use for control arrays. What is it?

17. What are the easiest kinds of programming bugs to fix, and why?

18. Is punctuation important in computer programming, and if so, why?

19. What does `On Error Resume Next` do?

20. Which debugging feature should you use if you want to skip over a `For...Next` loop and resume single-stepping just after that loop?

☑ **Friday**

☑ **Saturday**

☑ **Sunday**

PART

V

Sunday
Morning

Personal Data Manager: Designing a Useful Application

Session Checklist

✔ Create a list of features for your program

✔ Define the user interface

✔ Choose between Single Document (SDI) or Multiple Document Interface (MDI)

✔ Databases 101: Understanding records, fields, tables, and indexes

**30 Min.
To Go**

This, and the rest of the Sunday sessions, will bring together the Visual Basic techniques and programming skills you've been learning throughout this book. We'll create a functional, and rather handy, application: a personal data manager program.

Our goal is to design, then build, a general-purpose collection tracker. It's a database manager, designed to let you easily add, modify, search, and print information about every item in your collection. What collection? That's why it's called the *personal* data manager (PDM). It works with whatever kind of collection you have.

What do you collect? Books, videos, stamps, recipes, photos, buttons? Whatever it is that interests you, the PDM lets you type in a title, and as much additional data as you wish, about each item in your collection. And when you want to see a subset of that collection (such as a list of all recipes for Mexican food), that information is displayed swiftly.

We'll make it a free-form database — not a group of little cells to fill in, but instead a single large TextBox that you can fill with as much information about each item as you'd like. Studies have shown that approximately 80% of all Visual Basic applications manage a database, so it is a useful topic for you to spend time on. Additionally, in the process, you'll see how to sketch, then organize and build, a VB application of some sophistication.

Making Our Wish List

What do you want the program to do? The first step in designing an application is to make a list of the jobs it does for the user.

We'll want the items of data displayed alphabetically in a ListBox, so you can easily select which one to view or modify. They can also be scrolled, one at a time, forward or backward. You want a search feature, so users can see a list of all items matching a criterion. You'll want to provide some menus to allow the user to select various options to customize the PDM. There has to be a facility for adding a new record (each complete item in a database is known as a *record*). Each of the items in our database will have two elements in a record: the record's title and its description (the description field can include any information you want). The elements that make up a record are known as the record's *fields*. Our records will have two fields.

What else? There should be a way of deleting a record — including the usual dialog box asking, do you *really* want to delete this record. And we want to go even further by providing an Undo feature that restores the most recently deleted record, if you should change your mind.

There should be a backup feature. You don't want to have only one copy of your database — especially after you've spent a lot of time typing in the records. There should be a way to print a record, or set of records, to hardcopy. We should allow the reader to specify the font and font size for the TextBoxes that display the title and description fields.

What Shows, What Doesn't?

Now that we know all the things we want accomplished, let's divide them up into three categories:

- Things the user always sees:
    - A TextBox showing the Title field (If the user types in a title that duplicates an existing title, we'll alert them and require that each title be unique.)
    - A TextBox showing the Description field
    - A data control to help the user move through the database sequentially, or jump to the first or last record
    - A set of buttons for the common tasks: Search, Index, Add New Record, Delete Record, Undo Delete, and Exit
- Things the user sometimes sees:
    - The ListBox that displays an index (list) of each title so the user can quickly select an item from anywhere in the entire database
    - A second ListBox that displays the results of a search
    - A dialog box into which the user can type the query that begins a search
- Items on menus:
    - A File menu with New, Open, Close, Save, and Print
    - An Options menu with choices for automatic backup on exit (yes/no), form background color, and font selection

Now you know what should be on the main form (what the user always sees), what should be on separate, floating forms of their own (the two ListBoxes and the InputBox that the user sometimes sees), and the menu items.

**20 Min.
To Go**

Understanding SDI and MDI

When you're designing a project, one of your first decisions must be whether you want it to be a Single Document Interface (SDI) or Multiple Document Interface (MDI) style application.

In SDI mode, all windows are independent of the other windows, and can float free on the desktop, or can be dragged onto other windows. MDI, by contrast, has a large container window with one or more child windows within it. When you're using an MDI, the child windows can't be dragged outside the parent (application) window. This is the way that Word for Windows works — you can split the window, or see two or more open documents at once in child windows. But these smaller windows cannot be moved outside the Word container window. If you move the container window in Word, all of the child document windows move with it.

Visual Basic is something of a hybrid of MDI and SDI. Utility child windows like the Properties Window can be dragged outside the VB container, but forms behave like MDI children and cannot be dragged outside.

You can use either SDI or MDI when you create a new project in VB. Recall from Session 10 that one of the options offered by the Application Wizard was the choice between MDI and SDI. We ignored it then, but let's try it out now.

Choose File ⇨ New Project. Double-click the VB Application Wizard icon in the New Project dialog box. Click the Next button and you see the dialog box where you choose between MDI and SDI, as shown in Figure 21-1.

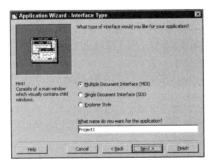

Figure 21-1
By default, the Application Wizard has the Multiple Document Interface selected.

Leave MDI selected and click the Finish button (this accepts the rest of the Wizard's defaults, which we don't care about in this example).

Now you can see that there are two forms: the parent container form titled (MDIForm), and a child form named frmDocument. You can add more child forms if you wish. During design time, you don't see the containment relationship, but press F5 and it becomes clear that you cannot drag frmDocument outside the container form, as shown in Figure 21-2.

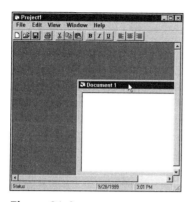

Figure 21-2
*During run time, it's obvious that this is an MDI-style application — you
cannot move Document1 outside of the container window.*

The MDI style enjoyed a few years of popularity, but now it seems to be losing
favor. Even the latest version of Word has abandoned it to an extent (rather than
using MDI, you can simply use full-screen documents. To switch between full-
screen documents, just press Alt+Tab).

One reason for the drift away from MDI is that new users apparently cannot
intuitively understand the concept of container/child. So for this reason, and to
give users as much freedom as possible to arrange their desktops the way they
want — we'll stick with SDI in our database program. The main window will not
contain the two ListBox forms.

Understanding Databases

Before taking the decisions we made earlier in this session and applying them to
building the user interface, let's first spend a little time on the concept of databases. The steps we'll take in future sessions will be clearer if you have a good
understanding of the fundamentals.

If you have a Rolodex" on your desk, you've got the essentials of a database. To
make it a real database, you need to type it into a computer program that stores it
as an orderly file. The key is *orderly*. The information shouldn't be merely a simple
list; it should have an underlying organization.

Records and fields

If you were designing a database to hold the information in your Rolodex, you would recognize that each card in the Rolodex is a single *record* and that each of those records is divided into perhaps eight *fields* (zones): Name, Address, City, State, Zip, Voice Phone, Fax Phone, and E-mail address. So you would design the database to give each record eight fields. But do you notice a little problem? How is the program going to sort these records? On which field? The Name field is the logical one, but it might be awkward to require that each last name be typed first (alphabetizing on the first names is impractical).

So you change your specs: nine fields now, with the previous Name field now divided into LastName and FirstName fields. Now the alphabetizing can be done on the LastName field. The field (or fields) that you choose to have the records sorted by is called the *index*.

In our database program, there will be only two fields. The Title field (the index) and the Description field. Users can type in any information they wish, in whatever fashion they wish.

Separate tables

In a complex database, there may be more than one group of records. If you have a huge Rolodex, you might divide the records into two categories: Personal and Business, for example. This kind of large-scale group of records is called a *table*. A database can have multiple tables — and they can be linked, searched, or otherwise interrelated in various ways. But I propose we don't worry our pretty heads about that stuff. Our database will have only a single table.

The key to indexes

When you specify that a field is to be indexed, it is maintained in alphabetical (or numeric) order by the database engine (the underlying, low-level support code that does jobs for a database).

If a user asks for a particular record (or set of records, such as *all coins in my collection older than 1890*) and the DateOfCoin field is not indexed, then each record must be searched individually. It's the equivalent of a box of coins — just a pile of them in a box and you have to pick up each one and look at its date. However, if the DateOfCoin field is indexed, then the computer can very quickly locate a record or set of records (called, appropriately enough, a *recordset*). Having the DateOfCoin field maintained as an index is the equivalent of having a coin album in which you've put each coin in plastic pockets ordered by their dates.

Searching hundreds of thousands of company records via an index is very efficient. However, indexing isn't all that much of an issue when dealing with the number of records likely to be stored in a personal collection database. A few thousand records can be swiftly searched, if necessary, even if an index isn't used. That many records can also be swiftly alphabetized by a ListBox. But we'll sidestep a ListBox, not use it, and simply make our Title field an index field — so it more quickly displays all the titles alphabetized in the Index ListBox. Can't hurt.

Our Goal

**10 Min.
To Go**

The main advantage of a free-form database program, like the one we're going to construct, is that it's up to the user how much, or what kind, of information is saved.

We want to give the user a powerful search engine. How powerful? Let's say that the user includes these lines in the Description field (the Description TextBox) of their recipe collection database:

Fry strips of cooked roast with onions and peppers. Sprinkle with chipotle pepper. Wrap in warmed tortillas.

leftovers Mexican appetizer

That last line, "*leftovers Mexican appetizer*", makes it possible to hit this recipe if we search on any of those three words.

We want to give the user a truly flexible search feature. That's our main goal. The user should be able to ask the search feature to find, for example, *Mexican*, and our program should respond by filling the Search ListBox with every recipe in the entire recipe database that includes the word *mexican* in either its title or description fields. Uppercase or lowercase will not matter (it'll be case-insensitive).

And, what's more, we want to let them search for a combination of terms: *mexican* AND *chipolte*; *mexican* OR *chipolte*; or a precise phrase such as "*mexican appetizer*".

That's our goal, and we'll achieve it. We'll employ some of the great database tools available in Visual Basic 6.

Done!

REVIEW

In this session, you saw how to sit yourself down and write yourself a list. When you're creating a new application in VB, you want to plan it. You want to see its parts and how they might fit together. I'm not saying that some gifted programmers can't build a program the way that Tennessee Williams wrote great plays: by wrestling them into existence with no original sketching. But most of us have to do at least a little outlining if we want the project to go smoothly and be logical. So, first you list all the things you want your program to do for the user. Then you decide which of those things are on menus, which are visible to the user at all times, and which require separate windows (forms) of their own. This session concluded with an overview of the primary terminology of databases: records, fields, tables, recordsets, and indexes.

QUIZ YOURSELF

1. What kinds of items should always be visible, and what should be subordinated and put into menus? (See "What Shows, What Doesn't?".)

2. Which style of application is now becoming unfashionable, SDI or MDI? (See "Understanding SDI and MDI".)

3. How does a record differ from a field? (See "Records and Fields".)

4. What is a table? (See "Separate Tables".)

5. If you specify that a field should be indexed, what happens to that field? (See "The Key to Indexes".)

Building a Bullet-proof User Interface

Session Checklist

✔ Putting the primary components on the form

✔ Learning how to size and position components via code

✔ Adding shortcut keys and specifying the TabIndex order

✔ Defining menus

✔ Writing some basic code

30 Min. To Go

Let's continue with the application we conceived in Session 21. It's time to put up a visible interface — the components that the user will interact with to view and modify the PDM database. We made a list in the previous session of things the user always sees, so let's start with that. These components will be on the main form of our application, the form that the user works with most of the time.

Adding the Main Components

Choose File ⇨ New Project, then double-click the Standard EXE icon. Stretch the form so that it nearly fills the VB design environment. Now put two TextBoxes and a Data control on the form. Stretch the TextBoxes and Data control so they fill about ¾ of the form, as shown in Figure 22-1.

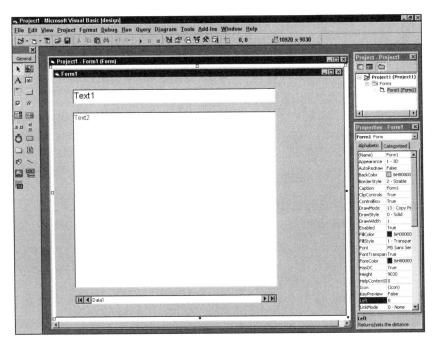

Figure 22-1
The TextBox on the top is for the title, and the larger one is for the description.

Change the small TextBox's Name property to txtTitle, its MultiLine property to True, and change its Font property to Arial, 12-pt. size (or whatever is readable at your screen resolution). Change the large TextBox's Name property to txtDesc, and its Font property to 16-pt. Arial (or what's best for you). Delete the Text property from both TextBoxes, so the user doesn't see the defaults, *Text1* or *Text2*.

Now put six CommandButtons over on the right side of the form. Drag your mouse around all of them to select them as a group. Change their Font property to 11-pt. Arial (or whatever looks best). Change their Left, Width, and Height properties so that they line up and look good. Finally, deselect them from the group and change their individual Name properties to cmdSearch, cmdIndex, cmdNew, cmdDelete, cmdUndo, and cmdExit. Change their Caption properties to name them as shown in Figure 22-2:

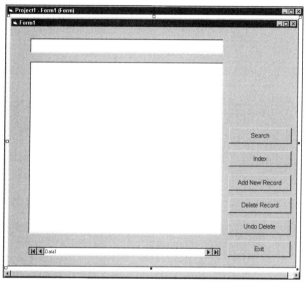

Figure 22-2
The main window your user will work with is now complete.

Saving your work

At this point, you might as well save this project so that you don't have to redo everything if the power fails or something. Use Windows Explorer to create a new folder named PDM. Then choose File ⇨ Save Project. Save Form1.Frm and Project1.Vbp to the PDM folder.

Adding the Secondary Interface

Recall from Session 21 that there were a couple of user-interface elements that were not visible by default. When the user clicks the Index button, all of the titles in the database are displayed in a ListBox. When the user clicks the Search button, an InputBox appears where they can type their search criteria; then, if they click its OK button, the subset of titles defined by their query (technically, the *record-set*) is displayed in a second ListBox.

Both ListBoxes permit users to click any title, and when they do so, the clicked record is immediately displayed, after which the ListBox closes. Using only one ListBox for both the Index and Search features might seem efficient to you. In some ways, it might be, but if you want to make anything particular to one of the ListBoxes, you will run into a problem. You then have to keep track of *which* mode (Search or Index) the current instance of the ListBox is in. This gets messy fast. So I suggest you simply use two ListBoxes; one dedicated to showing the Index and one dedicated to showing the results of a search query. Then you can customize each ListBox to your heart's content without worrying about which is which.

Put two ListBoxes on the form (don't worry where) and change their Name properties to lstSearch and lstIndex. Change both the ListBoxes' Font properties to 12-pt. Arial, or whatever is readable. Change both their Visible properties to False — we want them initially hidden during run time.

Sizing and positioning

Making secondary components the right size and putting them in the right position onscreen is often best done via code. Rather than stretching them and dragging them by eye, just use existing components' Top, Left, Width, and Height properties (or the Form's same properties) to make them line up and look smart when they become visible during run time.

It's good to put sizing and positioning code into the Form_Load events. That way, the code gets executed before the form is made visible, and it's executed only that one time when the form is first created.

We want the ListBoxes to cover all of the buttons on the right side of the form except for the Exit button. When displaying a secondary component to the user, it's often important that you disable, hide, or otherwise inactivate alternative input devices like CommandButtons. It gets messy if your program has to see, for example, if the user has clicked the Index button right after clicking the Search button and things like that. So, to simplify, we'll simply display the lstIndex or lstSearch ListBoxes right on top of most of the buttons — so the user simply cannot click them.

To position and size the ListBoxes, type the following code into the Form_Load event:

```
Private Sub Form_Load()

With lstSearch
```

```
        .Left = cmdSearch.Left
        .Top = txtTitle.Top
        .Width = cmdSearch.Width + 30
        .Height = txtTitle.Height + txtDesc.Height + 400
    End With

    With lstIndex
        .Left = cmdIndex.Left
        .Top = txtTitle.Top
        .Width = cmdIndex.Width + 30
        .Height = txtTitle.Height + txtDesc.Height + 400
    End With

End Sub
```

Notice the fudge factors (+ 30 and + 400) in this code. Adjust those as necessary to make your ListBoxes neatly cover the buttons (except the Exit button).

The ScaleHeight property is similar to the Height property, but ScaleHeight doesn't include the form's Title bar or frame—just the interior measurement. We added 400 to take into account the space above and below the CommandButton.

> The ListBoxes you put on your form cover up other components that you still want to work with. So, to make them invisible during design time, go to the Properties Window and change their Left properties to something like -8325. This moves them way off to the left of the screen—off into Virtual Land. (Just remember that you did this—so if you need them back for some reason, you can remove the minus sign.)

Making Life Easier for the User

20 Min. To Go

Users expect some shortcuts in their Windows applications, and woe be the programmer who forgets them. He or she will be thought unprofessional. Users expect an Alt+ shortcut key on each button, so they can press, for instance, Alt+S to activate the Search button without having to reach for the mouse.

They also expect to be able to press the Tab key to move among the components. The order of the TabIndex properties determines the order in which each component gets the focus. On this form, I would say that each button in turn going down should get the focus, followed by the Title TextBox and then the

Description TextBox. Also, you should figure out which component will have the default when the program first runs, and you should give it the TabIndex of 0. I think that after the user has entered the data, the first thing they will most often want to do when they fire up the application is search. So we'll give the Search button the default focus. That way, the only thing the user needs do when the program runs is press Enter to trigger the Search button.

Creating shortcut keys

Recall that you use the & symbol before the letter that you want to make the shortcut character. The Caption is then displayed with that letter underlined as a cue to the user. Change the Search button's Caption property to &Search and do the same for &Index, &Add New Record, &Delete Record, &Undo Delete, and &Exit.

Arranging the TabIndex properties

Change the TabIndex of cmdSearch to 0, then go down the list giving each button the next higher TabIndex (1 for the Index button, 2 for the Add New Record button, and so on), ending with 6 for the txtTitle and 7 for the txtDesc. Press F5 and press the Tab key repeatedly to make sure that the focus cycles as you planned.

Adding the Menus

You remember how to add menus: Just press Ctrl+E or choose Tools ⇨ Menu Editor. We want two menus: File and Options. So Press Ctrl+E, and then type **&File** in the Caption field and **mnuFile** in the Name field. Click the Next button, and then click the right-arrow button to make it possible to enter submenu items. Type **&New**, **mnuNew**, and press Enter to move down to the next entry. Repeat these steps until you've added &Open, mnuOpen, &Close, mnuClose, &Save, mnuSave, &Print, and mnuPrint.

Now press the left-arrow button to move back out to the main menu location, and type &Options, mnuOptions. Press the right-arrow button to get back to the submenus, and add these: &Automatic Backup, mnuAutomatic, &BackColor, mnuBackColor, &Fonts, and mnuFonts. Your Menu Editor should look like the one shown in Figure 22-3.

Figure 22-3
When you've finished adding your menus and submenus, the Menu Editor should look like this.

At this point, you probably want to save your work. You've done a lot to improve your project, and you don't want to have to repeat your efforts if the power goes out.

Sketching Some Crucial Code

One of Visual Basic's best qualities is that you can press F5 and easily see the effects of your programming. Then you can stop the program and make any necessary adjustments. To make this test/adjust cycle easier, we should now put in some elementary code that gives us the ability to quickly exit the program by clicking Exit (we can just put the End command in the Exit button's Click event). We'll also be able to quickly display the Search or Index ListBoxes by clicking their buttons. We'll also sketch in the basic code to configure the user interface to make it possible for the user to add new records.

We'll put additional code into these various events after we add database connectivity to the program. But for now, at least we'll have some things happening when we press F5. We can also see if the interface responds visually as it should.

Type in this code so that when the user clicks the Search button, several things happen: The caption on the Exit button changes, the ListBox is made visible, and the Data control is rendered temporarily disabled.

```
Private Sub cmdSearch_Click()
cmdExit.Caption = "&Click to Close List"
lstSearch.Visible = True
Data1.Enabled = False
End Sub
```

Now type in the following (quite similar to the above) code for the Index button:

```
Private Sub cmdIndex_Click()
cmdExit.Caption = "&Click to Close List"
lstIndex.Visible = True
Data1.Enabled = False
End Sub
```

When either ListBox is displayed, it covers all buttons except the Exit button. We want the caption of the Exit button to change while a list is displayed. The changed caption should read: &Click to Close List.

When the user clicks that button, we need to know whether the click means, "Exit the program" or "Close the ListBox". Here's code that tests the ListBoxes' Visible properties to see if either of them is currently visible. The program then knows the answer, and can behave as it should. Here's the code you should type into the cmdExit's Click event to test the Visible properties:

```
Private Sub cmdExit_Click()

If lstSearch.Visible Or lstIndex.Visible Then
    cmdExit.Caption = "&Exit"
    lstSearch.Visible = False
    lstIndex.Visible = False
    Data1.Enabled = True
Else 'they want to quit the program
    End
End If
End Sub
```

Remember that when you use a phrase like If lstSearch.Visible, what you're really saying is: If lstSearch.Visible = True.

In this code, if a ListBox closes, we change the button's Caption property back to &Exit, then make the ListBoxes both visible (we don't need to worry about which one is currently displayed — just set them both to False), and finally, we re-enable the Data control.

However, if the user clicks the button to shut down the program, we use the End command for that.

Now press F5 and try out the various buttons to see how things look. When you click the Search or Index buttons, your ListBoxes should appear as shown in Figure 22-4.

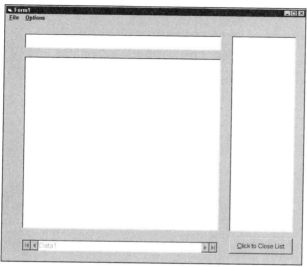

Figure 22-4
The ListBoxes cover the buttons, except for the lowest button that closes the list.

Coding the Visible Part of the New Record Feature

The final thing we will do at this point is provide a way for the user to add a new record to the database. All of the buttons should be made invisible (we don't want a mishap to occur, such as the user trying to delete a record while we're in the delicate process of adding a record). The Data control should be made invisible as well. Two new buttons should replace the Data control: *Cancel* and *Add This to the Database*.

Add two CommandButtons to the form (put them somewhere up above the other buttons; we'll move them into position with code). Change the Name property of one of them to cmdCancel, and set its Caption property to &Cancel. Name the other one cmdAdd, and set its Caption property to &Add This Record to the Database. Adjust both Font properties to make them readable, and set both Visible properties to False.

Now add the following code (in boldface) to the existing code in the Form_Load event so that the two buttons are correctly positioned:

```
Private Sub Form_Load()
```

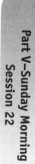

```
With lstSearch
    .Left = cmdSearch.Left
    .Top = txtTitle.Top
    .Width = cmdSearch.Width + 30
    .Height = txtTitle.Height + txtDesc.Height + 400
End With

With lstIndex
    .Left = cmdIndex.Left
    .Top = txtTitle.Top
    .Width = cmdIndex.Width + 30
    .Height = txtTitle.Height + txtDesc.Height + 400
End With

cmdAdd.Top = Data1.Top
cmdAdd.Left = Data1.Left
cmdAdd.Height = Data1.Height
cmdAdd.Width = (Data1.Width / 2) - 50

cmdCancel.Top = Data1.Top
cmdCancel.Left = cmdAdd.Left + cmdAdd.Width + 100
cmdCancel.Height = Data1.Height
cmdCancel.Width = (Data1.Width / 2) - 50

End Sub
```

Now, put the following code into the cmdCancel button. We want the two buttons to disappear, and all the other buttons to reappear if the user clicks this Cancel button:

```
Private Sub cmdCancel_Click()
Data1.Visible = True
cmdSearch.Visible = True
cmdIndex.Visible = True
cmdNew.Visible = True
cmdDelete.Visible = True
cmdUndo.Visible = True
cmdExit.Visible = True

cmdCancel.Visible = False
```

```
cmdAdd.Visible = False

End Sub
```

And put this same code into the cmdAdd button as well:

```
Private Sub cmdAdd_Click()

Data1.Visible = True
cmdSearch.Visible = True
cmdIndex.Visible = True
cmdNew.Visible = True
cmdDelete.Visible = True
cmdUndo.Visible = True
cmdExit.Visible = True

cmdCancel.Visible = False
cmdAdd.Visible = False

End Sub
```

Done!

Now press F5 to see what happens when you click the Add New Record button. That's it. You've built a nice user interface, and made some things happen when buttons are clicked. In the next session, you'll create a new database, and also connect your PDM program to that database.

REVIEW

This session launched you into the brave sea of building a sophisticated program. You learned how to add the major visible components, and then added the secondary components that are sometimes visible. You created the shortcut keys, massaged the TabIndex property for each major component, and added the menu stubs (empty procedures). Finally, you added the basic code to make several of the buttons respond to clicks — at least to respond with the correct visual reaction (they don't yet have all of the code they'll have when the project is finished).

Quick Quiz

1. What's usually the best way to size and position secondary components? (See "Sizing and Positioning".)

2. What symbol is used to display an underlined character to the user as a cue that pressing Alt+*that character* will trigger a response? (See "Creating Shortcut Keys".)

3. What is special about setting a component's `TabIndex` to 0? (See "Arranging the `TabIndex` Property".)

4. What does the code `If lstSearch.Visible` mean? (See "Sketching Some Crucial Code".)

Session Checklist

✔ Creating a database with the VisData utility

✔ Building a database with programming code

✔ Adding the Data Access Objects library to your project

✔ Testing the new database

**30 Min.
To Go**

You can create a database dynamically during run time using code, or you can create one during design time using VB's Visual Data Manager utility. We'll start off with the simpler approach: using the Visual Data Manager. Next, we'll see how to use the CreateDatabase command. I'll show you how to allow the user to bring a new database into existence from within the application. Recall that on our Personal Data Manager application's File menu we have a New option, which allows the user to start a new database if they wish.

VB ships with a Visual Data Manager utility that makes the creation of a new database effortless and makes the definition of its interior structure — its tables and fields — a snap. You can also use the Visual Data Manager to make adjustments to a database after it's created, if you wish.

Using VisData to Create a Database

Let's see how it works. We know that we want one table containing two fields: Title and Description. Armed with that knowledge, select Add-Ins ⇨ Visual Data Manager. Notice that it calls itself VisData in its title bar — so we'll use that nickname from now on.

In VisData, select File ⇨ New ⇨ Microsoft Access ⇨ Version 7.0 MDB. There are many different kinds of databases. We'll stick with the most tested and most popular database style in the world: the Access-style database. Visual Basic has a lot of built-in support for the Access-style database. These databases end in the extension .MDB, which stands for Microsoft Database.

The *Select Microsoft Access Database to Create* dialog box appears. You want to use this dialog box to give your new database a name and a place on your hard drive. Type **PDM** in the File name textbox. Our database file will be saved as PDM.MDB. Now use this dialog box to browse your hard drive until you locate the PDM folder that you created in Session 22 to hold this project's .FRM, .VBP, and other files.

Click the Save button. The dialog box closes, your new database is saved to \PDM\PDM.MDB, and the VisData utility displays two new windows: Database Window and SQL Statement, as shown in Figure 23-1.

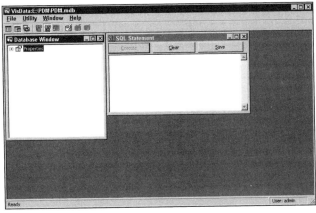

Figure 23-1
Your new database awaits your instructions; it's time to define the fields.

SQL means Structured Query Language. It's a language used to extract a recordset from a database. We'll deal with SQL more in Session 25.

Now we need to tell VisData which kind of database this is. There are three fla-vors. The Table-type recordset works with a single table, and we'll use that one because our database has only one table. The second flavor is the Dynaset-type recordset, which is used to access more than one table at a time. Finally, the Snapshot-type recordset is read-only — use that one for reports, but not if you need to manipulate the data in the database.

To choose the Table-type recordset, click the button on the far left on the VisData toolbar. This defines the Table-type recordset.

Defining a table

Now we'll create the table. Right-click the word *Properties* in the Database Window. From the context menu that pops out, choose New Table. There it is — the Table Structure dialog box appears, as shown in Figure 23-2.

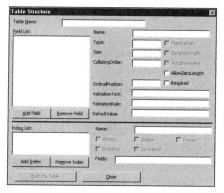

Figure 23-2
This is where you specify the fields, data types, indexes, and other qualities that define your database's structure.

Now type **tblCollection** in the Table Name field.

Defining fields

Every table has one or more fields. Click the Add Field button in the Table Structure dialog box. Boom. A new dialog box pops out, as you can see in Figure 23-3.

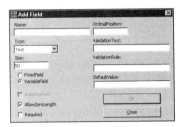

Figure 23-3
Define your database's fields in this dialog box.

Type **Title** as the name of your first field. Notice that by default a new field is a Text type (similar to a string variable) and it can be up to 50 characters long. It can also be zero ("Allow Zero Length"). Change the 50 to 100 to permit the user to enter a title of up to 100 characters. We'll also require that they do fill in this field — it will be our index — but we'll validate that in our code instead of here. Click the OK button.

The field is added to the Table Structure dialog box, but the Add Field dialog box remains open so you can add additional fields. We want one more. Type in **Description** as the Name, and then drop down the ListBox labeled Type and change it from Text to **Memo**. The Memo data type is a text-type field, but unlike the Text data type, the Memo type can be essentially as long as the user wishes (a memo can contain up to 1.2 GB of text data!).

Specifying a data type for each field enables the database to store its data more efficiently. If one of your fields asks for a simple either/or answer like Male/Female, there's no reason to waste space by storing this answer as a 50-character large piece of text data. You can just use the Binary data type (the equivalent of VB's Boolean variable type), which requires only one character (one byte) of storage space.

Defining the index

Click the OK button, and then click the Close button. Now, in the Table Structure dialog box, click the Add Index button. The *Add Index to tblCollection* dialog box opens. In the Name field, type **indxTitle**, and then double-click the word *Title* in the Available Fields list. This adds the Title field to the Indexed Fields list. Now the Titles will be maintained within the database in alphabetical order. Click OK, and then click Close to close the Add Index dialog box.

Building the table

Now click the *Build the Table* button on the Table Structure dialog box. After a little pause, the database is constructed according to your wishes. You can see it in the tree diagram in the Database Window, as shown in Figure 23-4.

Figure 23-4
Your table, and its fields and index, are illustrated in this tree diagram.

Close VisData. At this point, you have an empty database sitting on your hard drive.

Creating a Database Using Code

Although the VisData utility works fine, there are times when you want to let the user create his or her own database file. Our PDM offers the user this capability in the File ➪ New menu option. So let's now see how to create and define the structure of a database via programming.

Choose File ➪ Open Project in VB, and load your PDM project (it's the .VBP file in the PDM folder you created).

Adding the DAO library of commands

Before you can use database programming in a VB project, you must first add a special library of code to your project. It's called the DAO (Data Access Objects) library, and it contains procedures and commands not available by default in VB. To add this library to the PDM project, select Project ➪ References. When the References dialog box appears, find *Microsoft DAO 3.51 Object Library* in the ListBox. Click the checkbox next to this entry in the ListBox titled Available References. Now click the OK button to close the dialog box and add this library to your project.

If you have a version later than 3.51 listed (DAO 3.6, for example), do not use it. VisData can't handle any version beyond 3.51. Also, if when you click the OK button, you get the message, "Name conflicts with an existing module, project, or object library", this most likely means that you've already added a DAO library to this project. To see if that's the case, choose Project ⇨ References again and look at the very top of the Available References ListBox where all of the currently installed libraries are checked. You can uncheck the DAO library that's up there and select the other version, if you wish.

Adding the CommonDialog

It's also necessary to add the CommonDialog component to this project. So, select Project ⇨ Components. Locate Microsoft Common Dialog Control 6.0 in the Controls ListBox. Check its checkbox. Click OK to close the dialog box and add it to your Toolbox. Display the design window so you can see Form1 (double-click Form1 in the Project Explorer). Double-click the CommonDialog icon on the Toolbox to place it onto your form.

Go to the code window. Using the drop-down ListBox on the top left in the code window, locate the mnuNew_Click procedure. This menu option's procedure is where we'll put the code that allows users to create new databases. They can create new databases to their hearts' content and name them whatever they want, but we'll define the two fields and the index in code — they don't get to do that.

Type this code into the mnuNew_Click event:

```
Private Sub mnuNew_Click()

Dim dbNewDB As Database
Dim tdNewTable As TableDef
Dim fld As Field
Dim idx As Index

response = InputBox("Type in the name of your new database. Then
you can browse your hard drive and decide where to save it.")
If response = "" Then Exit Sub 'they clicked Cancel

If LCase(Right(response, 3)) <> "mdb" Then response = response &
".mdb"
```

```
CommonDialog1.FileName = response
CommonDialog1.CancelError = True 'detect Cancel button

On Error Resume Next
CommonDialog1.ShowSave    ' display the Save dialog
If Err = 32755 Then Exit Sub 'they clicked this Cancel button

Set dbNewDB = CreateDatabase(CommonDialog1.FileName,
dbLangGeneral)
Set tdNewTable = New TableDef

Set fld = tdNewTable.CreateField("Title", dbText, 100)
tdNewTable.Fields.Append fld

Set fld = tdNewTable.CreateField("Description", dbMemo, 50)
tdNewTable.Fields.Append fld

Set idx = tdNewTable.CreateIndex
     With idx
        .Name = "idxTitle"
        .Fields.Append .CreateField("Title")
     End With

tdNewTable.Indexes.Append idx


tdNewTable.Name = "tblCollection"
dbNewDB.TableDefs.Append tdNewTable

Set dbNewDB = Nothing

End Sub
```

The bulk of this code deals with objects, and we'll get to that topic in the final session. Rather than repeating the discussion of the Set command, and other object-related programming concepts, just type this one in monkey-see-monkey-do. We'll defer our dive into the world of objects until that final session. Nevertheless, you can easily *use* this code as a template for creating new databases, tables, fields, and indexes. Just substitute your file path for the .MDB file path here, and substitute your names for the tables, fields, and indexes.

A brief comment on detecting the Cancel button is in order, though. If the user clicks Cancel, we want to just exit this sub and not build the new database. It's easy enough to tell if the user clicks the Cancel button to close an InputBox because the returned variable is an empty string "". However, you have to set the CancelError property of a CommonDialog to True (it's False by default) to trigger an error condition if the user presses the Cancel button in a CommonDialog. It's cumbersome, but this code illustrates how to trap the Cancel button.

Done!

Testing Your New Database

To see that you can actually create a new .MDB database file, press F5 and then choose File ➪ New in your running program. Provide a filename and then use the CommonDialog to choose a location on your hard drive. Click the Save button to save the new database. Stop your program from running.

Now Choose Add-Ins ➪ Visual Data Manager. Choose VisData's File ➪ Open Database ➪ Microsoft Access. Locate your new .MDB file and double-click it. Use the Database Window to verify that the table, fields, and index have been created (click on tblCollection, Fields, and other objects in the tree diagram to expand the branches and see what you've got).

> **Warning: If you ever get an "unrecognized database format" error when trying to open a new database in VisData, it means that you ignored my warning earlier in this session and are using the DAO 3.6 library, which VisData cannot digest. Go back and dese-lect the *Microsoft DAO 3.6 Object Library* in the Project ➪ References dialog box, and instead select the *Microsoft DAO 3.51 Object Library*.**

REVIEW

This session showed you two ways to create a new Access-style database. You saw how to use the VisData utility that ships with VB 6 to define the tables, fields, and indexes in the new database, and then how to save it to disk. You then switched gears and built a database dynamically during run time via programming code using the world's most popular database language — the tried and true DAO library of database programming commands. Finally, you tested your new database by checking it out in VisData to see if the table, fields, and index you built in code actually made it into the database.

QUIZ YOURSELF

1. A Memo data type is unique — what's so special about it? (See "Defining Fields".)

2. What does "Allow Zero Length" mean when defining a new field in a database? (See "Defining Fields".)

3. What does the DAO Library offer to you as a programmer? (See "Adding the DAO Library of Commands".)

4. Why is it necessary to use the Project ⇨ References feature to add the DAO Library to your project? Why isn't it just always available for your use? (See "Adding the DAO Library of Commands".)

5. Why did we set the `CommonDialog1.CancelError = True`? (See "Adding the CommonDialog".)

Connecting to a Database

Session Checklist

✔ One way to add a record to a database

✔ Connecting to a database

✔ How to bind components to a Data control

✔ Opening a database and extracting data with programming

✔ Alternative file-access techniques

30 Min. To Go

Connecting to a database using the Data control is easy and straightforward. The project we've been building since Session 21, the PDM, already has a Data control on it, so now let's attach it to the PDM.MDB database we created in Session 23. After you do this, you'll actually see a record displayed in the PDM for the first time. It's a great moment.

Adding a Record

If it's not already loaded, open Project1.VBP, located in your PDM folder. Recall that although we designed the table and fields for the PDM.MDB database in the previous session, we did not put any records in it. A record contains the actual *data*. In this database, a record contains some data in the Title field and the Description field.

Because we're going to connect to this database and display data in our two TextBoxes, we should first put some real data into the database. That way, we'll see something in those TextBoxes after we make the connection. Seeing is believing, and when the record appears in the TextBoxes, we'll know for sure that we're connected to the database. So let's put a record into the PDM.MDB database.

Choose Add-Ins ⇨ Visual Data Manager. Open VisData's File menu and see if the PDM.MDB database is displayed at the bottom of the File menu. If it is, click it to load it; if not, choose File ⇨ Open Database ⇨ Microsoft Access and locate and load PDM.MDB.

Double-click tblCollection in the Database Window. The VisData data entry dialog box appears, as shown in Figure 24-1.

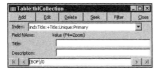

Figure 24-1
You can use this dialog box to add new records to a database.

Click the Add button in the data entry dialog box. Type in the title and description of a coin, a recipe, or anything that's part of the collection you want to create. (The Description field in VisData is limited to 255 characters, but don't worry — in the PDM you'll have the full Memo data-type's size of over 2GB.) When you finish, click the Update button. You've now added a record to the database. Close VisData.

Connecting to a Database

The Data control serves two purposes:

- During design time, it can be used to connect your project to a database.
- During run time, it can serve as a way for the user to navigate through the records in the database. Notice that the Data control has two pair of icons. The icons with an arrow plus line symbol take the user to the first or last record. The simpler arrow icons move the user back or forward by one record.

You connect a Data control to a database by setting its `DatabaseName` and `RecordSource` properties. Open the design window so you can see the Data control on the form. Click the Data control so its properties appear in the Properties Window. Double-click the `DatabaseName` property. A file browser dialog box appears, as shown in Figure 24-2.

Figure 24-2
Browse your hard drive to locate the database you want to connect to.

Double-click the PDM.MDB database filename in the PDM folder. The browser dialog box closes, and the full path to your database appears as the `DatabaseName` property in the Properties Window.

Now locate the Data control's `RecordSource` property and click the icon to drop down the list, as shown in Figure 24-3.

Figure 24-3
Once you've connected to a database, all of its tables will appear in the RecordSource property's listbox.

As you can see in Figure 24-3, setting the Database property automatically provides a list of the tables in that database in the RecordSource property. Click tblCollection to make that the table we'll work with (it's the only table we defined for our database anyway).

20 Min. To Go

Binding Components to a Data Control

Change the small TextBox's Name property to txtTitle, its MultiLine property to True, and change its Font property to 12-pt. Arial (or whatever is readable at your screen resolution). Change the large TextBox's Name property to txtDesc, and change its Font property to 16-pt. Arial (or what's best for you). Delete the Text property from both TextBoxes so the user doesn't see the defaults, *Text1* or *Text2*.

Now it's time to attach the two TextBoxes to the Data Control and, in the process, define which field is to be displayed in which TextBox. Click the top TextBox to select it (its name is txtTitle). Locate the DataSource property in the Properties Window and click the arrow icon to drop down its list. You see Data1, the Data control. Click it to select it as the source (think of it as a pipe) through which the database's records flow to the TextBox.

Now click the DataField property's icon and notice that its list contains both fields in the tblCollection: Title and Description. Choose Title for this TextBox.

Now select the larger TextBox named txtDesc. Set its DataSource property to Data1 and its DataField property to Description.

Press F5. There you are: The record is displayed as you'd hoped, with its Title and Description fields in the appropriate TextBoxes, as shown in Figure 24-4.

Programmatic Database Access

The Data control works great for the kind of database we're building — relatively small and simple. However, if you're going to do something heavy-duty (10,000 records, say, for a business), you'll also want to know how to connect to a database via programming.

We'll use a new, empty VB project to illustrate this technique, so save the PDM project and choose File ⇨ New Project. Select the Standard EXE project and add a ListBox to the blank Form.

Figure 24-4
You've now connected to a database and displayed one of its records.

You remember the routine: Choose Project ➪ References and locate *Microsoft DAO 3.51 Object Library* in the listbox. Click the box next to it in the Available References list. Click the OK button to close the dialog box and add the library to this project.

Double-click the form to get to the code window and type this into the Form_Load event:

```
Private Sub Form_Load()

Dim dbBiblio As Database
Dim rsWholeTable As Recordset
Set dbBiblio = OpenDatabase _
("C:\program files\vb98\biblio.mdb")
Set rsWholeTable = dbBiblio.OpenRecordset("Titles")

Do Until rsWholeTable.EOF = True
    List1.AddItem rsWholeTable.Fields("Title")
    rsWholeTable.MoveNext
Loop

End Sub
```

If you're using the Visual Studio version of VB 6, change the above file path to: C:\Program Files\Microsoft Visual Studio\VB98.

Press F5 and be patient (this is a large database of 8,569 records). After a second or two, the ListBox will be displayed and will contain the Title field of each record in the Titles table in the Biblio.MDB database, as you can see in Figure 24-5.

Figure 24-5
Filling a listbox with records requires only a few lines of code.

Biblio.MDB is a sample database that ships with VB 6 and can be used for practice and testing when database programming. It is usually located in the \program files\vb98 folder, but use the Windows Search feature to locate it if you don't find it there.

What's happening in the code we used for this? We first define two special variables: dbBiblio is a Database object, and rsWholeTable is a Recordset object. Then we use the Set command and the OpenDatabase method to assign the database to the Database object, and we use the OpenRecordset method to assign the Titles table to the Recordset object. At this point, rsWholeTable "contains" (actually is a pipeline to) the records in the Titles table.

Now we use the Do Until loop structure to continually test the EOF property of the recordset until it reaches the end (EOF means *End of File*). Then, the current record's Title field's contents are added to the ListBox. Finally, the MoveNext method of the Recordset object is used to point to the next record in the table.

**10 Min.
To Go**

Simple File Access

A few years ago, simple data was saved and retrieved directly using a few elementary file management commands. These days you get more power and much more flexibility using the database language and database-related components that are now available in VB.

However, sometimes you merely want to save and retrieve something simple, like the contents of a TextBox or the user's choice of BackColor. Creating a formal database for this amount of data would be overkill. In such cases, you should be aware how the Open and Close commands work with files, and how the Write or Print commands work with data.

The Open command is your gateway to the computer's disk drive and the files there. Using Open is like pulling a file drawer open — now you can put new folders (files) into the cabinet or take out existing files for inspection or modification.

Disk files hold all kinds of information — pictures, budget data, even programs that can be run. However, the Open command works with *data* (information of some kind), not programs that can be run. And you would use the LoadPicture and SavePicture commands for images.

What's left? Information, usually in text form — records of tax payments, lists of birthdays and anniversaries, short stories, or whatever kinds of data a program generates or manipulates and the user wants to save for later retrieval.

Opening a file

How many characters an application reads in, or writes to, a file depends both on the mode with which the file was opened and the particular command you are using to read from, or write to, the file. Line Input # reads in a whole sentence at a time (a line that ends with a carriage return, linefeed codes), Get # can read a single byte, and Input can read an entire text file into a single text (string) variable. Here's a simple example:

```
Open "C:\MyFile" For Input As #1
n = LOF(1) 'the whole length of this file
a = Input(n,#1)
Close 1
```

LOF tells you the length of the file (the total number of characters it contains). After the preceding commands are carried out, the variable a holds all of the characters in the disk file named MyFile. Note that you can use a variable instead of specifying the file path with a literal like "C:\MyFile".

In place of For Input, you can use For Append, which adds data to the end of the file, or For Output, which either replaces the contents of an existing file or, if no file exists by that name, creates a new file. You give each opened file an ID number (#1) as in the above example, and it identifies the file until you use the Close command. (The # symbol is optional.)

Writing to a file

The Print # command sends *an exact copy* of text to an opened file. A copy of text saved to disk with Print # can later be read off a disk file and sent into a TextBox with any original line-break formatting intact.

To me, Print # is usually preferable to the alternative, Write #, because Write # inserts commas between the individual pieces of saved text and adds quotation marks to text (string) variables. All of these extra symbols have to be extracted by your program before the data can be properly manipulated by your program. However, if you are saving variables or arrays in a kind of mini-database manager application, you might want to investigate the capabilities of Write #.

Here's how to save the contents of a TextBox, including any line breaks (where the user pressed Enter to move to the next lower line):

```
Private Sub Command1_Click()

Open "C:\MyFile" For Output As #1
Print #1, Text1
Close 1

End Sub
```

To read this data into your program and place it into a TextBox (with line breaks preserved), use the code example in the previous section, "Opening a file".

Deleting a file

Visual Basic uses the colorfully named Kill command to delete a file:

```
Kill "C:\MyFile"
```

or

```
FilePathVariable = "C:\MyFile"
Kill FilePathVariable
```

Done!

REVIEW

In this session, you found out how to use the VisData utility to add records to a database, then how to connect a Data control to a database file. Next, you saw how to bind TextBoxes to a Data control so you can display records to the user. An alternative to using a Data control is to write programming that opens a database — a technique you used to fill a ListBox with records from one of VB's sample databases, Biblio.MDB. Finally, you worked with several VB commands that let you manipulate files: open, save, append, replace, retrieve, and delete data. This approach is useful for small, simple data storage and retrieval — but it's not a substitute for the more robust database tools provided via VB's proven database programming language (DAO), or the various components that can be used with databases.

QUIZ YOURSELF

1. What are the two jobs that a Data control does? (Hint: One happens during design time and one during run time.) (See "Connecting to a Database".)

2. A TextBox has a `DataSource` property. What is it used for? (See "Binding Components to a Data Control".)

3. The `Set` command is used with object variables. What does it do? (See "Programmatic Database Access".)

4. How can you make use of the `EOF` property? (See "Programmatic Database Access".)

5. Which is a better command to use — `Write #` or `Print #` — when saving the contents of a TextBox, and why? (See "Simple File Access".)

Session Checklist

✔ Adding records to a database

✔ Deleting records from a database

✔ Providing a safety net: adding an undo feature

✔ Permitting the user to edit records

**30 Min.
To Go**

It's time to provide the code for the four buttons in our PDM application. Those buttons are captioned: Add New Record, Add This to the Database, Delete Record, and Undo Delete. We'll give each of them the programming necessary to make them do the jobs their captions promise. So load PDM into VB.

Adding New Records

In Session 24, you learned how to use VisData to add a new record to your database, but that's not a practical approach for your user. It's unlikely they will even have Visual Basic and its VisData utility. But even if they do, they'll expect to be able to add records using your application rather than some outside program.

Double-click the Add New Record button to see its code. Recall that we already put some code into that event. The existing code hides all of the buttons, and then displays two new buttons captioned *Cancel* and *Add This to the Database*. However, we must add a couple of lines to the Add New Record button's code. The following lines in boldface should be added:

```
Private Sub cmdNew_Click()

If Data1.DatabaseName = "" Then Exit Sub

rsBookmark = Data1.Recordset.Bookmark
Data1.Recordset.AddNew

Data1.Visible = False
cmdSearch.Visible = False
cmdIndex.Visible = False
cmdNew.Visible = False
cmdDelete.Visible = False
cmdUndo.Visible = False
cmdExit.Visible = False

cmdCancel.Visible = True
cmdAdd.Visible = True

End Sub
```

The first new line of code tests to see if the Data control is in fact connected to a database. It's possible that the user has clicked the Close option on the File menu (the code for the Close option will be added in Session 27), so there is no database currently attached to the PDM. In such a case, we Exit Sub.

The rsBookmark variable holds the pointer to the current record (the one the user sees in the TextBoxes). The Bookmark property of the Recordset object is useful when you want to restore the current record after some activity has moved you to a different record. In this situation, you're adding a new record (the TextBoxes will empty), but if the user clicks the Cancel button, you want to return to the record that was being displayed when he or she clicked the Add New Record button. To make this work, you also need to add a form-wide variable, so type the following into the General Declarations section of the form:

```
Dim rsBookmark As String
```

And add the line in boldface to the `cmdCancel_Click` event. This line restores the proper record:

```
Private Sub cmdCancel_Click()

Data1.Recordset.Bookmark = rsBookmark

Data1.Visible = True
cmdSearch.Visible = True
cmdIndex.Visible = True
cmdNew.Visible = True
cmdDelete.Visible = True
cmdUndo.Visible = True
cmdExit.Visible = True

cmdCancel.Visible = False
cmdAdd.Visible = False

End Sub
```

The `AddNew` method creates a brand-new record in the database, but it's only a provisional record. Unless the `Update` method is later used to actually save the record into the database, the new record is discarded. `AddNew` causes any components that are bound to the Data control (like our TextBoxes) to become empty and blank. This is because these data-bound components are showing a new, and currently empty, record.

You use the `AddNew` and `Update` methods of the Data control's *recordset object*. When your program starts running, a recordset is automatically generated based on the `DatabaseName` and `RecordSource` properties of the Data control. Thereafter, this recordset can be referred to in code as `Data1.Recordset`. The Cancel button has little to do — it merely reverses what the Add New Record button did: Cancel hides itself and the *Add This to the Database* button, and makes visible all the other buttons and the Data control. We already wrote the code that does this.

However, if the user clicks the *Add This to the Database* button, we must add the new record to the database. So we must put some new code into the *Add This to the Database* button to make this work. Type in the additional code (shown in boldface):

```
Private Sub cmdAdd_Click()
```

**20 Min.
To Go**

```
If txtTitle = "" Or txtDesc = "" Then
    MsgBox "You must put something into both TextBoxes"
    Exit Sub
End If

If InStr(txtTitle, "'") Or InStr(txtDesc, "'") Then
MsgBox _
"Alas, single quotation marks are not allowed. Please remove them"
Exit Sub
End If

On Error Resume Next


With Data1.Recordset

    .Fields("Title") = txtTitle
    .Fields("Description") = txtDesc

End With

If Err Then
    MsgBox (Error): Exit Sub
Else
    Data1.Recordset.Update
End If

If Err = 3022 Then 'duplicate title
n = txtTitle
MsgBox "You already have a record with the title: " _
& n & ". Please type in a unique title."
Exit Sub
End If

If Err Then MsgBox (Error) 'some other error

Data1.Recordset.MoveLast

Data1.Visible = True
cmdSearch.Visible = True
```

```
cmdIndex.Visible = True
cmdNew.Visible = True
cmdDelete.Visible = True
cmdUndo.Visible = True
cmdExit.Visible = True

cmdCancel.Visible = False
cmdAdd.Visible = False

End Sub
```

The new code starts off by checking to see if the user has left either the Title or Description field empty. If so, our program refuses to save the record. The Title field is used as an index, so it's supposed to have unique data in each record (so it can be sorted properly). One record with an empty Title field would be OK, but two would generate an error in the database. So we simply require that the field have something in it. The Description field was defined as requiring some data — so rather than have an empty txtDesc TextBox display a database-generated error, we provide a more helpful error message. We also check to see if the user used a single-quote ('), which confuses the database (single-quotes are used as punctuation for queries and searches, so embedding one in the text itself confounds the search commands).

Then we ensure that the program won't crash if an error occurs by adding On Error Resume Next. Then we use the With structure to modify the two fields in the current record (a new record) of Data1's Recordset. If an error occurs, we display it to the user and go no further in this sub (in other words, we don't commit the record to the database because the Update command is never carried out).

However, if there is no error, the Update command is executed. It's possible that the user might enter a duplicate title, and that would trigger error #3022. If so, the database will refuse to actually carry out the Update. So, we can tell the user the problem and exit this sub, again without committing the faulty record to the database.

Finally, so user doesn't see a blank pair of TextBoxes (which always panics them), we use the MoveLast method. This way, the last record in the table will be displayed to the user, which will be the record they just typed in because a newly added record is always appended to the "end" of the table, not automatically alphabetized within it.

Deleting Records

The process of deleting a record is straightforward. You use the Recordset object's Edit method to make it possible to modify or delete the current record. Then you get rid of it by using the Delete method.

We'll need two string variables with form-wide scope to hold the deleted Title and Description fields, in case the user changes his or her mind and clicks the Undo button. So, go to the General Declarations section at the top of the code window and type this:

```
Dim RemovedTitle As String, RemovedDescription As String
```

Put the following code into the Delete button's Click event:

```
Private Sub cmdDelete_Click()

RemovedTitle = txtTitle: RemovedDescription = txtDesc

On Error Resume Next
With Data1.Recordset
    .Edit
    .Delete
End With

If Err Then MsgBox (Error): Exit Sub


'try to move to the next higher record
Data1.Recordset.MoveNext

'test for "no current record error"
n = Data1.Recordset.Fields("Title")


If Err = 3021 Then
' no current record (they deleted highest record)
Data1.Recordset.MovePrevious

End If
End Sub
```

In this code, you save the data first in case the user later wants to undo the delete, and then you provisionally `Edit` and `Delete` the current record. If there's an error (the deletion didn't happen for some reason), you display the error message to the user and exit from this procedure. However, if things went well, your code then attempts to move to the next higher record in the database (so users don't see a confusing pair of empty TextBoxes, which would require them to click the Data control to move to an actual record). Then your code checks the Title field to see if it's still empty. Error 3021 means "no current record", and that tells you that the `MoveNext` command tried, but failed, to go to a higher record. This means that the user deleted the highest record in the table. If this is the case, the `MovePrevious` command shows the user a record. If he or she emptied the database entirely, a "No current record" message will be displayed and the user will realize that he or she emptied it.

Handling an Undo Request

**10 Min.
To Go**

The Undo Delete button restores the most recently deleted contents of the two TextBoxes. Type this into the Undo Delete button's `Click` Event:

```
Private Sub cmdUndo_Click()

If RemovedTitle = "" Then
MsgBox "There is nothing to undo.": Exit Sub
End If
Data1.Recordset.Edit
Data1.Recordset.AddNew

txtTitle = RemovedTitle: txtDesc = RemovedDescription

'so they can't undo twice
RemovedTitle = "": RemovedDescription = ""
cmdAdd_Click 'do a normal add-record

End Sub
```

This procedure first checks to see if there is any text in the `RemovedTitle` variable — if not, the user either hasn't deleted anything yet, or already used the Undo feature for a record. How do we know if the user already used the Undo feature for a particular record? Look a little lower in this procedure to where we store an empty "" value into the `RemovedTitle` variable. We empty the contents of that variable each time we run this `Undo` procedure, precisely to prevent the user from repeating an Undo.

After checking for an empty `RemovedTitle` variable, we prepare the Data control's recordset for a change (`Edit`), and then add a new record provisionally (`AddNew`). Then, our code triggers the `cmdAdd_Click` event. Note this: If part of what you need to do in one procedure has already been coded in another procedure, just call that other procedure. In this situation, we've added the Title and Description text, and we want to "pretend" that the user clicks the *Add this to the Database* button. So we simply write `cmdAdd_Click` in our source code, and that procedure is carried out just as if the user had clicked its button.

Editing Records

Allowing the user to change records in a database is a central feature of any database application, and our PDM is no different. However, you'll be pleasantly surprised that you need write no code to enable editing. The Data control, and the two TextBoxes bound to it, are capable of detecting, and then committing to the database, any changes that the user makes to existing records. If the user makes a change to the Title or Description TextBoxes, the change is updated and committed to the database as soon as the user moves to a new record by clicking one of the four buttons on the Data control, or by shutting down the program.

Done!

REVIEW

In this session, you added the main programming code that allows the user to manipulate the data in a database. You learned how to use the Data control's recordset object to add new records, delete records, and undo deletions if the user changes his or her mind. Finally, you saw that record editing requires no code when you bind components to a Data control. The changes are automatically committed to the database when the user moves to a different record, or exits the program.

QUIZ YOURSELF

1. You use the `AddNew` method to provisionally add a new record to a recordset, but what method actually saves the new record to the database? (See "Adding New Records".)

2. Are you required to execute the Edit command before you use the Delete command? (See "Deleting Records".)

3. If part of what you need to do in one procedure has already been coded in another procedure, what should you do? (See "Handling an Undo Request".)

4. Do you need to use the Update command to commit changes a user makes to existing records? (See "Editing Records".)

Creating and Searching Recordsets

Session Checklist

✔ Displaying all the records in a table

✔ How to search for a record

✔ Searching for a group of records

✔ Building a SQL query string

30 Min.
To Go

Two more buttons remain that need code from you before they can perform their jobs: Index and Search. These two features are similar: The Index button fills a ListBox will all the records in the tblCollection table. The Search button allows the user to specify a subset of the records.

Both of these features bring in a recordset — a set of records — from the database. The difference between the two is that the Index feature doesn't exclude any of the records, whereas a Search usually seeks only those records that match a pattern or otherwise satisfy a user's criterion.

Adding an Index Feature

You saw how to fill a ListBox with a table of records in Session 24, in the section "Programmatic Database Access". Doing the same thing using a Data control is quite similar. However, instead of creating Database and Recordset objects with code, as you did in Session 24, in this session you simply adjust the Data control's Recordset object.

To fill the ListBox (named lstIndex) with all of the records, use a Do...Loop structure. Where to put the loop, though? At first, you might think it's a good idea to put it into the Index button's Click event. But let's back off a minute and consider where it would be best to put this loop in our program.

Fill the ListBox only once

Once you get a couple hundred records typed into your database, there will be a noticeable delay each time you click the Index button. After users have filled their databases with data, usually they will use the PDM program simply to look up existing data (rather than adding or deleting records). Since the data in the database will not change most of the time this program is used, it would be inefficient to slavishly refill the Index ListBox every time the user asks to see it. The only time the PDM program needs to refill the ListBox is if the user has added or deleted a record.

A better solution is to fill the ListBox once (invisibly) when the program first starts up. Then, if the user clicks the Index button, the list will be instantly available. What if the user does add or delete a record? You can keep track of that by creating a variable with form-wide scope called IsDirty. Every time the user adds or deletes a record, you set IsDirty to True. But every time the user clicks the Index button (to see the Index ListBox), you set IsDirty to False. That way, the Index button will refill the ListBox only when a record has been added or deleted, and as a result, the table is different from the previous time the ListBox was displayed.

In the General Declarations section, type this:

```
Dim IsDirty As Boolean
```

Use Form_Initialize to contact the Data control

So, you might now think to put your Do...Loop into the Form_Load event. Unfortunately, Form_Load executes before the Data control is brought into existence, so you'll get an error message if you try to use it. Instead, put your loop into the Form_Initialize event.

When you refer to a component in your source code (like the Data control), if the form it's on has not yet been loaded, VB goes ahead and loads that form.

In the code below, when the line of code `lstIndex.AddItem Data1.Recordset.Fields("Title")` **is executed, the** `Form_Load` **event is triggered. At that point, the Data control becomes real —** *instantiated* **is the technical term for an object that has been brought into existence. You'll find out more about this concept in Session 30. For now, just note that you want to employ the Data control's services in the** `Initialize` **event rather than the** `Load` **event. If you try to put it in the** `Load` **event, you'll get a not-very-helpful error message that an "object variable or with block variable not set".**

The problem is that the Data control doesn't yet exist — but you're referring to it in your code. VB doesn't know what you're talking about. (One day, *all* error messages will be specific, explicit, and helpful. That day is in the future.)

However, do memorize this: The error message "object variable or with block variable not set" usually means an object has not yet been instantiated, or that you failed to add it to your project using Project ⇨ Components or Project ⇨ References.

```
Private Sub Form_Initialize()
Do Until Data1.Recordset.EOF = True
    lstIndex.AddItem Data1.Recordset.Fields("Title")
    Data1.Recordset.MoveNext
Loop
Data1.Recordset.MoveFirst
IsDirty = False
End Sub
```

Doubtless you remember the description of how this code works from Session 24, but notice that by the time the loop finishes, the MoveNext command has put you at the end of the recordset. So you use the MoveFirst command so the user sees the first record when the program starts.

Now add the following code (in boldface) to the cmdIndex button's existing code:

```
Private Sub cmdIndex_Click()

If IsDirty = True Then

lstIndex.Clear
```

```
Data1.Recordset.MoveFirst

    Do Until Data1.Recordset.EOF = True
        lstIndex.AddItem Data1.Recordset.Fields("Title")
        Data1.Recordset.MoveNext
    Loop

    IsDirty = False
End If

cmdExit.Caption = "&Click to Close List"
lstIndex.Visible = True
Data1.Enabled = False

End Sub
```

The new code cmdIndex (in boldface above) does two necessary things. First, you clear the ListBox so it's empty (and you don't just add more items to the existing ones). Then you move the Recordset to its first record (the pointer can be anywhere in the Recordset, depending on which record the user was viewing when they clicked the cmdIndex button).

And in the cmdAdd procedure, change this line:

```
Data1.Recordset.Update
```

to:

```
Data1.Recordset.Update: IsDirty = True
```

Finally, in the cmdDelete procedure, add the line in boldface following the line containing the MoveNext command:

```
Data1.Recordset.MoveNext
IsDirty = True
```

Now you've fixed it so IsDirty switches to True any time a record is deleted or added.

**20 Min.
To Go**

Searching for an Individual Record

It's nice that the user can see all of the records' titles in the Index ListBox, but it would be useful if they could click any title in the ListBox and instantly go to that record so that it's displayed in the two TextBoxes.

To do that, you must take the clicked Title and search the entire Recordset for a match. Remember that the Title fields are unique in each record — we ensure this when accepting a new record in the cmdAdd_Click() procedure by seeing if an error was triggered (If Err = 3022 Then). Therefore, because the Title fields are unique, the FindFirst method will locate the *only* match that exists in the entire recordset. We don't have to worry that there might be additional matches.

Type this into the lstIndex_Click event:

```
Private Sub lstIndex_Click()

Selected = lstIndex.List(lstIndex.ListIndex)

Target = "Title = '" & Selected & "'"    ' Set the criteria.

Data1.Recordset.FindFirst Target   ' Find first matching record.

End Sub
```

This code puts the Title they clicked in the lstIndex ListBox into the variable Selected. Then it uses that variable to create a variable named Target that (if the user clicks a title named *Indiana 1992*) contains this value: Title = 'Indiana 1992'

You can use the Recordset's FindFirst method to search the Recordset. To do that, create a string (text) variable (the variable Target in the code above). First, name the variable, followed by an = sign. Then, use single quotes around the actual data for which you're searching.

Then, just execute the FindFirst method, using the string variable. The record is located and automatically displayed in the two TextBoxes bound to the Data control, as shown in Figure 26-1. This figure shows how the PDM looks after you've added a lot of records to it — the ListBox is bulging with recipes in this example:

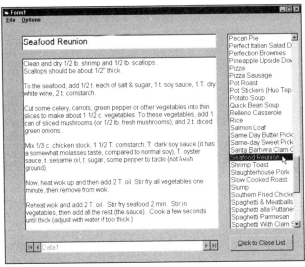

Figure 26-1
The user can click on any record in the Index ListBox to display that record immediately in the TextBoxes.

Searching for a Set of Records

If the user wants to see only those recipes that contain the words *Chinese* and *pork*, you want to permit them to get that list of titles. You want to let the user enter search criteria, and then you want to display a ListBox displaying all of the matches. The user can click any title in the list to see the full record, including the description. (The target words can appear anywhere in the title or description fields — but if the user enters two words, *both* words must appear for a match.)

The user can type in as many words as they wish, with each additional word narrowing the search and further limiting the number of matches. *Chinese* and *pork* likely result in more recipes in the returned recordset, for example, than *Chinese* and *pork* and *shrimp*. Technically, this is an *and* style search (as opposed to an *or* style with which a match of any of the words would add that record to the list).

The first part of this job is to get the user's input, and then parse it to see which word(s) they've typed in as their query. Then, you use those words to construct a formal query string. Finally, you go through Data1's recordset using the FindFirst and FindNext methods to locate each match.

This is industrial-strength programming, but don't be daunted. Type this new code (in boldface) into the `cmdSearch_Click` event:

```
Private Sub cmdSearch_Click()

If Data1.DatabaseName = "" Then Exit Sub

Dim targets(1 To 25) 'holds the users search words
Dim cnt As Integer ' holds the count of the search words

On Error Resume Next

response = InputBox _
("Please enter one or more search words, separated by spaces...")

If response = "" Then Exit Sub

'parse the words
l = Len(response)

For i = 1 To l
    p = InStr(i, response, " ")
        If p = 0 Then Exit For 'no space found
            tem = Mid(response, i, p - i): cnt = cnt + 1
            If cnt > 5 Then GoTo Toomuch
            targets(cnt) = tem

    i = p 'set the counter forward
Next i

tem = Mid(response, i, l - p): cnt = cnt + 1 ' final word
targets(cnt) = tem

Toomuch:
If cnt > 5 Then 'too many
    MsgBox ("If you have more than five search criteria, the
search becomes too narrow.  Please use fewer search words."), 48,
"WARNING"
    Exit Sub
End If
```

```
'construct query string:

For i = 1 To cnt
If quer <> "" Then quer = quer & " AND "
quer = quer & "[Description] Like '*" + targets(i) + "*'"
Next i

If quer <> "" Then


quer = "(" & quer & ")" & " OR"


End If

'define second query
For i = 1 To cnt
If quer1 <> "" Then quer1 = quer1 & " AND "
quer1 = quer1 & "[Title] Like '*" + targets(i) + "*'"
Next i

If quer1 <> "" Then
quer1 = " (" & quer1 & ")"
End If

quer = quer & quer1

lstSearch.Clear


'now run the search

Data1.Recordset.FindFirst quer      'Find first matching record.


Do Until Data1.Recordset.NoMatch
    d = Data1.Recordset.Fields(0).Value
    lstSearch.AddItem d
    Data1.Recordset.FindNext quer
Loop
```

```
cmdExit.Caption = "&Click to Close List"
lstSearch.Visible = True
Data1.Enabled = False
End Sub
```

**10 Min.
To Go**

Understanding the code

The first line in the above code tests to see if the Data control is in fact connected to a database. It's possible that the user clicked the Close option on the File menu (this code will be added in Session 27), and there is no currently active database. In that case, we Exit Sub, which means that no further lines of code in this sub are executed — we just jump right out of the procedure entirely.

In the For...Next loop that begins with For i = 1 To 1, you pick apart the user's text, looking repeatedly for a space character, until you've isolated all of the words he or she typed. Each word is placed separately into the Targets() array. The variable cnt keeps track of just how many words the user typed. If the user types in more than five, the search is deemed too narrow, and the user must start again.

You search a recordset using a query string. There's a whole language, SQL, that offers many ways to define querys. It's beyond the scope of this book to explore SQL, but we'll look at the query we develop here. It's a typical query, and you can use it in your own programming for many kinds of searches.

We define two query strings, and then join them together into one big query string using the & operator. Here's how we build the first query that works on the Description field:

```
For i = 1 To cnt
If quer <> "" Then quer = quer & " AND "
quer = quer & "[Description] Like '*" & targets(i) & "*'"
Next i
```

This code adds each word in the targets() array to a query string. Each word is described like this: [Description] Like '*word*' AND, which means look in the Description field for the word. The word is surrounded with * characters *, which means it can be embedded. For example, if the user entered *son*, it would match if the word *reasonable* is anywhere in the Description field of any of the records. Each search word is joined to the next by the AND. Here's an example: Say that the user entered *Arena Sand Lion* as the search terms. The code above would process these words into this formal SQL query:

Part V–Sunday Morning
Session 26

[Description] Like '*Arena*' AND [Description] Like '*Sand*' AND [Description] Like '*Lion*'

Then we add an OR to the end of the first query so we'll get a hit if either the Description field *or* the Title field contains the search words.

Next, the same process is repeated, only this time it builds the query string for the Title field. Then the two query strings, joined by the OR, are concatenated: quer = quer & quer1.

Finally, the FindFirst and FindNext commands are used to locate any records that match the query criteria.

Notice the If cnt > 5 Then GoTo Toomuch. **This line means that if the** cnt **variable grows larger than 5, the execution should *jump* over (not execute) any following lines of code until it comes upon the "line label"** Toomuch:. **A line label can be any word (other than words already used as the names of variables or procedures, or by VB's set of commands, such as** Print **or** End**). The line label must be on a line all by itself, and must end with a colon (:). The line label is a place marker. It says, pick up execution following this line label.**

Responding to a ListBox selection

All that remains for you to do now is to make it possible for the user to click one of the items in the Search ListBox, and then have that record displayed in the TextBox. The following code is precisely the same as what you put into the Index ListBox's Click event, with the exception that the name lstSearch is now used instead of lstIndex:

Done!

```
Private Sub lstSearch_Click()
Selected = lstSearch.List(lstSearch.ListIndex)
Target = "Title = '" & Selected & "'"    ' Set the criteria.
Data1.Recordset.FindFirst Target   ' Find first matching record.
End Sub
```

REVIEW

This session contains the most challenging programming example you've yet encountered in this book. True, it started out less formidably with a simple bit of code that uses the `MoveFirst` and `MoveNext` methods to fill a ListBox with every record in a recordset. Then you learned how to use the `FindFirst` method to locate a single record in a recordset. Finally, you explored the complicated code that takes apart a string input by the user, and then builds those individual words into a complex query string. You used that string to then find each record in a recordset that matches the user's words.

QUIZ YOURSELF

1. Why fill a ListBox only once, rather than refill it each time a user chooses to see a whole recordset? (See "Fill the ListBox Only Once".)

2. When should you use the `Form_Initialize` event rather than the `Form_Load` event? (See "Use Form_Initialize to contact the Data Control".)

3. How are single quotation marks used when building a query string? (See "Searching for an Individual Record".)

4. What is the difference between the AND and OR commands in a SQL query? (See "Searching for a Set of Records".)

5. What is a line label and when is it used? (See "Searching for a Set of Records".)

PART

V

Sunday Morning

1. What do the acronyms SDI and MDI mean?

2. Which style of application is now becoming unfashionable, SDI or MDI?

3. Define the terms *record* and *field* when used with database programming.

4. Define the term *table* when used with database programming.

5. What is an *index* in a database?

6. If you plan to size and position components during run time, what is an advantage of putting the code that does this into the Form_Load event?

7. How do you define shortcut keys for your components, which will the user press Alt+ShorcutKey to activate that component?

8. What is the purpose of the TabIndex property?

9. What makes the Memo data type different from all other data types?

10. What does DAO mean and what does it offer a programmer?

11. When you define a new field in a database, what does "Allow Zero Length" mean?

12. What is VisData?

13. What does the DataSource property do?

14. What does EOF mean?

15. Which is a better command to use — Write # or Print # — when saving the contents of a TextBox to a disk file, and why?

16. The AddNew method provisionally adds a new record to a recordset, but what method actually saves the new record to the database file on the hard drive?

17. Is it necessary to use the Update command to commit changes a user makes to existing records in a database?

18. When should you use the Form_Initialize event instead of the Form_Load event?

19. In an SQL query, what is the difference between the AND and OR commands?

20. What does the following line of code do?

```
Toomuch:
```

PART

VI

Sunday Afternoon

Letting the User Customize an Application

Session Checklist

✔ Adding a feature to open new databases

✔ How to close a database

✔ Saving a recordset

✔ Printing the current record

✔ Saving user preferences to the Registry

✔ Restoring user preferences

**30 Min.
To Go**

In previous sessions, you wrote the code to make all of the buttons in the PDM application do their duty. The buttons work well. Now it's time to finish the application by providing code for the menu items.

The File menu we added in Session 22 offers these features: New, Open, Close, Save, and Print. The Options menu includes Automatic Backup, BackColor, and Font choices. When writing the code that provides these features to the user, you'll benefit quite a bit by using the CommonDialog component.

Switching to a Different Database

The CommonDialog should be on your Toolbox (and its icon should be on your form) because we used it when we added the necessary code for the mnuNew menu item in Session 23.

Now it's time to provide the code for the mnuOpen_Click event. This feature opens a previously created .MDB database file. Type the following code into the mnuOpen_Click event:

```
Private Sub mnuOpen_Click()

CommonDialog1.CancelError = True 'detect Cancel button

On Error Resume Next
CommonDialog1.ShowOpen    ' display the Save dialog
If Err = 32755 Then Exit Sub 'they clicked this Cancel button

'close current connection to previous database

Data1.DatabaseName = CommonDialog1.FileName

Data1.Refresh

Form_Initialize

End Sub
```

This code is fairly straightforward. You display the Open dialog box to the user and then set the Data control's DatabaseName property to the path of the .MDB file that the user chose. The key to making this code work is the Refresh command. If you change databases, you must use Refresh to disconnect the previous database and connect the new one. Finally, you want to use the same loop you used in the Form_Initialize event to fill the Index ListBox. So you simply call the Form_Initialize event procedure.

(Note that the Data control's RecordSource property is already set to the name of the table: tblCollection. This is done during design time and cannot be changed by the user. We're hard-wiring this because every database created or viewed with the PDM always has the same internal structure: a tlbCollection table and its two fields — Title and Description.)

Closing the Current Database

You also offer the user the option of closing the currently opened database. Essentially, this merely means setting the Data control's `DatabaseName` property to nothing (""), using the `Refresh` method to disconnect from the currently open database, then clearing each TextBox by setting its Text value to "" and using the `Clear` method to empty the Index ListBox. To do these things, type the following code into the `mnuClose_Click` event:

```
Private Sub mnuClose_Click()
On Error Resume Next

Data1.DatabaseName = ""
Data1.Refresh
txtTitle = ""
txtDesc = ""
lstIndex.Clear

End Sub
```

Saving the Database

This File menu option allows the user to explicitly force the current recordset to be committed to the disk file. When you use a Data control, there's really no reason to have a Save feature. Each time the user moves to a new record — and there are many ways in this application that the user moves to a new record (editing, viewing, deleting, and so on) — the previous record is committed to the database. Likewise, if the program is shut down, or if the New or Open menu items are used, any changes to any records are saved.

However, if someone is typing in a huge Description field and is afraid a power failure might cause their work to be lost, he or she might feel the need to explicitly force the current work to the disk. Type the following code into the `mnuSave_Click()` event to allow this:

```
Private Sub mnuSave_Click()
    On Error Resume Next
    Data1.Recordset.Edit
    Data1.Recordset.Update
End Sub
```

Printing the Current Record

This simple routine merely prints the current record to the printer. To print an entire recordset, you'll need to take a more complicated approach. A printed recordset, or group of recordsets, is known in database lingo as a *report*. (If you're interested in printing reports, you might want to check out VB's DataReport Designer — choose Project ⇨ Components, and then click the Designers tab on the dialog box and select Data Report. Press F1 to get assistance in using it.)

However, the following code enables the user to simply print the currently displayed record:

```
Private Sub mnuPrint_Click()

If txtTitle = "" Then Exit Sub

Printer.Print
Printer.Print txtTitle
Printer.Print
Printer.Print
Printer.Print txtDesc

End Sub
```

If there is no currently displayed record, don't do anything. The `Printer.Print` command prints a carriage return by itself (moves down one line on the page).

By the way, if you want to make the title boldface and center it, here's code that does it:

```
Printer.FontBold = True
sx = Printer.ScaleWidth / 2
tx = Printer.TextWidth(txtTitle) / 2
Printer.CurrentX = sx - tx
Printer.Print txtTitle
Printer.Print
Printer.FontBold = 0
```

You used the `ScaleWidth` command in a previous session to find out the interior width of the form (less its frame). You can use the same command to get the measurement of the paper in the printer by merely querying the `ScaleWidth` property of the `Printer` object, as we do in this line: `sx = Printer.ScaleWidth / 2`. The variable `sx` now holds the value of the precise midpoint of the paper. The

`TextWidth` command tells you the measure of a string variable (at the current font settings). So the variable `tx` is given the value of the precise middle of the text in the Title TextBox when it gets printed. (If you want to find out the width of text onscreen, just omit the reference to the `Printer` object.) Finally, use the `CurrentX` property to position the "insertion cursor" a little to the left of center, which has the effect of precisely centering the title on the paper. The Printer object's `CurrentX` property defines where, *horizontally*, the next printing or drawing will take place on the paper in the printer. There is a comparable `CurrentY` property that can move the insertion point vertically.

Preserving Options

**20 Min.
To Go**

If you let the user customize your application, you also have to save those customizations and then reload them each time the user starts your application running. If the user changes the `BackColor` of the form to bright blue, they expect it to be bright blue the next time they run the application.

Preferences used to be saved in an .INI file, but that approach has been abandoned in favor of storing customizations in the Windows Registry (a huge database maintained by the operating system).

Visual Basic has several commands you can use to access the Registry, including the `SaveSetting` and `GetSetting` functions. You'll see how to use them in the following example.

Allowing the User to Choose Color

To save a user's color preference to the Registry, type the following code into the `mnuBackcolor_Click()` event:

```
Private Sub mnuBackcolor_Click()

CommonDialog1.CancelError = True 'detect Cancel button

On Error Resume Next
CommonDialog1.ShowColor
If Err = 32755 Then Exit Sub 'they clicked this Cancel button

Form1.BackColor = CommonDialog1.Color
```

```
'now save to the registry:

SaveSetting appname:="PDM", section:="UserPrefs", _
    Key:="BackColor", setting:=Form1.BackColor
End Sub
```

After the color dialog box is displayed to the user, the form's `BackColor` is changed to his or her selection. Then the `SaveSetting` function is used to store the color in the Registry. If this is the first time you've used `SaveSetting` for this PDM entry, the keys and fields will be created *automatically* for you in the Registry. If they already exist, the value will simply be stored in the *setting:* field. This makes accessing the Registry from within Visual Basic quite easy.

Later in this session (after we've finished with the other customization options), we'll add the following line to the `Form_Initialize` event so the color preference is retrieved when the application starts running:

```
colr = GetSetting _
(appname:="PDM", section:="UserPrefs", Key:="BackColor")
```

As you can see in Figure 27-1, the PDM Registry entry is ready to be queried by the `GetSetting` function or modified by the `SaveSetting` function:

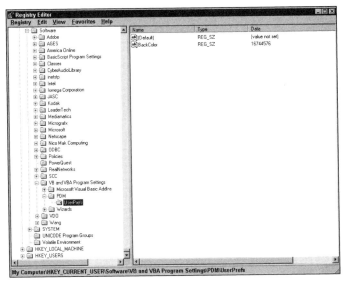

Figure 27-1
Here is the preferences section in the Registry, ready to accept new data or report the current backcolor preference.

Choosing Automatic Backup

Some users like the security of knowing that their work is being regularly saved to disk. To allow them to do this, first create a form-wide variable named AutoBack. It will hold the user's choice of backup intervals (in minutes), and because its scope is form-wide, it can be set in the mnuAutomatic menu event, and accessed by the Timer that does the backing up.

Create the AutoBack variable by typing the following code into the General Declarations section of the form:

```
Dim AutoBack As Integer 'minutes for automatic backup interval
```

Then type this into the mnuAutomatic_Click( ) event:

```
Private Sub mnuAutomatic_Click()

response = InputBox("You can specify how often, in minutes, you
want your database saved to disk automatically. Currently, it is
set to " & AutoBack)

If response = "" Then Exit Sub

AutoBack = response

SaveSetting appname:="PDM", section:="UserPrefs", _
Key:="AutoBack", setting:=AutoBack

If AutoBack <> 0 Then _
Timer1.Interval = 60000 'set it to one minute

End Sub
```

In the above code, you ask users to specify the backup interval; if they don't press the Cancel button, you save their chosen interval to the Registry. Finally, you start the Timer if they have chosen an interval. The AutoBack variable tells the Timer how many times it should execute (this timer has a one-minute interval because you set it to 60,000 milliseconds).

Now put a Timer component onto your form, and then type this code into the Timer's Timer event:

```
Private Sub Timer1_Timer()

Static switch As Boolean
Static counter As Integer

If switch = False Then 'first time into this procedure
switch = True
counter = AutoBack 'set counter
End If

If switch = True Then
    counter = counter - 1
        If counter = 0 Then 'reset and save
            switch = False
            mnuSave_Click 'save the recordset
        End If
End If

End Sub
```

Using variables inside a Timer can be a bit tricky because the Timer keeps executing (at its interval). So, we cannot simply assign the value in AutoBack to a variable and then use that variable to count down each minute until we get past the final minute (minute zero) and perform our backup.

The reason we cannot simply assign the value in AutoBack to counter is that the same value would be *reassigned* each time this event triggers. Therefore, the counter variable would never reach zero. It would keep being reset to the number of minutes the user wants as the backup interval (this value is held in the AutoBack variable). See the problem?

To solve this, we use a second variable, switch. It goes between True and False (starting out False). So, the first time the event is executed, switch is set to True, and the value in AutoBack is assigned to the variable counter. Thereafter, as long as switch remains True, the counter variable is decremented and tested for zero. Once it reaches zero, switch is toggled back to False, and the mnuSave_Click procedure is called (it saves the current recordset).

Permitting the User to Adjust the Fonts

The code that lets the user choose new font properties is quite a bit longer than the other option procedures we've worked on in this session. There are two reasons for this:

1. We're dealing with two separate font selections: one for the Title TextBox and the other for the Description TextBox.

2. Multiple properties can be changed. We've offered the user the ability to change three font properties: Name, Size, and Bold. We will ignore Italic, StrikeThrough, Color, and Underline.

Type the following code into the mnuFonts_Click() event:

```
Private Sub mnuFonts_Click()

CommonDialog1.CancelError = True 'detect Cancel button

On Error Resume Next

MsgBox "Please first choose the font for the Title field..."

CommonDialog1.Flags = cdlCFScreenFonts

CommonDialog1.FontName = txtTitle.Font.Name
CommonDialog1.FontSize = txtTitle.Font.Size
CommonDialog1.FontBold = txtTitle.Font.Bold

CommonDialog1.ShowFont
If Err = 32755 Then Exit Sub 'they clicked this Cancel button

txtTitle.Font.Name = CommonDialog1.FontName
txtTitle.Font.Size = CommonDialog1.FontSize
txtTitle.Font.Bold = CommonDialog1.FontBold


SaveSetting appname:="PDM", section:="UserPrefs",
Key:="TitleFontName", setting:=CommonDialog1.FontName
SaveSetting appname:="PDM", section:="UserPrefs",
Key:="TitleFontSize", setting:=CommonDialog1.FontSize
```

```
SaveSetting appname:="PDM", section:="UserPrefs",
Key:="TitleFontBold", setting:=CommonDialog1.FontBold


MsgBox "Now choose the font for the Description field..."

CommonDialog1.Flags = cdlCFScreenFonts

CommonDialog1.FontName = txtDesc.Font.Name
CommonDialog1.FontSize = txtDesc.Font.Size
CommonDialog1.FontBold = txtDesc.Font.Bold

CommonDialog1.ShowFont
If Err = 32755 Then Exit Sub 'they clicked this Cancel button

txtDesc.Font.Name = CommonDialog1.FontName
txtDesc.Font.Size = CommonDialog1.FontSize
txtDesc.Font.Bold = CommonDialog1.FontBold


SaveSetting appname:="PDM", section:="UserPrefs",
Key:="DescFontName", setting:=CommonDialog1.FontName
SaveSetting appname:="PDM", section:="UserPrefs",
Key:="DescFontSize", setting:=CommonDialog1.FontSize
SaveSetting appname:="PDM", section:="UserPrefs",
Key:="DescFontBold", setting:=CommonDialog1.FontBold
End Sub
```

First you tell the user they're choosing the Title font, and then (remember?) you must set the `Flags` property before you use the `ShowFont` command (`CommonDialog1.Flags` = `cdlCFScreenFonts`). Next, you set the three CommonDialog properties so they reflect the current font settings for the Title TextBox. This way, when the dialog box opens, the user sees the name, style, and size of the font currently in use. Finally, you display the Fonts dialog box to the user. After they make their selections, you set the Title TextBox's font properties to the user's choices, and then save those choices to the Registry. The whole process is then repeated for the Description TextBox.

Getting Preferences from the Registry

To load the user's preferences from the Registry into your application, you must make the following changes (in boldface) to the Form_Initialize event:

```
Private Sub Form_Initialize()
On Error Resume Next

Do Until Data1.Recordset.EOF = True
    lstIndex.AddItem Data1.Recordset.Fields("Title")
    Data1.Recordset.MoveNext
Loop

Data1.Recordset.MoveFirst

colr = GetSetting(appname:="PDM", section:="UserPrefs",
Key:="BackColor")
If colr <> "" Then
Form1.BackColor = colr
End If

N = GetSetting(appname:="PDM", section:="UserPrefs",
Key:="AutoBack")
If N <> Null then AutoBack = N

If AutoBack <> 0 Then
Timer1.Interval = 60000
End If


n = GetSetting(appname:="PDM", section:="UserPrefs",
Key:="TitleFontName")
If n <> "" Then

txtTitle.Font.Name = n
txtTitle.Font.Size = GetSetting(appname:="PDM",
section:="UserPrefs", Key:="TitleFontSize")
txtTitle.Font.Bold = GetSetting(appname:="PDM",
section:="UserPrefs", Key:="TitleFontBold")
```

```
End If


n = GetSetting(appname:="PDM", section:="UserPrefs",
Key:="DescFontName")
If n <> "" Then

txtDesc.Font.Name = n
txtDesc.Font.Size = GetSetting _
(appname:="PDM", section:="UserPrefs", Key:="DescFontSize")
txtDesc.Font.Bold = GetSetting _
(appname:="PDM", section:="UserPrefs", Key:="DescFontBold")

End If

End Sub
```

Following each use of the GetSetting function, you check to see if the user
has stored a preference (if the variable colr, for example, isn't empty (""), that
means the GetSetting function returned a color value). So, if the variable does
contain a value, you use that to restore the user's backcolor, backup interval, or
font preferences.

Extending and Enhancing the Application

You can, of course, continue to refine this application. Here are some ideas.
Perhaps you want to improve the error trapping by adding On Error Resume Next
to more procedures, and providing more elaborate error messages. You might want
to expand the offerings on the Options menu to include password protection (so
nobody but you can get into your database unless they know the secret word). A
simple InputBox can be used to request the password. Or perhaps you want to add
a wallpaper feature so the user can specify a background for the form (see the
LoadPicture command); allow the user to specify font settings for the Printer
object (Printer.FontSize, for example); display the current record's position
in the database in the form's title bar (Form1.Caption = Data1.Recordset.
AbsolutePosition + 1); or display the total number of records in the database

(Data1.Recordset.MoveLast: Form1.Caption = Data1.Recordset.
RecordCount). You have to use the MoveLast method to get an accurate count.

One final point. During design time (in the Properties Window), you set the
DatabaseName property for the Data control to point to a particular .MDB file
(C:\PDM\PDM.mdb). This is what programmers call *hard-coding* or *hard-wiring*
the path to a specific file.

This approach is uncommon and generally frowned upon by programming theo-
rists. What if your word processor was hard-wired to always load the same .DOC file
every time you started the word processor running? Pretty inefficient.

The advantage, though, of this hard-wiring is that when you fire up the PDM
application, you don't have to face the tedious job of accessing File ⇨ Open to
locate the particular .MDB database file you want to work with. Also, if you only
work with that one database all the time, you'll enjoy not having to choose it each
time. (You might want to make this hard-wiring an option the user can select on
your Options menu. Save the last-used .MDB file into the Registry and automatically load it. In this case, you don't hard-wire it during design time; you just permit the most recently used .MDB file to be the one that's automatically loaded at
startup.)

It's up to you if you want to avoid assigning the DatabaseName property during
design time. If you *do* choose to omit that property, you must make the following
change (in boldface) to the Form_Initialize event:

```
Private Sub Form_Initialize()
On Error Resume Next

Do Until Data1.Recordset.EOF = True
If Err = 91 Then Exit Sub
    lstIndex.AddItem Data1.Recordset.Fields("Title")
    Data1.Recordset.MoveNext
Loop
```

Without this new line of code, your program will go into the dreaded *endless
loop* state: This Do...Loop will never end because there is no recordset for Data1
(Data1 is not connected to a database, thus no recordset). In this sad situation,
the End of File (EOF) test can never become True because the recordset is just
not there!

Error number 91 represents that notoriously misleading "Object variable or with
block variable not set" error message that we decried in Session 26.

Done!

REVIEW

In this session, you finished programming the Personal Database Manager — an application I hope you'll enjoy using and polishing. You saw how to Open, Close, and Save a database. You also saw how to store user preferences to the Windows Registry so they can be retrieved the next time the user runs the application.

QUIZ YOURSELF

1. When you change the DatabaseName property of a Data control, what method must you also use to actually force the control to connect to the new database? (See "Switching to a Different Database".)

2. What are three commands or user behaviors that cause a Data control's recordset to be saved to disk? (See "Saving the Database".)

3. The Printer.Print command causes what to happen on the paper in the printer? (See "Printing the Current Record".)

4. How would you describe the Windows Registry, and when should you use it? (See "Preserving Options".)

5. What command can you use to access information stored in the Registry? (See "Getting Preferences from the Registry".)

Off to See the Wizard

Session Checklist

✔ Turning your application into an executable Windows program

✔ Understanding how to deploy a project

✔ Using the Package and Deployment Wizard

**30 Min.
To Go**

V B boasts many wizards — question-and-answer dialog boxes that step you through the process of accomplishing some goal. In this session, we'll look at one of the best wizards, the Package and Deployment Wizard.

Compiling an Application

In Session 27, you finished your marvelous Personal Data Manager application. However, you don't want to merely run it from within the VB design environment — you want to make it into a normal Windows executable (.EXE) file so you can run it independently of the VB IDE. In other words, when you're happy with the application and consider it ready to send into the world, you must transform your source code into an actual Windows program.

Not surprisingly, there's a Make Exe option on the VB File menu. The process of transforming source code into an executable file is called *compilation*. So that's what you will do, compile your project.

To see how to create an executable version of your PDM application, load it into VB and then choose File ⇨ Make Project1.exe. A disk browser dialog box appears, as shown in Figure 28-1.

Figure 28-1
Choose where you want to save your new .EXE file.

Browse your hard drive until you find the PDM folder. Then change the name from Project1 (as shown in Figure 28-1) to PDM.EXE in the Filename TextBox. Then click OK. The dialog box closes, the hard drive whirls, and, in a few seconds, the deed is done. You now have a PDM.EXE file in your PDM folder. At this point, you can shut down VB if you wish — it's no longer needed to run your PDM application.

Run Windows Explorer and double-click PDM.EXE, and you'll see that your source code has indeed been transformed into a regular Windows program such as Word or Flight Simulator. You can create a shortcut to it and put it on your Desktop or your Start menu. The VB IDE is no longer needed to run this program. Happy day.

Deploying Your Application

It's fine to compile your application into an .EXE file on your hard drive, but what if you want to give it to other people to use: sell it, pass it around to grateful coworkers, or make it available on the Internet? Publishing your application — making it available to others — is called *deployment*.

Deploying one of your applications involves more than the mere compilation of the source code. Compilation works fine on your machine — you can double-click your compiled .EXE file, and it will run just fine. However, it might not run at all on somebody else's machine.

You see, there can be a problem when your application is loaded onto someone else's hard drive. You cannot assume that a user has the necessary *dependencies*. Dependencies are files that your application needs in order to run: things like components (such as the CommonDialog component) or .DLLs (dynamic link libraries) that are in *your* hard drive, but may be missing from the user's hard drive.

For one thing, VB itself stores many of its built-in functions (like `InStr` or `MsgBox`) in a huge file called the VB run-time library. What if the user doesn't own the VB language and doesn't have this necessary library? No VB program can run without it.

The solution is that you must use VB's Package and Deployment Wizard to bundle a set of files — along with a SETUP.EXE file that installs them on a user's machine. The package will contain PDM.EXE, plus all components and libraries that PDM.EXE requires.

If you're distributing your application via CD or diskette(s), all dependencies will be bundled and stored on the medium of your choice. If you're deploying your application over the Internet (or a company intranet, for that matter), the user's hard drive will be checked first to see if they already have the latest version of each dependency file. If they do, that file will not be downloaded to them. You know how slow Internet downloads can be — no sense sending users stuff they've already got.

**20 Min.
To Go**

Using the Package and Deployment Wizard

The new VB 6 Package and Deployment Wizard is an improvement over VB's previous setup utilities. The Wizard has a variety of new features, including the ability to create compressed .CAB files that can be downloaded by a visitor to your Web site. After the download, the set of files is checked for tampering; any libraries or components are registered; and then your VB program does its job right there in the user's browser.

In addition to packaging a VB project for Internet deployment, the Wizard can also create packages for deployment on other media: CDs, floppy disks, a workstation, or server hard drive.

To learn how to use the Package and Deployment Wizard, let's create a deployment package for the PDM application you built over the previous several sections. Follow these steps:

1. Load the PDM project into VB's IDE.
2. Select Add-Ins ⇨ Add-In Manager.
3. Double-click Package and Deployment Wizard to load it.

4. Click the OK button to close the dialog box (the Wizard is now listed as an option on the Add-Ins menu).

5. Select Add-Ins ⇨ Package and Deployment Wizard.

6. The Wizard's first screen appears, as shown in Figure 28-2.

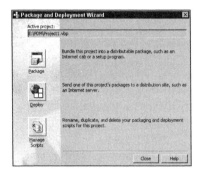

Figure 28-2
On this page, you choose whether you want to create a distributable package, deploy an existing package to a server, or modify scripts you saved from previous sessions.

7. Click the top icon titled Package. If you've made improvements to the source code (or design) of your application since it was last compiled, you'll see the dialog box shown in Figure 28-3.

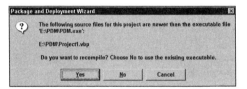

Figure 28-3
The Wizard kindly asks if you want to use the latest version of your project.

8. Choose Standard Setup Package, and then click Next.

9. If your project hasn't been compiled, click Yes. The Wizard then compiles your project and continues to search for dependencies and to create a provisional package.

10. You're now asked if you want to actually create a setup package, or to merely create a list of dependencies.

11. Select Standard Setup Package and click Next.

12. At this point, you see a page where you define the location where the Setup Package should be saved.

13. Click the New Folder button, shown in Figure 28-4.

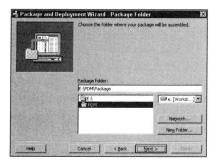

Figure 28-4
You can save your Setup Package to your own hard drive or to a network location.

14. The new folder will be created as a subfolder under the current directory. Name the new folder *Setup*, and you'll later be able to find the results of the Wizard's efforts in the \PDM\Setup folder.

15. Click the OK button to close the dialog box, and then click the Next button on the Wizard.

16. You're now shown a list of drivers, as you can see in Figure 28-5.

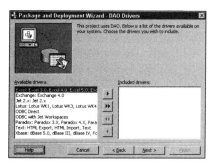

Figure 28-5
Add any necessary specialized drivers with this page in the Wizard.

You used Project ⇨ References to add Microsoft's DAO (database language) feature to the PDM application. At this point, you must decide if you want any specialized DAO drivers included in your setup package (in case a user doesn't have the necessary

DAO support). However, your project is not expected to work with Excel, Paradox, or the other features listed, so you can ignore these drivers. The ordinary DAO support libraries *will* be added to your package, as you'll see in step 19 below.

17. Click Next. *If* there are any files the Wizard plans to include that do not describe *their* dependencies, you're told about them at this time, as you can see in Figure 28-6. (You may not see Figure 28-6; it is shown only if a file, or files, doesn't explicitly list its dependencies.)

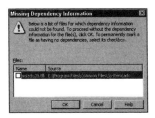

Figure 28-6
You're warned that this file doesn't identify its own dependencies. Click the checkbox if you don't want to see this warning in the future.

Dependencies can, in turn, have their own dependencies. Newer files contain data about any dependencies, but older files might not.

18. Click OK to close the Missing Dependency Information dialog box.

19. You now see the list of dependencies that the Wizard intends to bundle into your Setup Package, as shown in Figure 28-7.

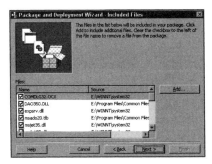

Figure 28-7
You used the CommonDialog component, so its support file will be included in the Setup Package — along with various other dependency files.

A total of approximately 18 files will be included in the Setup Package, including PDM.EXE; various setup and uninstall files; support libraries for DAO and components; and the general VB6 run-time library. The package isn't going to be small.

Note that in the dialog box shown in Figure 28-7 you can add or remove any dependencies. If you're positive that a coworker, for example, already has the latest versions of some of these files, go ahead and deselect them to reduce the size of the Setup Package. But in general, you can trust that the Wizard knows which dependencies are required to run your application — just leave them as is.

20. Now click Next. You're asked if you want to build one huge setup file, or if you want multiple smaller files that can fit on floppy diskettes.

21. Select the Single cab option button and click Next.

22. Change the Installation Title from *Project1* to *Personal Data Manager*. Then click Next.

23. You now see a dialog box asking how you want your project displayed on the user's Start menu. Leave the Wizard's default choice as is and click Next.

24. Now you have the opportunity to change where certain files will be saved on the user's system. Ignore this option and click Next.

25. Finally, you have the option of permitting your application to be used by more than one file. However, the PDM isn't an ActiveX component; it's a standard EXE Windows application. So you can ignore the sharing issue. (You *can* build components in VB that can be used by applications or browsers just the way a TextBox is used by VB projects. You'll see how to use a special Wizard to do just that in Session 29.)

26. Click Next. You're asked to name the settings (script) that you chose for this session with the Wizard. If you're creating many similar setup packages, the scripting feature is useful. However, you can just click Finish and let the Wizard build the package.

    A brief report tells you how to manually adjust a batch file if you make some changes to your project. Ignore this — it's better to start the Wizard all over again. The Wizard doesn't take that long to do its job (and you can even use the script the next time).

Done!

You're now back where you started — the Wizard's first screen. Click Close and use Windows Explorer to take a look at the \PDM\Setup folder. Look in \PDM\Setup\ Support to see all of the files used to install your PDM application. Try running \PDM\Setup\Setup.exe. You'll see the results shown in Figure 28-8.

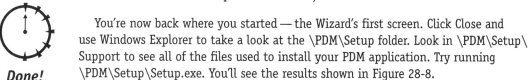

Part VI—Sunday Afternoon
Session 28

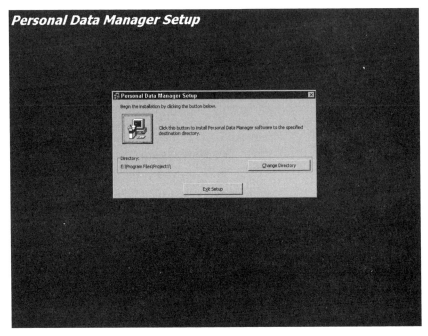

Figure 28-8
Your project installs just like any other professional Windows application.

REVIEW

After you finish creating a Windows application in VB, you want to turn it into an official, executable program so it can be run outside the VB editor — you want it to become a normal Windows .EXE program. In this session, you saw how to compile a project from source code into an executable application. Then you learned that the Package and Deployment Wizard can bundle your project together with all of its dependency files. You learned that there are several ways to bundle: for the Internet, a destination on a network, a CD, or a set of diskettes. Finally, you stepped through the process of creating a typical Windows Setup utility for the PDM application and all of its dependencies.

QUIZ YOURSELF

1. The word *compilation* means what? (See "Compiling an Application".)

2. When would you choose to create a compressed .CAB file? (See "Using the Package and Deployment Wizard".)

3. What is a script in the Package and Deployment Wizard? (See "Using the Package and Deployment Wizard".)

4. What are *dependencies*? (See "Using the Package and Deployment Wizard".)

5. When should you worry about whether or not your project can be *shared*? (See "Using the Package and Deployment Wizard".)

Internet Conversion

Session Checklist

✔ How to transform a standard Windows utility into a component

✔ Seeing your ActiveX component run in the browser

✔ Understanding how to make your component downloadable

✔ Providing database access on an Internet or intranet site

**30 Min.
To Go**

How hard do you think it would be to translate a standard Windows program you wrote so that it would run within a browser?

You guessed right! With VB, it's not hard at all. There's a Wizard that pretty much does the work for you. In this session, you'll write a traditional little Windows utility that converts between British pounds and American dollars. Then you'll see how to offer that same utility to the entire online world by putting it into an Internet Web page. Going from Windows to browser was never supposed to be this easy.

The techniques described in this chapter are most useful for smaller Web sites or intranets. If you are attempting to set up a large, sophisticated Web site, or if you require serious scalability or security, look into other techniques such as IIS Applications or ASP.

Creating a Windows Utility

To create the currency converter utility, choose File ⇨ New Project and double-click the Standard EXE icon. Put one TextBox, one Label, and two CommandButtons on the form. Using the Properties Window, change Command1's Caption property to "Covert into Dollars" and change Command2's Caption property to "Covert into Pounds". Delete the TextBox's Text property. Adjust the components' font properties to suit yourself.

Then change the Label's Caption property so it reads: "Type in a cash amount here, then click the appropriate button to convert it...". Your project should now look like Figure 29-1.

Figure 29-1
This simple currency converter will later be added to a Web page.

Now program the code. Double-click Command1 and type the following into the Command1_Click event:

```
Private Sub Command1_Click()
'convert pounds to dollars
pounds = Text1
answer = pounds * 1.65
```

```
Text1 = pounds & " Pounds equals $" & answer

End Sub
```

Put this code into the `Command2_Click` event:

```
Private Sub Command2_Click()
'convert dollars to pounds
dollars = Text1
answer = dollars * 0.6055

Text1 = "$" & dollars & " equals " & answer & " Pounds"

End Sub
```

Use Windows Explorer to create a new folder named *Converter* on your hard drive. Choose File ⇨ Save As to save your project and form into the Converter folder.

20 Min. To Go

Using the ActiveX Document Migration Wizard

VB's ActiveX Document Migration wizard is the fastest way to transform an ordinary traditional Windows application into a browser-ready object. An ActiveX document is similar to the components you've been working with on VB's Toolbox — Labels, CommandButtons, and all the rest. Simply put (very simply put), these objects are self-contained little programs (often including a user interface) that *can be dropped into other "container" programs.*

In this example, we'll translate the Converter utility into an object that can be dropped into a Web page. To change the Converter from an executable Windows program into an object, follow these steps:

1. With the Converter you created earlier in this session already loaded into the VB editor, choose Add-Ins ⇨ Add-In Manager.
2. Double-click VB 6 ActiveX Document Migration Wizard to select it, and then click the OK button to close the dialog box.
3. Select Add-Ins ⇨ ActiveX Document Migration Wizard.

4. Click Next to get past the opening screen, and then click the CheckBox next to Form1, which indicates that this is the form you want to "migrate" into an ActiveX object.

5. Click Next to get to the Wizard's Options page, shown in Figure 29-2.

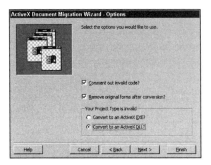

Figure 29-2
You can ask the Wizard to change bad code into a comment.

6. Choose both options shown on the Options page, and select Convert to an ActiveX.DLL (don't worry about the distinction between .EXE- and .DLL-style objects — that subject is beyond the scope of this book).

   A browser or other container (such as a VB application containing a component) does not like to contain objects to execute certain code (such as the End or Show commands). That kind of code is the responsibility of the container program, not the contained object. So, any lines in your program that contain those forbidden commands will be commented out by the Wizard so you can take a look at the bad code and see if you need to revise it.

7. Click the *Remove Original Forms after Conversion?* checkbox. This means that the browser-compatible ActiveX object won't need the VB Form once the object itself is created. (However, the VB project's forms are not erased from the hard drive, so you can make modifications later and then re-use the Wizard if you wish.)

8. Click Next and agree to see the Summary the Wizard provides.

Like the "script" option you saw with the deployment Wizard you used in Session 29, the Document Migration Wizard has a feature that remembers your choices: the *Save Current Settings As Default* option. If you do make changes to your original VB project and want to re-run the Migration Wizard, this feature is helpful because it saves all of the choices you made (DLL or EXE, remove original forms, and so on). The next time you run the Wizard, all of your choices will be the defaults.

9. Click Finish, and agree to save Form1. Click OK to close the dialog box that tells you the Wizard is finished.

Glance at the provided report if you're interested. It's not about your project in particular; it just explains how you can test the new object you just created, and how to find more information about these kinds of components.

Testing Your ActiveX Component

Things have changed in the VB IDE. Take a look at the Project Explorer. You see that UserDocuments has replaced the Forms category. Double-click Form1, and you'll see that it is now borderless — it's not really even a form any more. It's now a component that can be added to a Web page.

Press F5. Instead of simply running like an ordinary Windows program (in the VB IDE), you now see the dialog box shown in Figure 29-3.

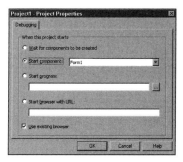

Figure 29-3
The default options here are exactly what you want.

The dialog box permits you to specify a different starting location, or to change the container from Internet Explorer to a different Start program or to a specific URL. Ignore those options and click OK.

Depending on your Internet Explorer security settings, you may see the dialog box shown in Figure 29-4.

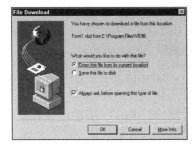

Figure 29-4
Agree that this is a safe file to be opened in your browser.

Click the OK button to close the dialog box shown in Figure 29-4.

Now your component is loaded into Internet Explorer, as shown in Figure 29-5.

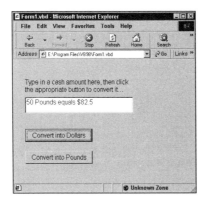

Figure 29-5
There it is — your transformed component has been loaded into Internet Explorer.

If Internet Explorer (IE) doesn't automatically display your component, make sure that you are using Internet Explorer 4 or higher. Then try shutting IE down and pressing F5. IE might start up and then load your component. If that doesn't work, start IE running, switch to VB, and then press F5 to see if it will load into a running IE. If all that fails, choose File ⇨ Open from IE's menu bar, and then click the browse button. Locate your document file (its name is FORM1.VBD). Click OK to load it into IE.

Deploying a Component in a Web Site

You've now successfully transformed your VB project into a component and tested it. To actually add it to a Web page, however, you must mix it in with some real HTML code (HTML is the language used to define the look of a Web page). To drop your component into a Web page, you must compile it into a .DLL, and also provide a way for the person who visits the Web page to get any necessary dependencies.

To do this, make sure that the Converter project is loaded in VB's editor, and then follow these steps to use the Package and Deployment Wizard to create a downloadable package:

1. Choose Add-Ins ⇨ Add-In Manager.
2. Double-click Package and Deployment Wizard to select it (if it's not already selected), and then click the OK button to close the dialog box.
3. Select Add-Ins ⇨ Package and Deployment Wizard.

Using .CAB Files

A .CAB file (*cabinet*) holds the files necessary to download a component over the Internet. Prior to the download, the user's browser can check to see which dependencies it doesn't have — rather than downloading the entire set of files. The browser can then decompress the files in the .CAB file, register any new dependencies or other needed files, and finally run your component in its Web page in the browser. Recall from Session 28 that some dependencies can be quite large — and, over the Internet, it

Continued

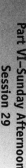

Using .CAB Files
Continued

might take a very long time to download everything. The only thing you need for your converter is the VB run-time library, but it's huge. As connections get faster, this problem will fade, but right now it's a serious consideration unless a visitor to your Web page already has the latest (VB 6) version of the VB run-time library.

However, setting up sites on an intranet is increasingly popular. One big advantage of providing other people in your company with utilities and applications in their browsers via a Web page is that upgrading is ridiculously simple. If you must frequently upgrade your VB programs because of bug repairs or new features, an intranet Web page is the way to handle a large number of users efficiently. A *single copy* of your ActiveX Document program resides on the server. When you want to replace it with a new version, you merely replace that single ActiveX Document component on the server. However, everyone connected to the intranet automatically gets the upgrade. As soon as user gets to the page holding your component, the version on their hard drives is checked and found to be older than the version on the server. Their local version is immediately replaced with the new version automatically. So, you don't have to run around changing the component on each person's local hard drive (as you would with a standard Windows .EXE application).

**10 Min.
To Go**

4. Click the Package button on the first page of the Wizard. You're asked if you want the project compiled into a .DLL. Agree that you do by clicking the Compile button. If you see a message box that asks you to save your current project, go ahead and do it.

5. After spending a little time getting itself together, the Wizard then asks what kind of deployment package you want. Select Internet Package and click Next.

6. Choose the \Converter\Package subfolder as the location on your hard drive to store the package.

7. Click Next and agree that the subfolder should be created.

8. Agree that your component (Project1.DLL) and the VB run-time library are the only dependencies required. Don't deselect these dependencies; just click Next.

9. You're informed that your component can be included in the CAB (or downloaded from your Web site), but the VB run-time library will be downloaded from the Microsoft site. If you're setting up on an intranet, you would likely want to change this and download both from your local server (which you can do at much higher speeds than downloading from Microsoft).

10. Click Next.

 A dependency such as msvbvm60.dll (the VB 6 run-time library) can be sent to the user in .CAB files that have been *digitally signed* by Microsoft from the Microsoft Web site. Some people feel that digitally signed components are safe (guaranteed to be virus-free). I have my doubts about a security system based on *trust*. Seems oxymoronic to me. I rarely see any digitally signed components when surfing the net. I don't think this is the ultimate solution to virus attacks.

11. Click Next, and the Safety Settings page is displayed. Ignore this page.

12. Click Next, and then click Finish.

The Wizard builds your .CAB file. You see a brief report telling you the location of the package you've just created. Use Windows Explorer to find the subfolder in \Package. Notice that there's an .HTM (HTML Web page) file. If you look at this file with Notepad, you'll see a lot of comments and some HTML, but the really significant HTML code is this: `<a href=Form1.VBD>Form1.VBD</a>`. This is a hyperlink that loads your component when the user clicks the link. (Your UserDocument file must always be kept in the same folder as this .HTM file because no actual path is provided to your .VBD component.)

The definition of your object (component) is also important, but you can let the Wizard deal with that huge CLASSID number. Don't mess with it. However, you can add new HTML to your heart's content to reformat this page, as long as you don't disturb the object definition, the brief script, and the other HTML that the Wizard already provided to make your component work in this page.

Now try double-clicking Project1.HTM in Windows Explorer. It loads into Internet Explorer, as you can see in Figure 29-6.

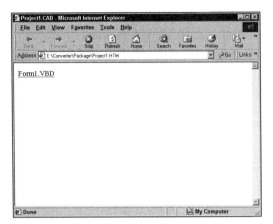

Figure 29-6
Your component will pop up any time the user clicks this hyperlink.

Now click the Form1.VBD hyperlink. You'll probably see the warning dialog box asking if you want to open or save this download. Open it. Immediately, your converter utility is loaded into the browser, as previously shown in Figure 29-5.

Done!

Adding Database Access to a Web Page

It's easy to provide access to a database in a component. Follow the steps earlier in this session to create the Converter utility, but instead, add a Data control and some data-bound TextBoxes as necessary for the fields in your database. (See Session 24 if you need a refresher on how to set the DatabaseName, RecordSource, DataSource, and DataField properties.)

Then follow the steps in this session to convert the project into an ActiveX Document, bundle it into a downloadable .CAB file, and create a reference to it in an .HTM Web page. Be aware, though, that you probably won't want to permit strangers to actually edit or delete the fields in your database — make it read-only by changing the Data control's RecordsetType property to Snapshot.

REVIEW

Given the increasing importance of the Internet — and the increasing use of browsers as hosts for intranet applications — it's important to make your programs Internet/intranet-accessible. This session explored how to transform a traditional

Windows program into a component. Once transformed, it can be tried out in a browser, and then formally compiled into a .DLL and put into a .CAB file for downloading. Finally, you saw how easy it is to add database access to a Web page, using the techniques you learned in this, and earlier, sessions.

QUIZ YOURSELF

1. What is an ActiveX Document? (See "Using the ActiveX Document Migration Wizard".)

2. Name one of VB's standard commands that cannot be used in a browser environment. (See "Using the ActiveX Document Migration Wizard".)

3. Why can't the standard command you named in question #2 be used in a browser? (See "Using the ActiveX Document Migration Wizard".)

4. What is a *container* application? (See "Using the ActiveX Document Migration Wizard".)

5. A .CAB file is used for what purpose? (See "Deploying a Component in a Web Site".)

Understanding Classes and Objects

Session Checklist

✔ Understanding the main components of an object

✔ Using encapsulation to avoid bugs and facilitate reusability

✔ Validating data sent to properties

✔ Working with the Class Builder to create properties more easily

✔ Creating, then accessing, an object

**30 Min.
To Go**

I n Session 29, you used a wizard to change a traditional Windows utility into an object. What, you might well ask, is an *object*?

The items on the VB Toolbox are objects. Put an OptionButton on a form, and you have an OptionButton object. How does an object differ from a variable? An object is more powerful and sophisticated — it's like a self-contained mini-program. A variable contains a value, a single piece of data. An object, on the other hand, usually contains several pieces of data. An object's data are known as its *properties*, such as the OptionButton's Left property, which describes its horizontal location within its container form, or its Caption property, which specifies the text the user sees next to the button.

In addition to its data, an object also includes programming — things it knows how to do with its data, such as the OptionButton's Move method, which changes its Left and Top properties, thereby relocating the OptionButton on its form. The object's programming that manipulates its data is known as its *methods*.

Finally, objects can (but don't necessarily) have events — a place for a programmer to define how the object behaves if some outside action (such as a mouse click) happens to that object.

Also note that an object can (but doesn't necessarily) include a visible user interface. An OptionButton component does have a visible user interface, but a Timer component does not.

However, don't get the idea that objects are limited to components. True, all components are objects, but not all objects are components. As you'll learn in this session, you can create objects that are intended to be used only within a single program. This kind of object isn't compiled into a component (such as an ActiveX Document object) to make it possible to drop it into other programs. Instead, using objects can merely be a useful way of organizing your programming.

Object-oriented Programming

Some programmers believe that *all* Visual Basic programs should be written using OOP (Object-oriented Programming). I'm not one of them. I feel that objects are most useful with large, complex programs, and also when you're writing a program with other programmers, as a group effort. Programming objects forces you to follow some strict rules that can help avoid problems that are commonly encountered when group programming or working with complex applications.

The PDM you built did not use OOP techniques because it was a relatively simple project, and because you didn't write only parts of it that later had to be blended in with parts written by other programmers. But if you've never been exposed to it, you might find this session helpful. I will show you some of what OOP can do for you, should you need to use it.

Encapsulation

A primary benefit of OOP is known as *encapsulation*. This means that an object doesn't permit outside programming to directly manipulate its data. (None of an object's variables should be declared Public — they're all Private.)

Any properties that you want to permit outside code to read (query) or set (change) are "exposed" to the outside code in a special way, using *property proce-*

dures. The outside code must contact these procedures, and then the procedures deal directly with the object's data. The outside code doesn't get to manipulate an object's actual data directly.

To illustrate the idea of encapsulation, let's say that you decide to permit outside code to change a property called `StateTax`. First, in the General Declarations section, you declare a variable that's private to the object:

```
Private StateTax
```

This variable will hold the actual value. Then you write a special kind of procedure to provide a way for outside code to request a change to the `StateTax` property:

```
Public Property Let StateTax(ByVal Amount As Variant)
If Amount > 10 Or Amount < 1 Then
    MsgBox "No state has tax higher than 10% or lower than 1%"
    Exit Property
End If
StateTax = Amount
End Property
```

Notice that I said *request* a change to this property. If the outside code doesn't provide what your object considers a valid value, the request is refused.

Did you see the `ByVal` command in this example? Using this command is a way of building an additional wall between an object and outside code. `ByVal` means that only a copy of the outside value *Amount* is passed to this procedure — not the actual location in memory. Therefore, the procedure cannot make any changes to the outside value. The opposite command, `ByRef`, is the default in VB and *does* provide the actual address of the passed variable, exposing it to potentially being changed by code within the procedure.

Validation

Notice that your object intercepts the outside request to change the `StateTax` property. This gives the object the option to *validate* the requested change — as we did in this example by refusing (`Exit Property`) to change the tax if the amount is greater than 10 or less than 1.

20 Min. To Go

This validation prevents errors — perhaps a programmer who wrote the outside code didn't realize that the `StateTax` property doesn't accept percentages expressed as fractions, such as .03, but wants it expressed as a whole number, 3. You can see how useful this kind of protection against bad data is when several programmers are working together on the same project and must eventually join their pieces of code together into one harmonious large application. Data validation is one of the primary benefits of OOP.

Another side benefit of OOP is that the other programmers don't need to know the details of how the code in your object works. Let's say that you have a method named AddTax in your object that adds the state tax to the retail price. Outsiders need not be bothered to look at your code (indeed cannot look at it) to try to figure out if the math involved in your AddTax method uses .03 or 3 as the percentage. Does the AddTax method look like this?

```
Public Function AddTax(RetailCost)
Percent = STax / 100
AddTax = RetailCost * (Percent + 1)
End Function
```

This code takes 3 as the percent value and therefore divides it by 100 before doing the calculation.

Or does the AddTax method's code look like this?

```
Public Function AddTax(RetailCost)
AddTax = RetailCost * (STax + 1)
End Function
```

Here, the outside code provides the state tax percent in the form .03.

It doesn't matter. The outside programmer need not be concerned with precisely how an object's methods work. The validation code for the properties should catch any errors — all the outsider need know is which properties are exposed, what they mean, and how to use the object's methods to get results. Needless to say, the outside programmer has no access to an object's programming code directly. No tampering is allowed.

Note that you program a method in an object quite simply as a Public Function or Public Sub, like Public Function AddTax in the example above.

Have you been wondering how the outside code accesses the properties or methods of an object? You already know. Any time you access a VB component, you're accessing an object — so, you've used the correct syntax throughout the previous sessions. You query an object's properties like this:

```
n = MyObject.StateTax
```

and you change an object's property like this:

```
MyObject.StateTax = n
```

Finally, you execute an object's method (if it is a function) like this:

```
n = MyObject.AddTax (RetailCost)
```

Or, if it's a sub, you execute it like this:

```
MyObject.AddTax (RetailCost)
```

This encapsulation concept can be compared to a receiver you might buy for your stereo system. It has publicly exposed properties (such as the loudness or tone knobs) and methods (such as a button to scan for the next FM station). However, it doesn't permit you to turn the volume knob below zero or up to 1,400 — you are permitted a range of 1-10 for the loudness. Though, as Spinal Tap famously revealed, some really expensive audio equipment goes up to 11.

Additionally, the receiver doesn't let you see, or, worse, adjust, the internal programming that executes the Scan method. Put another way, it's a *black box* with some public properties and events you can mess around with — and lots of stuff inside that you cannot get to. That's just as well.

Note too that objects simplify code maintenance. Programmers often have to go back and make adjustments to a program perhaps a year after they wrote it. Maybe you want to add new features, or improve the user interface. In cases such as that — unless you have a perfect memory — *you* become the outsider to your own code. You'll then be glad that encapsulation relieves you from the necessity of having to interpret the programming inside an object, and that validation helps you avoid feeding bad data to the object. You also avoid having to search throughout an entire application's source code to see if there are *other* places in the code where, for example, state tax is added to retail tax.

One final point: Objects are more easily reused in future programs than ordinary source code. You write one object that accepts passwords, and you can reuse it in future projects as often as you wish. As you've seen, objects are, to a considerable extent, self-contained. Therefore, you can usually add them to other projects quite quickly — without worrying that a constant, variable, or codependency exists somewhere outside the object.

Using the Class Builder

For those getting started with OOP, VB includes a Class Builder utility that does some of the tedious coding for you (property procedures and their associated `Private` variables require fairly repetitive code).

What's a class? It's a blueprint, the code that describes how an object performs. There's code in the VB run-time library for the TextBox class. When you add a TextBox to a form, you've *instantiated an object of the TextBox Class*. An important feature of objects is that you can instantiate (bring into existence) as many of them as you need. You can create two dozen TextBox objects if that's what you want.

Let's assume you start a real-estate business and need to write a program that keeps track of customers. You can create a customer class, and then create a customer object for each customer.

Just as it's a good idea to plan the jobs that an application is supposed to accomplish before you start writing code, it's also a good idea to think through the properties and methods before you start coding a class.

Our customer object should contain the following properties: name, address, phone number, annual salary, location preferences, house preferences, and perhaps others. To keep this example easy to follow, let's limit ourselves to programming only one property: the `AnnualSalary` property.

As for methods, we'll limit ourselves to one as well: `AffordToPay`, a method that looks at the customer's annual salary and calculates how high a monthly payment this customer can comfortably manage. The general rule is to multiply the customer's monthly salary by a factor of .28.

A class is defined in a special kind of VB module called a *class module*. Follow these steps to create the Customer class:

1. Start a new Standard EXE VB project.

2. Choose Add-Ins ➪ Add-In Manager and double-click VB 6 Class Builder Utility. Then click OK.

 You can also start the Class Builder using Project ➪ Add Class Module, but I prefer to put the Class Builder on the Add-Ins menu because it's easier to reopen it from that menu.

3. Choose Add-Ins ➪ Class Builder Utility to open it, as shown in Figure 30-1.

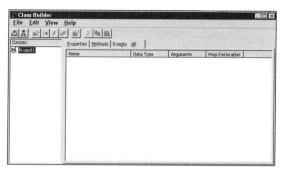

Figure 30-1
This utility does some of the coding for you when you're defining the properties, methods, or events of a class.

4. Click the button on the far-left side of the Class Builder's toolbar. A new class dialog box appears, as shown in Figure 30-2.

Figure 30-2
Use this dialog box to give your class a name.

5. Change the default name from `Class1` to `Customer`. If you have other classes already defined, you can base this new class on one of them, and merely modify it. But that's not the case here, so click OK to close the dialog box.

6. Add the `AffordToPay` method by clicking the fourth button from the left on the Toolbar (the icon that looks like a flying green eraser, which is quite obviously the right visual cue to symbolize the concept *method*).

The Method Builder dialog box appears, as shown in Figure 30-3:

Figure 30-3
Specify the name of the method, its arguments, and other qualities in this dialog box.

Name this method `AffordToPay`. It has no arguments. However, change the Return Data Type field to `String`. (It would have been made a `Sub` procedure if you'd left the Type field set to None.) By specifying a data type, the Method Builder will make this method a function because only a function can return a value to the outside code. Click OK to close the dialog box.

7. Click the third button from the left, showing a hand holding a videotape. That, as you doubtless guessed, represents the Add New Property feature. The Property Builder dialog box opens, as shown in Figure 30-4.

Figure 30-4
You're supposed to avoid using the third option here — an object's properties should never be simple public variables.

The `Friend` **command is similar to** `Public`, **but container applications cannot access an item given** `Friend` **scope — it is only available to the various modules or forms in your project.**

8. Name the property `AnnualSalary`, and click OK to close the dialog box.

9. Close the Class Builder Utility. It asks if you want to update the project with changes. Answer yes.

Now look at the code window for the Class Module. You'll notice that the Class Builder Utility created a private variable for your property, and it created three property procedures to provide a public interface for (to expose) the property to outside code.

The `Property Let` procedure is explained earlier in this session. `Property Get` merely lets outside code read the value of your property. `Property Set` is used if a property can accept an object variable. You can delete the whole `Property Set` procedure from this application — this property doesn't work with object variables.

Object Variables **are a special variable type. They can be used to assign references to particular objects or to copy references from one object variable to another. The way the** `Set` **command works is similar to the way in which the equal (=) symbol works with regular text or numeric variables. We'll use** `Set` **shortly when we demonstrate how to create an object in code.**

You must provide any validation code you want in the property procedures, and also add code to the methods to make them do their jobs. Here's what you need to type into the `AffordToPay` method:

```
Public Function AffordToPay() As Currency
Monthly = AnnualSalary / 12
AffordToPay = Monthly * 0.28
End Function
```

The client's monthly salary is calculated, and then multiplied by a factor of .28 and returned to the caller.

**10 Min.
To Go**

Creating an Object

To create an object of the Customer class — and then use its `AffordToPay` method — double-click Form1 in the Project explorer, and then double-click Form1 to get to its code window. You are now writing *outside code*: code that instantiates — and then can access the public properties and methods — of a Customer object.

Type the following code into the `Form1_Load` event:

```
Private Sub Form_Load()

Set cCustomer = New Customer

cCustomer.AnnualSalary = 45000

MsgBox cCustomer.AffordToPay

End Sub
```

Try running this to see that everything works as it should.

The line that begins with the `Set` command says to assign a new instance of the Customer class to the object variable named `cCustomer`. And from now on in this procedure, whenever I use the word `cCustomer`, I'm referring to this Customer object. Specify an object variable's scope the same way you define the scope for any other variable. For example, to make an object variable form-wide, `Dim` it in the General Declarations section of the form:

```
Dim cCustomer as Object
```

Be sure you remember that you must always create an object variable before you can write code that accesses an object. You can't set a property, for instance, until you have an object variable that represents the object. It's not possible to directly call on an object in code, like this:

```
Customer.AnnualSalary = 45000
```

Done!

There are other ways to take advantage of objects in addition to the ones we've covered in this session. For instance, you can manage groups of objects by putting them into *collections* — array-like structures — which facilitates saving or loading all of the Customer objects in a disk file. If you suspect that OOP techniques would come in handy in your work, I recommend the book *Concepts of Object-oriented*

Programming with Visual Basic by Steven Roman. It's not a big book, but it's in-depth and it's clear.

REVIEW

You were exposed to an important programming philosophy in this session: object-oriented programming. You learned that, in VB, the primary virtue of OOP derives from encapsulation — sealing off data and code from the outside world (including other programmers or even yourself a year later). In addition to preventing various kinds of bugs, reusing objects is simpler than attempting to read and understand ordinary source code. Objects also help prevent errors by validating changes made to their properties. Then you saw how to use VB's Class Builder Utility to avoid having to type in all the variables and procedures required for properties. Finally, you switched tactics and wrote outside code to instantiate, then use a method of, an object.

QUIZ YOURSELF

1. How do property procedures differ from ordinary procedures? (See "Encapsulation".)

2. Why is validation a useful feature of encapsulation? (See "Validation".)

3. Define the difference between a class and an object. (See "Using the Class Builder".)

4. Explain the concept of instantiation. (See "Using the Class Builder".)

5. What VB command do you use to assign an object to an object variable? (See "Creating an Object".)

PART

VI

Sunday Afternoon

1. What does the `Printer.Print` command accomplish?
2. What is the main value (for a VB programmer) of the Windows Registry?
3. What VB command do you use to access information stored in the Registry?
4. What code do you use to close a database that's been opened with a Data control?
5. What does *deployment* mean when used with a VB project?
6. What are *dependencies*?
7. Can VB 6's Package and Deployment Wizard create .CAB files for downloading over the Internet?
8. What is *compilation*?
9. What does VB's ActiveX Document Migration Wizard do?
10. What is the purpose of a "script" in wizards such as the Package and Deployment Wizard, or the ActiveX Document Migration Wizard?
11. After you've created an ActiveX component using the ActiveX Document Migration Wizard, what happens when you press F5 to test it?
12. What is a .CAB file?
13. What does a *digitally signed* component do?
14. Name one of VB's standard commands that cannot be used in a browser environment.
15. Why can't the standard VB command you named in the previous question be used in a browser?

16. What is a *container* application?

17. Do all objects have user interfaces?

18. What is *encapsulation*?

19. How is VB's Class Builder feature useful?

20. Define the difference between a class and an object.

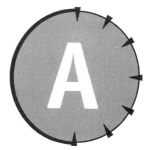

Answers to Part Reviews

Following are the answers to the Reviews at the end of each Part of the book. Think of these Reviews as mini-tests, designed to help you prepare for the final — the Assessment Test on the CD.

Friday Evening Review Answers

1. Answers will vary based on how you do the exercise.

2. Answers will vary.

3. The Project Explorer works in VB somewhat the way Windows's Explorer works in Windows. The Project Explorer shows the overall organization of the project or projects you're currently working on — a tree view of the forms, or other elem ents in your projects such as modules, class modules, user controls, user documents, property pages, and designers.

4. Text1 and Text2. VB provides a shorthand version (CommandButton becomes Command) of the component's Toolbox name, and then appends a number to distinguish multiple components of the same type.

5. chk, lst, lbl, and img

6. It's always possible — just choose File⇨Add Project. The reason to work on two projects at once is that you can create your own components with VB, and there must be a way to test them. To test components, one project needs to be a container application, and the second project needs to be the component you want to test. (Components designed to be used in Web pages are tested in Internet Explorer — you'll work with just such a Web component in Session 29.)

7. IDE means Integrated Design Environment — a fancy phrase for the VB editor. RAD means Rapid Application Development. The VB IDE was the first, and many still consider it the best, of the RAD environments.

8. F5 starts it running. There is no key to stop a running program in the VB IDE. You must click the X icon in the upper-right corner of the program's active window, press Ctrl+Break, or choose Run ⇨ End.

9. It specifies the order in which components on a window get focus as the user presses the Tab key.

10. In arithmetic, when you say a = b, you mean that both a and b are the same number. What you mean by Text1.Text = "Helloooo!" is, when this line is executed, the contents of this TextBox will change to Helloooo!. An equals sign used this way in programming signifies assignment rather than equality. It means, if this line of programming executes, the text "Helloooo!" will be placed (assigned) to this TextBox. However, in other contexts, the equals sign in programming means the same thing as it does in arithmetic — that is, equality. In a line of programming that tests something, the equals symbol really does mean equals. Here's an example: If X = 12 Then DoSomething. That means, if X equals 12, then carry out the assigned job.

11. The design window is the form's user interface surface — where you add, position, and size components; and adjust their various properties. The code window is "underneath" the components and the form; you put your programming in the code window.

12. A sub is a little program within a program (sub is short for subroutine). The programming you put between the Sub and End Sub will sit there and wait to be activated by some outside event. Subs, or functions, are called procedures.

13. Press Ctrl+T, and then select one of the components in the Components dialog box.

14. It is used to display familiar, standard Windows dialog boxes to the user — File Open, Save, Font, Color, and so forth.

15. VB looks at lines of code as a single, cohesive statement of your wishes. If a logical line is quite long, you might want to break it into two physical lines so you can view the whole thing without having to scroll the editor horizontally. You can break a logical line of code into two physical lines by using a space character followed by an underscore character. Here's an example of a single logical line of code broken into two physical lines:

```
If CommonDialog1.FileName <> "" Then _
   Text1.Text = CommonDialog1.FileName
```

16. CommonDialog1.ShowOpen

17. This code puts the contents of the file the user selected with the CommonDialog's Open dialog box into the TextBox named Text1. However, if the user clicked the Cancel button, the CommonDialog's Filename property will be empty (""), and your code continues on without attempting to open a no-name file.

18. An empty text variable

19. End

20. It's something that happens to a component or a form. I'd compare it to a summer's day. Seriously, folks, think of a toaster. Pressing its bar down (to start toasting) is one event. Pulling up on the bar to abort toasting is the other event. A typical toaster has two events — two things that an outside agent can do to it, and to which it should respond.

21. Double-click the CommandButton. You then see its Click event in which you can write some code if you wish. The event you see when you double-click a component is the event that VB thinks is the most often used of all of that component's events. So it's most likely the one you want to write programming for, too.

Saturday Morning Review Answers

1. Auto Syntax Check watches as you type in each line of code. As soon as you finish a line, it checks the line to see if you mistyped anything, or if you made some other kind of error such as leaving out something necessary.

Auto List Members provides you with a quick list of all of the properties and methods of an object. As soon as you type the period following Text1. in the code window, you see the Auto List Members feature pop into action. (When you type an object's name, such as Text1, followed by a period (.), you're telling VB that you are going to specify a property of that object next, or perhaps a method.)

2. It starts Windows Notepad running. The Shell command launches applications, just as if you had double-clicked the application's filename in Windows Explorer.

3. Choose Project ➪ Add Form to add a new form to a project. Many applications include more than a single window. You might, for example, want to allow the user to specify customizations to your project, and you could display a form with various option buttons or checkboxes where they can make such choices.

4. Grouped OptionButtons work together to be mutually exclusive. If the user clicks one of them, the rest become unselected. In other words, only one OptionButton in a group can be selected at a given time. This is useful for such choices as the `BackColor` of a form — it can be only one color at a time.

5. CheckBoxes are never mutually exclusive. The user can select none, one, some, or all of any CheckBoxes displayed.

6. The `Enabled` property, if set to False, prevents users from typing anything into a TextBox (it is said to be *disabled*). Its text will appear light gray rather than black to indicate that the TextBox is disabled. Components are disabled when it makes no sense for the user to try to use them. Other components — such as the OptionButton — can also be disabled and turn gray, refusing to respond to mouse clicks or keyboard actions.

7. The `ToolTipText` property is a small help window that pops up to inform the user about the purpose of a component. It pops up when the user pauses the mouse pointer on top of a component.

8. When you select multiple components, the Properties Window displays only those properties that all the selected components have in common and that make sense to change to the same thing. When you change the `Font` property with several components selected, for example, that property changes for *each* of the selected components.

9. Just what it sounds like: to describe to the user the purpose of some other component

10. `AutoSize` causes a label to grow or shrink to fit whatever text is inside. This can be useful if you plan to dynamically add text (to add it during run time) and you do not know in advance how much text there will be.

11. Yes, set the label's `BackStyle` property to `Transparent`.

12. To alphabetize, change the ListBox's `Sorted` property to True in the Properties Window.

13. Use the `RemoveItem` command.

14. Set the ListBox's `Columns` property to any number greater than one, and you get multiple columns — and a horizontal ScrollBar, if a ScrollBar is needed.

15. A ComboBox has a small TextBox at the very top. The user can select from the items in the list by typing only the first letter or first few letters, and then pressing enter. The typical ComboBox only displays one item — the user doesn't see the list unless the down-arrow button next to the TextBox is clicked.

16. An Image control draws onscreen faster; an Image control uses fewer of the computer's resources (such as memory) because it is less complex and has far fewer properties than a PictureBox. Graphics placed in an Image can be freely resized, and other components — such as OptionButtons — can be *grouped* or contained within a PictureBox (the Frame control can do this as well).

17. It erases whatever graphic is currently displayed in the PictureBox named `Picture1`.

18. The VB Application Wizard

19. `mnuCut.Enabled = False`

20. VB includes many built-in constants. Constants are predefined values for such things as colors, keypresses (`vbKeyF10 = 121`, for example), and other elements used in programming. Instead of using 121 in your programming, you can make your source code far clearer and more understandable if you use the constant `vbKeyF10` instead, like this:

```
Private Sub Command1_KeyDown(KeyCode As Integer, Shift As
Integer)
If KeyCode = vbKeyF10 then SaveDocToFile
End Sub
```

Saturday Afternoon Review Answers

1. An argument is data passed to a procedure, such as "Display This Message" passed to the `MsgBox` function.

2. Sometimes. Some arguments are optional and can be omitted from an argument list. For example, the Title argument for the `MsgBox` function is optional. However, if you do leave out an optional argument, you must still insert a comma in the argument list to indicate that an argument is missing from the list.

3. A function returns information to the source code that calls it.

4. Open, Save, Color, Font, and Printer

5. Font

6. Assign the data to the function's name.

7. Pressing F8 steps you line by line through your program — executing each line, and then stopping and waiting for you to press F8 again. This is an excellent debugging tool.

8. No. A function must be called from within an expression, such as X = FunctionName (), and a function call also requires a pair of parentheses around any arguments. Even if there are no arguments, the parentheses (though empty) are still necessary.

9. Text (or string) and numeric

10. The value is the contents of the variable. In the code, X = "Moosie", *Moosie* is the value.

11. It must start with a letter, not a digit. It cannot be one of Visual Basic's own command words like For or Height. It cannot be larger than 255 characters. It cannot contain any punctuation marks or spaces.

12. When you need to use a variable in a program, you can simply assign a value to a valid variable name, and the variable will come into existence. The following code implicitly creates the variable Z:

    ```
    Z = "Darby"
    ```

13. Dim, ReDim, Public, Private, or Static

14. One. There are specialized kinds of variables, such as arrays, that hold multiple values. An ordinary variable can hold only a single value at any given time.

15. Yes, in essence, they are. However, they are predefined by the creator of each component. You can adjust their values, but you cannot define new properties for a component.

16. The variant

17. It can contain only two values: True or False.

18. When you declare a variable inside a procedure, *the variable only works within that procedure*. While the program executes the procedure or event, the variable comes to life, does its thing, but then dies (disappears) as soon as the End Sub line is executed. Variables that live only within a single procedure are called *local* variables. Their *scopes* are limited to a single procedure. Variables declared with the Dim or Private

command in the General Declarations section of a form are accessible within that form. They have form-wide scope. Variables declared with the `Public` command in a module have project-wide scope.

19. An expression is a compound entity that VB evaluates at run time. An expression can be made up of literals, variables, or a combination of the two. In the following code, "Hello" + `MyVariable` is an expression, and it evaluates to "Hello Sandra":

```
MyVariable = " Sandra"
Response = MsgBox ("Hello" & MyVariable)
```

20. Operators are used in expressions to compare two elements (like two variables), to do math on them, or to perform a "logical" operation on them. The plus sign, for example, is an operator in this example: 2 + 4. The greater-than symbol (>) is an operator in this example, which says *n* is greater than *z*: n > z.

Saturday Night Review Answers

1. An array is a set of variable values that have been grouped together. Once inside an array structure, the values share the same variable name, and are individually identified by an *index number*.

2. Yes. Break the line by using a space character, followed by an underscore. However, you cannot use this technique within a text literal, like this:

```
MsgBox "Toron _
to"
```

3. By grouping many values under the same variable name, you can manipulate the `values` by individual index number. This means you can work with the values in a loop, using the loop's counter to reference each value by its index number. This technique permits you to accomplish certain jobs using fewer lines of code.

4. `Step` can be attached at the end of the `For...Next` structure to allow you to skip numbers — to *step* past them. When the `Step` command is used with `For...Next`, `Step` alters the way the loop counts. By default, `For...Next` increments by one.

5. It tests the truth of an expression, and then executes appropriate lines of code based on the answer to the question posed by the `If`. `If...Then` is a decision-making mechanism and is also sometimes referred to as *branching* because it can take one or more alternative paths in the code.

6. The lines of code that are carried out based on the results of the `If` expression are indented. Put another way, indent any line of code within an `If...Then` structure that does not begin with `If`, `Else`, `ElseIf`, or `Then`. This indenting helps clarify the structure and makes it easier to read and understand the code.

7. `If...Then` is great for simple, common testing and branching. But if you have more than two branches, `If...Then` becomes clumsy. Fortunately, there's an alternative decision-making structure in VB that specializes in multiple-branching — `Select...Case`, which should be used when there are several possible outcomes.

8. `Case Else` describes what the program should do if none of the other `Case` commands matches the `Select Case` expression.

9. Yes. `Case Is < 200`

10. Yes. `Case "n" To "z"`

11. The Timer component has several uses. It can make things happen at intervals (for instance, animation), remind people that it's time to do something, measure the passage of time, or cause a delay.

12. Most controls have more than a dozen properties; Timers have only seven. Most controls have at least ten events they can respond to; Timers have only one event. Most controls are visible and can be accessed and triggered by the user of the program; Timers work in the background, independent of the user. They are always invisible when a program runs. Most controls' events are triggered instantly; Timers don't carry out the instructions you've put into their events until their Interval (the duration) passes. Most controls' events are only triggered once; Timers will repeatedly trigger their event until you either set their `Interval` property to 0 or their `Enabled` property to False.

13. They generally don't have any effect; the Timer keeps on ticking independent of whatever else is happening in Windows. In rare cases, an application might freeze the system, but for all practical purposes, you can consider Timers isolated from outside influence.

14. The millisecond

15. The default property is nearly always the most commonly used property. For a TextBox, it's the `Text` property, and for a Label, it's the `Caption` property. A default property need not be typed into your code. You can often simplify your code by stripping off the reference to the default property, like this:

```
Text1.Text = "Rasmati"
```

can be simplified to:

```
Text1 = "Rasmati"
```

16. Using a control array is the only way you can create a new control (such as a brand-new TextBox) during run time.

17. Typos, because Visual Basic can generally alert you to them

18. Very. A misplaced comma can crash a program.

19. `On Error Resume Next` tells VB not to shut down the program if an error occurs. Rather, VB should *resume* execution of the *next* line of code following the line that caused the error.

20. The feature is called *Run to cursor*. Click in the code where you want execution to stop, press Ctrl+F8, and the code between the original and new locations is executed fast.

Sunday Morning Review Answers

1. Single Document Interface and Multiple Document Interface. In SDI mode, all windows are independent of the other windows and can float free on the desktop, or can be dragged onto other windows. MDI, by contrast, has a large container window with one or more "child" windows within it.

2. MDI

3. If you were designing a database that would hold the information in your Rolodex, you would recognize that each card in the Rolodex is a single *record*, and that each of those records is divided into perhaps eight *fields* (zones): Name, Address, City, State, Zip, Voice Phone, Fax Phone, and Email address. In other words, a record is a set of data (the actual name, address, and so on of an individual), and fields are the categories that define what data should go into the records.

4. In a complex database, there may be more than one group of records. If you have a huge Rolodex, you might divide the records into two categories: Personal and Business, for example. This kind of large-scale group of records is called a *table*. A database can have multiple tables — and they can be linked, searched, or otherwise interrelated in various ways.

5. When you specify that a field is to be indexed, it is maintained in alphabetical (or numeric) order by the database engine (the underlying, low-level support code that does jobs for a database). An index makes it easier to search for information in a database.

6. It's good to put sizing and positioning code into the Form_Load event. That way, it gets carried out before the form is made visible, and it happens only that one time when the form is first created.

7. Use the & symbol before the letter that you want to make the shortcut character. The Caption property is then displayed with that letter underlined as a cue to the user. Change a search button's Caption property to &Search, for example, and the user will see Search as the visible caption.

8. It determines the order in which components on a form get the focus as the user presses the Tab key to cycle through them.

9. It holds a huge amount of data. The Memo data type is a text-type field, but can be essentially as long as the user wishes (a memo can contain up to 1.2 GB of text data!).

10. DAO (Data Access Objects) is a library containing many database-programming commands not available by default in VB.

11. This option means that the field need not contain any data.

12. VB ships with a Visual Data Manager utility that makes the creation of a new database effortless, and makes the definition of its interior structure — its tables and fields — a snap. You can also use the Visual Data Manager to make adjustments to a database later on if you wish.

13. It specifies the Data control through which a database's records flow into a component.

14. End of File. This VB command is used to test to see if all data has been extracted from a file, and therefore you can exit a loop in your code. Here's an example:

```
Do Until rsWholeTable.EOF = True
```

15. The Print # command sends *an exact copy* of text to an opened file. A copy of text saved to disk with Print # can later be read off a disk file and sent into a TextBox with any original line-break formatting intact. To save the contents of a TextBox, Print # is usually preferable to the alternative, Write #, because Write # inserts commas between the individual pieces of saved text and adds quotation marks to text (string) variables.

16. The AddNew method creates a brand-new record in a database, but it's only a provisional record. Unless the Update method is later used to actually save the record into the database, the new record is discarded.

17. You don't need to write any code to permit editing. A Data control — and a TextBox bound to it — are capable of detecting, then committing to the database, any editing that the user does to existing records.

18. You want to reference a Data control in the Initialize event rather than the Load event of the form on which that control sits. If you try to put code that references a Data control in the form's Load event, you'll get this not-very-helpful error message: "Object variable or with block variable not set." The problem is that the Data control doesn't yet exist when the Form_Load event's code is executed. You are, therefore, referring to a non-existent component. VB doesn't know what component you're talking about. By the time the Initialize event executes, however, the Data control has come into existence.

19. If the user wants to see only those recipes that contain the words *Chinese* and *pork*, use the AND command to permit them to get a list of only those titles that contain *both* words. If the user wants to see all recipes containing *either* of the words, use the OR command.

20. A single word on a line of code ending with a colon is a *line label*. You use it as a place marker. For example: If cnt > 5 Then GoTo Toomuch:. This line (earlier in the code) means that if the *cnt* variable grows larger than 5, the execution should *jump* over (not execute) any following lines of code until it comes upon the line label Toomuch:.

Sunday Afternoon Review Answers

1. It moves the printing to the next line down in the printer. It's the equivalent of pressing the Enter key when typing text into a word processor.

2. You can save user preferences there, so when the user next runs your application, the user's favorite background color, for example, is still there. The Registry is a place to save the data if you offer the user the option of customizing your VB application.

3. GetSetting

4. Data1.DatabaseName = ""
Data1.Refresh

5. If you want to give your VB application to other people to use — sell it, pass it around to grateful coworkers, or make it available on the Internet — that's called *deployment*.

6. Dependencies are files that your application needs in order to run. Examples of dependencies are components (such as the CommonDialog component) and .DLLs (dynamic link libraries).

7. Yes

8. The process of transforming source code into an executable file is called *compilation*. There is a Make Exe option on the VB File menu that compiles the current project.

9. Using VB's ActiveX Document Migration Wizard is the fastest way to transform an ordinary traditional Windows application into a browser-ready object.

10. The "script" option remembers your choices as you move through the question-and-answer format of a wizard. If you later want to re-run a wizard, the scripting feature is helpful because it has saved all of the choices you made the previous time you ran the wizard. The next time you run the wizard, all your choices are the defaults.

11. The component is loaded into Internet Explorer, so you can see how it works in the browser environment.

12. A .CAB file (*cabinet*) holds the files necessary to download a component over the Internet. Prior to the download, the user's browser can check to see which dependencies it doesn't have, rather than downloading the entire set of files. The browser then decompresses the files in the .CAB file, registers any new dependencies or other needed files, and finally runs your component in its Web page in the browser.

13. A dependency such as the VB 6 run-time library can be sent to the user in .CAB files that have been *digitally signed* by Microsoft from the Microsoft Web site. This means that the files are guaranteed to originate from Microsoft and therefore should be safe (free of viruses).

14. End or Show cannot be used.

15. Commands such as Show or End govern behaviors that are controlled by the browser, not by objects displayed within it. The browser decides when a component is displayed or shut down, not the component itself.

16. An ActiveX document is similar to the components you've been working with on VB's Toolbox — Labels, CommandButtons, and all the rest. These objects are little programs, often including a user interface, which *can be*

dropped into other "container" programs. When an ActiveX document is loaded into a browser, the browser is the *container*.

17. No. VB's Toolbox components are objects. An OptionButton object does have a visible user interface, but a Timer does not.

18. *Encapsulation* means that an object doesn't permit outside programming to directly manipulate its data. None of an object's variables are declared `Public`; they're all `Private`.

19. VB's Class Builder utility writes some of the tedious object-oriented programming code for you. Property procedures and their associated `Private` variables require fairly repetitive and predictable code.

20. A class is a description of an object; the object is the result of following that description to create an actual, working entity. A class is similar to a blueprint. There's code in the VB run-time library, for example, for the TextBox class. This code describes the qualities and behaviors of a TextBox. However, when you add a TextBox to a form, you've instantiated a TextBox *object* (*instantiated* means *created*).

What's on the CD

This book's CD-ROM includes all the source code from all the examples in this book, the Visual Basic 6 Weekend Crash Course Assessment Test, and the Visual Basic® 6 Working Model from Microsoft, as well as several demo versions of popular Visual Basic add-ons, components and sets of tools for developers.

Professional Software

Demos from three manufacturers are included. To try out these products, switch to the manufacturer's direcory on this CD and run the Setup program. Read any Readme.Txt files you see for additional information. You'll find demo versions of VBAssist 5.0 and Data Widgets from Sheridan Software; demos of a set of imaging tools from LEADTOOLS; and demos of seven useful products from VideoSoft.

Code Listings

The sample code developed for the book has been included on the CD-ROM. There is a folder for each of the 30 sessions in the book. In each folder you'll find all the source code from all the examples in that session—regardless of how few lines there were in the example. The source code examples are listed in the CD file in the same order that they appear within the session. Each example is separated from the others by several blank lines.

The Personal Database Manager (PDM) application built in the Sunday sessions is also included in its entirety in the folder named, you guessed it, PDM.

Visual Basic® 6 Working Model

The Visual Basic® 6 Working Model is provided by Microsoft and presents an opportunity for you to work with Visual Basic and create some programs without needing the full Visual Basic 6. The Working Model presents you with the Visual Basic working environment, minus some of the more advanced features and choices of the full version.

Limitations of the Working Model

There are some things with Visual Basic for which you need the full version; the Working Model won't do everything. If you want to create programs to market, distribute and sell to others, you'll eventually need to upgrade one of the full versions of VB: the Standard, Professional, or Enterprise edition. Here's a quick rundown of some of the key limitations of the Working Model:

- No online help: clicking any command on the Help menu gives you a dialog that informs you no help is available; you'll need to buy the commercial version for that.

- No compiler: you can create, edit, and run programs using the Working Model, but you can't compile them into an executable .EXE file for distribution.

- Fewer project types: The only project types the Working Model offers are the Standard EXE, VB Application Wizard, and VB Working Model types. The commercial versions provide several additional types, including ActiveX controls and IIS files among others.

- Fewer available form templates: The Working Model has a limited selection of templates for designing forms.

- Manual class modules: If you want to play around with object-oriented programming, the Working Model makes you build your own class modules by hand. The commercial versions of VB include wizards for creating class modules automatically.

- No Windows CE: you can't use the Working Model to create programs for Windows CE.

Installing the Visual Basic® Working Model

You'll find the Working Model setup files in the VBModel folder on the companion CD-ROM. Open an Explorer window. Browse to the CD-ROM and open that folder; then double-click on the Setup.exe file. (Depending on your Windows preferences, you may not see the .exe extension.)

The Installation Wizard will start up and take you step by step through the installation process. You should take note of the following:

- When you get to the screen that displays the Product ID, it's a good idea to write it down and save it for later reference.

- You'll be given the option of either a Typical or Custom installation. Typical should cover everything you need for most purposes: however, if you want to install the associated graphics library, you'll need to choose Custom.

- The Installation Wizard expects that you already have Internet Explorer 4.01 or later. If you don't, it's better to acquire IE and install it first; otherwise, the Installation Wizard for the Working Model will interrupt the process to try and take you through an IE installation, which could fail for any number of reasons.

- The Working Model will take about 50MB of hard disk space to install.

- When the installation completes, you'll be prompted to register your copy over the Internet. Assuming you've got Internet Explorer and an ISP account set up, you'll be automatically connected to the Microsoft Web site and registered. If you don't want to bother, clear the Register Now checkbox before clicking Finish.

Index

Continued

IDG BOOKS WORLDWIDE, INC.
END-USER LICENSE AGREEMENT

READ THIS. You should carefully read these terms and conditions before opening the software packet(s) included with this book ("Book"). This is a license agreement ("Agreement") between you and IDG Books Worldwide, Inc. ("IDGB"). By opening the accompanying software packet(s), you acknowledge that you have read and accept the following terms and conditions. If you do not agree and do not want to be bound by such terms and conditions, promptly return the Book and the unopened software packet(s) to the place you obtained them for a full refund.

1. **License Grant.** IDGB grants to you (either an individual or entity) a nonexclusive license to use one copy of the enclosed software program(s) (collectively, the "Software") solely for your own personal or business purposes on a single computer (whether a standard computer or a work-station component of a multiuser network). The Software is in use on a computer when it is loaded into temporary memory (RAM) or installed into permanent memory (hard disk, CD-ROM, or other storage device). IDGB reserves all rights not expressly granted herein.

2. **Ownership.** IDGB is the owner of all right, title, and interest, including copyright, in and to the compilation of the Software recorded on the disk(s) or CD-ROM ("Software Media"). Copyright to the individual programs recorded on the Software Media is owned by the author or other authorized copyright owner of each program. Ownership of the Software and all proprietary rights relating thereto remain with IDGB and its licensers.

3. **Restrictions On Use and Transfer.**

   (a) You may only (i) make one copy of the Software for backup or archival purposes, or (ii) transfer the Software to a single hard disk, provided that you keep the original for backup or archival purposes. You may not (i) rent or lease the Software, (ii) copy or reproduce the Software through a LAN or other network system or through any computer subscriber system or bulletin-board system, or (iii) modify, adapt, or create derivative works based on the Software.

   (b) You may not reverse engineer, decompile, or disassemble the Software. You may transfer the Software and user documentation on a permanent basis, provided that the transferee agrees to accept the terms and conditions of this Agreement and you retain no copies. If the Software is an update or has been updated, any transfer must include the most recent update and all prior versions.

4. **Restrictions On Use of Individual Programs.** You must follow the individual requirements and restrictions detailed for each individual program Appendix C of this Book. These limitations are also contained in the individual license agreements recorded on the Software Media. These limitations may include a requirement that after using the program for a specified period of time, the user must pay a registration fee or discontinue use. By opening the Software packet(s), you will be agreeing to abide by the licenses and restrictions for these individual programs that are detailed Appendix C and on the Software Media. None of the material on this Software Media or listed in this Book may ever be redistributed, in original or modified form, for commercial purposes.

5. **Limited Warranty.**

   (a) IDGB warrants that the Software and Software Media are free from defects in materials and workmanship under normal use for a period of sixty (60) days from the date of purchase of this Book. If IDGB receives notification within the warranty period of defects in materials or workmanship, IDGB will replace the defective Software Media.

   (b) **IDGB AND THE AUTHORS OF THE BOOK DISCLAIM ALL OTHER WARRANTIES, EXPRESS OR IMPLIED, INCLUDING WITHOUT LIMITATION IMPLIED WARRANTIES OF MERCHANTABILITY AND FITNESS FOR A PARTICULAR PURPOSE, WITH RESPECT TO THE SOFTWARE, THE PROGRAMS, THE SOURCE CODE CONTAINED THEREIN, AND/OR THE TECHNIQUES DESCRIBED IN THIS BOOK. IDGB DOES NOT WARRANT THAT THE FUNCTIONS CONTAINED IN THE SOFTWARE WILL MEET YOUR REQUIREMENTS OR THAT THE OPERATION OF THE SOFTWARE WILL BE ERROR FREE.**

   (c) This limited warranty gives you specific legal rights, and you may have other rights that vary from jurisdiction to jurisdiction.

6. **Remedies.**

   (a) IDGB's entire liability and your exclusive remedy for defects in materials and workmanship shall be limited to replacement of the Software Media, which may be returned to IDGB with a copy of your receipt at the following address: Software Media Fulfillment Department, Attn.: *Visual Basic(r) 6 Weekend Crash Course,* IDG

Books Worldwide, Inc., 7260 Shadeland Station, Ste. 100, Indiana-polis, IN 46256, or call 1-800-762-2974. Please allow three to four weeks for delivery. This Limited Warranty is void if failure of the Software Media has resulted from accident, abuse, or misapplication. Any replacement Software Media will be warranted for the remainder of the original warranty period or thirty (30) days, whichever is longer.

(b) In no event shall IDGB or the authors be liable for any damages whatsoever (including without limitation damages for loss of business profits, business interruption, loss of business information, or any other pecuniary loss) arising from the use of or inability to use the Book or the Software, even if IDGB has been advised of the possibility of such damages.

(c) Because some jurisdictions do not allow the exclusion or limitation of liability for consequential or incidental damages, the above limitation or exclusion may not apply to you.

7. **U.S. Government Restricted Rights.** Use, duplication, or disclosure of the Software by the U.S. Government is subject to restrictions stated in paragraph (c)(1)(ii) of the Rights in Technical Data and Computer Software clause of DFARS 252.227-7013, and in subparagraphs (a) through (d) of the Commercial Computer — Restricted Rights clause at FAR 52.227-19, and in similar clauses in the NASA FAR supplement, when applicable.

8. **General.** This Agreement constitutes the entire understanding of the parties and revokes and supersedes all prior agreements, oral or written, between them and may not be modified or amended except in a writing signed by both parties hereto that specifically refers to this Agreement. This Agreement shall take precedence over any other documents that may be in conflict herewith. If any one or more provisions contained in this Agreement are held by any court or tribunal to be invalid, illegal, or otherwise unenforceable, each and every other provision shall remain in full force and effect.

my2cents.idgbooks.com

Register This Book — And Win!

Visit **http://my2cents.idgbooks.com** to register this book and we'll automatically enter you in our fantastic monthly prize giveaway. It's also your opportunity to give us feedback: let us know what you thought of this book and how you would like to see other topics covered.

Discover IDG Books Online!

The IDG Books Online Web site is your online resource for tackling technology — at home and at the office. Frequently updated, the IDG Books Online Web site features exclusive software, insider information, online books, and live events!

10 Productive & Career-Enhancing Things You Can Do at www.idgbooks.com

- Nab source code for your own programming projects.

- Download software.

- Read Web exclusives: special articles and book excerpts by IDG Books Worldwide authors.

- Take advantage of resources to help you advance your career as a Novell or Microsoft professional.

- Buy IDG Books Worldwide titles or find a convenient bookstore that carries them.

- Register your book and win a prize.

- Chat live online with authors.

- Sign up for regular e-mail updates about our latest books.

- Suggest a book you'd like to read or write.

- Give us your 2¢ about our books and about our Web site.

You say you're not on the Web yet? It's easy to get started with IDG Books' *Discover the Internet,* available at local retailers everywhere.

CD-ROM Installation Instructions

The CD-ROM that accompanies this book contains the complete code examples from the text as well as evaluation versions of the following tools for Visual Basic programming:

- VBAssist 5.0 and DataWidgets 3.1 from Sheridan Software
- LEADTOOLS ActiveX from Lead Technologies
- VS-OCX, VSVIEW, VSFlexGrid Pro, VSSPELL, VSREPORTS, VSDOCX, and VSFORUM from VideoSoft.

These are stored on the CD in their own subfolders. To install, open each vendor's folder and run the installation program. See Appendix B for further information.

Microsoft Product Warranty and Support Disclaimer

The Microsoft program on the CD-ROM was reproduced by IDG Books Worldwide, Inc. under a special arrangement with Microsoft Corporation. For this reason, IDG Books Worldwide, Inc. is responsible for the product warranty and for support. If your CD-ROM is defective, please return it to IDG Books Worldwide, Inc. which will arrange for its replacement. PLEASE DO NOT RETURN IT TO MICROSOFT CORPORATION. Any product support will be provided, if at all, by IDG Books Worldwide, Inc. PLEASE DO NOT CONTACT MICROSOFT CORPORATION FOR PRODUCT SUPPORT. End users of this Microsoft program shall not be considered "registered owners" of a Microsoft product and therefore shall not be eligible for upgrades, promotions or other benefits available to "registered owners" of Microsoft products.